Praise for *THE RIGHT LEADER*

"In my various roles as a former corporate division president as well as current chairman of a not-for-profit organization and board director, I am keenly aware of issues around CEO succession and found the principles discussed very relevant for all types of organizations."

—Rita V. Foley
Director, **Dresser Rand, PetSmart** Chair, **Pro Mujer**
2007 NFP Director of the Year

"What greater challenge can there be than hiring right the first time? *The Right Leader* gives every leader a step-by-step guide to making sure you get the proper Match-Fit for your organization—saving you time and money."

—Robert Rigby-Hall
SVP Human Resources
LexisNexis

"Following the principles in *The Right Leader* will bring about a true metamorphosis in the hiring decision. It crystallizes the process, creating a way to reduce the costs and risks of leadership failures plaguing business—by selecting the right leaders in the first place."

—Mary E. Kier
Vice Chairman
Cook Associates, Inc.

"Put this book on your reading list. *The Right Leader* presents a true paradigm shift and changes how we think about selecting leaders. It replaces a framework that provides only short-term solutions for making decisions about key people with a pragmatic way to balance cultural and business needs."

—Hy Pomerance
Global Head, Talent Management, Human Resources
UBS

"No single board responsibility looms larger than selecting the right leader to compete in today's fast-paced, global economy. *The Right Leader* provides a comprehensive, yet practical, way to identify the leadership every business organization needs to excel. Congratulations on writing a first rate book!"

—William E. Stevens
Chairman, **BBI Group**
Director and Chair of the Compensation Committee
McCormick Inc.

"For the first time I was really able to see the limitations of the traditional interview process and to understand why some selections just didn't work out. The Match-Fit model is one that I know will make a profound difference to the executives I hire, to those I coach, and to the Agency as a whole."

—Susan R. Symington
Senior Executive at **Central Intelligence Agency** and Executive Coach

"As the CEO of a public corporation who was selected through the exact process described in *The Right Leader*, I can say without any reservations that (IT WORKS)! It takes the guessing and uncertainty out of early decision-making and gets everyone focused and on the proper page quickly."

—Finbarr J. O'Neill
SVP and GM, International Operations
J. D. Power and Associates
Former CEO, **Reynolds and Reynolds, Inc.**

"The Right Leader puts 'fit' not just into perspective but into practice so even the most seasoned, top executives can get it right . . . even deans."

—James B. Thomas
Dean, Smeal College of Business
The Pennsylvania State University

"Having recently been through succession planning, (my own), I heartily agree that the normally missing elements so clearly, concisely, and logically presented in *The Right Leader* are essential for success."

—Timothy F. Leatherman
Co-founder
Leatherman Tool Group

"The Right Leader constitutes a significant advancement in understanding how leaders and cultures interact."

—Richard Barrett
Author, *Building a Value-Driven Organization* and
Liberating the Corporate Soul
Chairman and Founder
Barrett Values Centre

"I think this book will be very valuable to executives, boards, recruiters and HR for decades to come."

—Marcella Arline
Retired Chief People Officer, **Hershey Company**

THE RIGHT
LEADER

THE RIGHT
LEADER

Selecting Executives
Who Fit

Nat Stoddard
with
Claire Wyckoff

WILLEY

John Wiley & Sons, Inc.

For their years of selfless listening and enduring presence, this book is dedicated to:

Mark W. Smith
Former Dean of Men, *Denison University*

Barbara L. Bridendolph
President and CEO, *Crenshaw Associates*

Contents

List of Illustrations   xi

Foreword   xiii

Acknowledgments   xv

Preface: The Why's and Wherefore's Behind This Book   xvii

1 Introduction   1

**Part One: The New Paradigm for Leadership
        Selection**   **21**

2 Design for a New Selection Model   23

3 The Abilities Bucket   41

4 The Personality and Energy Bucket   61

5 The Character Bucket   73

6 The Company's Needs   97

7 Corporate Culture   111

Part Two: Fixing a Flawed Selection Process   **137**

8 The New Hiring Process—"Hit My Smoke!"   139

9 Changing the Way Candidates are Vetted   149

10 The Missing Links to Selecting the Right Leader   167

11 The FAC Process at Work: The Case of SDI, Inc.   197

12 Putting It All Together: A Recipe for Success   211

Part Three: Conclusion   **235**

13 Why Boards Should Care   237

14 "You're Cleared in Hot"   259

Notes   279

Appendix A. Assessment Tools Matrix   293

Appendix B. Cross-Cultural Virtues   297

Appendix C. Book Figures   303

Bibliography   307

Index   317

LIST OF ILLUSTRATIONS

Figure

1.1	U.S. CEO Departures 2002–2007	4
2.1	Traditional Selection Process	14
2.1	The Traditional Selection Model—v.1	29
2.2	The Traditional Selection Model—v.2	31
2.3	The Match-Fit Model—v. 1	35
2.4	The Match-Fit Model—v.2	36
2.5	The Match-Fit Model—v.3	38
4.1	Comparison of Traditional and Match-Fit Model	67
5.1	Universal Character Traits of Leaders	80
10.1	Eliza's Predisposition vs. Corporate Culture	186
11.1	SDI Needs and CultureCompany Overall	200
11.2	James's Predisposition vs. Company Culture	203
11.3	James's Predisposition vs. Company Climate	204
11.4	James's Predisposition vs. Company Values	205
11.5	James's Predisposition vs. Company Senior Management Subcultures	207
11.6	James's Predisposition vs. Company Senior Management Subculture Climate	208
11.7	James's Predisposition vs. Company Senior Management Subculture Values	208
12.1	Accelerated Leader Selection Process	215
12.2	Advice/Adviser Matrix	227
13.1	Global CEO Turnover Rates 2001–2007	240
13.2	Nine Steps on CEO Succession Planning	248
13.3	Extended Leader Selection Process	249
14.1	The Complex Leadership Situation	271

Tables

1.1	Estimated Costs of CEO Failures at 18 Months in Job ($000)	9
7.1	Debunking the Myths of Culture	121
10.1	Mapping the Corporate Lay of the Land Original Survey Design	185
10.2	Mapping the Corporate Lay of the Land Current Survey Design	187
13.1	Ten Best Practices for CEO Succession Planning	251
13.2	The NEW Best Practices for CEO Succession Planning	251

Foreword

Almost every company in almost every industry claims that its people are its most valued asset. Yet our understanding of how to pick the right people has lagged behind the development of other management tools, such as approaches to allocating financial capital, offsetting risk, and even redesigning the organizational structures in which these most valued assets—people—operate. As a result, even the otherwise most sophisticated companies often stumble when it comes to picking their top leaders.

We live in an era when there is greater scrutiny than ever of the core responsibilities of boards of directors and other representatives of owners, yet there is widespread agreement that few companies do a good job at the central duty of picking the right leaders. As a result, almost two-thirds of all chief executives are replaced within four years—some 40 percent within eighteen months.

This book is the first systematic analysis of the problem, with a solution that is both innovative and simple to apply. Like many business issues, it turns out that the key to success in picking leaders is defining the problem correctly.

The Right Leader notes that we have learned a lot about what it takes to be an effective leader in general, and we try to apply that understanding carefully when reviewing candidates. The problem is that few companies have looked closely at the positions they are trying to fill, especially the sometimes amorphous, but often critical, cultural issues. In other words, companies need to know the shape of their "holes" if they are to do a better job of finding square pegs for square holes and round pegs for round holes.

Some of those holes turn out to be exceedingly difficult to fill because of the nature of the environment in which the new leader is expected to operate. A new focus on the actual job to be done—not the paint-by-the-numbers approach of many job specification memos—is required. So too is understanding leaders in a deeper way, including topics that are so old-fashioned that they are nearly taboo, but that, as our grandmothers could have told us, can also make all the difference. Character, this book claims, turns out to be a critical factor, but one that we too often fail to explore adequately.

Most executives have seen this issue from both sides of the table. As pegs, we have positioned ourselves for particular jobs. As participants in hiring decisions, we have been responsible for defining the hole to be filled. If your experience is anything like mine, you will recall the more than occasional disconnect between the job description and the actual job, for ourselves, for our peers, and (despite our best efforts) for our team. It does not always have to be this way.

The experts at Crenshaw Associates have great experience in avoiding peg-hole mismatch—especially relevant for situations where the new leader is likely to come from the outside. Job candidates have their skills, increasingly including career strategies and campaigns based on sophisticated self-assessments. Now companies can become as skilled, by understanding what Nat Stoddard and his colleagues call Mapping the Corporate Lay of the Land.[1] This includes identifying the true executional and directional needs of the company that a new leader will encounter. The approach defines, describes, and measures the overall organization's culture—what the author calls the "implicit, explicit, rational, irrational and nonrational, guides for behaviors that exist within all organizations." And of course each team within each company has its own related subculture, with which the new leader also needs to fit.

This is not a theoretical exercise, so do not be misled by the reference to topics we have been trained to minimize or even dismiss as soft and non-quantifiable, such as culture. The book recounts, example after example, how a poor fit can undermine leaders and damage companies. It is time to take culture out of the "that's soft stuff" category into the realm of hard facts and data-driven decision-making. Think of the "Match-Fit Model" as just as revolutionary a way of looking at finding the right leader as Six Sigma was to quality control. Both are tools to allow leaders to make better decisions, and both are systems that increase the likelihood of success.

Whichever side of the table you are currently on—hiring or being hired—the lessons in this book can make the difference between a great fit and a misfit.

—L. Gordon Crovitz, former Publisher,
The Wall Street Journal

Acknowledgments

One of the responsibilities of leadership is to assemble a strong team. In the course of writing this book, we were fortunate to be able to draw on the resources of a team of individuals whose knowledge and support are reflected throughout the book. We are extremely grateful to each and every one of them for their unique and generous contributions.

From the beginning we felt it was important to supplement our own experience and that of Crenshaw Associates with the knowledge of executives from other organizations who have in-depth knowledge of this field. To this end, we created an HR Advisory Council. It is made up of six outstanding executives who have been gracious enough to take time out of already packed schedules not only to read the manuscript but to provide detailed criticism and suggestions. They include: Marcella Arline, the former Senior Vice President, Chief People Officer at The Hershey Company; LeighAnne Baker, Senior Vice President and Chief Human Resources Officer for the Hertz Corporation; John Corness, Vice President of Human Resources at Polaris Industries; Peter Mani, former Vice President of Global Human Resources for Warnaco; Hy Pomerance, Director of Learning and Development for UBS; and Robert Rigby-Hall, the Senior Vice President of Human Resources for Lexis-Nexis.

Our Crenshaw team provided equally strong support and expertise of a different kind. For this we are especially grateful to: Natasha Taylor, for her creative figures, being a sounding board, spiritual support, and sharing an occasional good cigar; Phebe Annan, for her 10,000 administrative support activities, friendship, and dedicated patience; Mary Green for an incredible job of coordinating our Web-based Mapping beta test; Nitza Jones, for her attention to detail; Erin Worth, for being our true "Type-Thing" transcriber for nearly all 100,000 words in this work; Marisol Luna, for many extra hours of inputting our edits; and Kim Stoddard, for early comps of book jacket promo materials and coining the term "field guide."

For contributing to the content itself, we are most deeply indebted to the original pioneers of the Mapping concept: Barbara Bridendolph, Crenshaw CEO; Bob Aquilina, for early Mapping project leadership; Beth Powers, for research expertise in early stages of Mapping; and Dr. Kerry Sulkowicz, for counsel, support, insight, and encouragement. Helping us to keep the details current and accurate also required a great deal of specialized knowledge. Those whom we need to thank especially for serving as advisers in this way include: Dr. Gary Hayes, for his critique of Appendix A; Alan Renne, for numerous tips on today's search practices; Bill Rogers, for editorial insights; Bill Stevens, for his review and input regarding boardroom realities and practices; Ken Suelthaus, for detailed governance advice and experience; Lt. Col. (Ret.) Mike "Scoop" Jackson, for his technical guidance and his service to our country as a true FAC; Wendi Lazar for timely input on points of employment law; Tom Pomeroy, for his experience and accounts about transitioning; and The Genesys Team: George Weathersby, Geoff Weathersby, and Suzanne McBride, for the patient and persistent partnership in taking the Mapping Process to new heights. Others who have read the contents from cover to cover and shared their thoughts on how we could make it clearer, more informative, and a better read all the way around include: Fred Pugh and Bob Bean, who read, edited, and critiqued our manuscript; and Jack Stoddard, for proofreading, inputting content, and structural ideas. Thanks to you all!

From the start, we were honored that such a venerable firm as John Wiley & Sons would have lent their support to our work by agreeing to publish us. They have lived up to their great reputation throughout. In particular, we have been fortunate to have had excellent editorial guidance from Editors Lauren Lynch and Emily Conway and Publishers Larry Alexander and Matt Holt. Our thanks also to Brian Neill, Maureen Drexel, and Christine Kim for sorting out all the production matters for the book and support materials.

Before anyone ever read a page, however, there were others we turned to for guidance of a more general sort. They were the people who advised us where to set out on various stages of the journey and encouraged us to try it. They include: Kathy Berlowe, for opening doors and providing thoughtful guidance and spiritual support; Dr. Dan Fisher, for input on Appendix A; Mike Rice, our questionnaire straw man and long-time friend; Jack Wilson, for starting the ball rolling with his original Match-Fit Model concept; Marcia Markland and Ellen Scordato, for their earliest encouragement and guidance; and Gordon Crovitz, for his support, encouragement, and eloquent Foreword.

In any creative endeavor, families always deserve a special mention for their patience and tolerance of the process. My daughter Kim and my son Jack certainly do, as do Claire's daughter, Jenny, and husband, Dan Maguire.

Preface

If you have ever been involved in the search for a C-Suite executive (whether on the company or the candidate side), you know how difficult it can be to find a winning person/situation. We all want the outcome to be a success—where what was expected at the start is what actually occurs. But achieving the right combination is rarely the case today. In 2007 the estimated turnover rate of North American CEOs alone was 15.2 percent—roughly 50 percent higher than a decade earlier.[1] During the same ten-year period the terminations of CEOs for performance-related reasons increased threefold.[2] According to a number of reliable sources, 40 percent of all leaders fail in their new roles and are replaced or retired in their first eighteen months on the job.[3] Clearly success at the top is becoming more and more difficult to achieve.

No matter at what level, executive turnover is exacting an enormous toll on American business. Although not within the scope of the research undertaken to write this book (we have limited our focus primarily to the U.S. workplace, where we have a unique vantage), many overseas companies are being affected as well. In this country severance packages make headlines regularly. In addition there are hidden costs, such as the expense of finding replacements, lost market capitalization, stock price volatility, missed opportunities, and the loss of confidence that turnover engenders within the organization. For the companies, the individuals and, in the case of CEO failures, for the directors on the board, there is the cost of damaged reputations too.

The full impact of this phenomenon came into stark clarity soon after I became the chairman of a small but established New York consulting boutique Crenshaw Associates. Ultimately my experience at Crenshaw has led to an effort to redesign an improved process for selecting leaders, which is what this book is about.

When my business partner and Crenshaw's CEO Barb Bridendolph and I acquired the company in 2001, its only line of business was providing outplacement services to very senior-level executives. As we listened to our clients' accounts of why they left their organizations, we began to wonder if maybe there was not more to the rapidly increasing failure rates of senior executives than some latent deficiency on the parts of the leaders. On the whole, our clients were highly capable and personable men and women of high character—the stuff of excellent leaders. When subsequently placed in different situations, they were all invariably successful. If it was not entirely the leaders' fault, then what was it about the situations that contributed to their failure? Ultimately we were compelled to look critically at the selection process that put them in their jobs in the first place.

Lucky for us, a principal with Career Science, Inc. named Jack Wilson was a Crenshaw subject-matter expert at the time. Jack had created a framework for looking at the transition process that he dubbed the Match-Fit Model. This model fit the pieces of the selection puzzle together in a whole new way. It created a paradigm that, as we have worked with and modified it, has shown us its potential to lead to a significant reduction in leadership failures. We determined that the Traditional Selection Process places too much emphasis on the candidate's abilities and, in most instances, virtually none on the substance of the individual's character (such as the values, beliefs, and philosophies that drive decisions and shape behavior). On the other side of the coin, the Traditional Selection Process used by most companies today generally lacks any current, factual declaration of the company's true needs expressed in terms of actions rather than outcomes. Nor does it rely on any solid information about that so-called "soft stuff"—culture. Thus, hirers have no real way of gauging whether one candidate is truly better suited for a particular situation than another.

In the ensuing years we have modified Jack's original model and derived from it a new Leader Selection Process. This process accounts for what we have found to be gaps in the way most organizations select leaders. In addition we have experimented with, developed, and refined a methodology for gathering the necessary data to support the new Leader Selection Process. It works.

The Territory Ahead

As Crenshaw gained more knowledge and experience in our new approach, the importance of writing a book to get the message into the hands of the people who could put it to good use became increasingly evident. For help in this process, I turned to a friend and former publisher Claire Wyckoff for assistance. Together we have designed this book to introduce you to these processes and methodologies—to new ways of thinking about, and action steps for, selecting leaders so that you end up with the right leaders for your organization.

Part One explains the Match-Fit Model and examines how it changes the way we view the relationship of the leader to the organization. It discusses in detail those elements the Match-Fit Model has revealed as missing from the Traditional Selection Process. Chapter 1 provides additional data on executive turnover and its cost to the organization. Chapter 2 will clarify why we believe the current selection process is not working, contrasting the Traditional Selection Model with the new Match-Fit Model. In Chapters 3 through 7, we will look at the five basic components of the Match-Fit Model in depth and the role they will play in shaping the Leader Selection Process of the future.

Although Part Two is the "how to" section of the book, it is written more as an owner's manual than a technical handbook. It is intended to help "hirers"—that is, anyone who has a stake in the selection of senior executives, from HR heads to sitting CEOs, directors, and other senior executives to recruiters. It details the tools to use to transform the current selection process into a process that works. In particular it discusses the steps necessary to determine whether the candidate's abilities, personality, energy, and character align with the company's true needs and the specific nature of its various cultures. We will explain how to do what we call "Forward Assessment Consulting" and then use it to create "Culturemaps" to plot your organization. By Mapping the Corporate Lay of the Land, you will learn what the candidate's true fit is. The data collected in this part of the process can also be extremely valuable to both the right new leader—and the company—in successful onboarding.

In addition to a conclusion, Part Three contains a chapter devoted to the unique needs of independent directors interested in developing those meaningful succession plans that are strongly encouraged (although not yet required) by the Securities and Exchange Commission (SEC), the Financial Industry Regulatory Authority (FINRA), and the New York Stock Exchange (NYSE).

Setting Expectations

There are four distinct groups for whom this book is intended. The first, as previously indicated, is made up of those people who have any ownership stake in the hiring of leaders of any organization at any level, but particularly those at senior levels (board members, incumbent CEOs, HR leaders, and executive search professionals).

The second audience for *The Right Leader* is comprised of senior executives themselves, especially those who may already be, or aspire to be, candidates for leadership positions of increased responsibility. When such positions involve making a change to a new company or organization, or into a distinctly different operating unit within a parent organization or group, the relevance of what this book has to offer becomes all the more important.

The third group of readers who will benefit from *The Right Leader* are those who are involved in mergers and acquisitions, especially those responsible for the post-acquisition integration of multiple organizations. While we do not go into detail about the applicability of this work in conjunction with mergers and acquisitions, the principles and processes used for selecting leaders are just as applicable when merging cultures under consolidated leadership. With the failure rate of mergers and acquisitons even higher than those of newly appointed CEOs, the benefits of what this book has to offer are possibly greater in this area than elsewhere.

Independent directors of companies involved in Succession Planning constitute the fourth audience for this book. Chapter 13, "Why Boards Should Care," brings together a new set of principles, process changes, and best practices recommended for boards. Regardless of the role directors play in the CEO Succession Planning Process, all should have an awareness of the leading edge advantages of the new Leader Selection Process described in this book.

The Right Leader describes a multipurpose tool with a total of ten important advantages over the current and traditional hiring process. It offers specific benefits both to the organization and to all those that have a stake in hiring a new senior leader, as well as to the leader him- or herself. And, in this instance, if one wins, so does the other.

Benefits to the Organization (and the New Leader)

- It reduces the costs and risks of a new leader not measuring up to expectations (commonly called "leadership failure").
- It provides the data necessary for selecting the "best-fit" leader. When properly approached, the new Leader Selection Process generates information hirers can use to fine-tune their final interviews and really focus in on a factual basis for selecting the new leader.
- The new process serves as a retention tool for those who are not selected for the leadership position. It provides timely opportunities for their input, as well as specific, tangible feedback for them as to why they were not selected and where they will fit in the new plans going forward.
- It creates the backdrop (called Culturemaps) for all senior-level succession planning and individualized executive development plans for years to come. The understanding of the cultural elements will help develop specific action plans for executives being groomed for succession within the organization.
- It can be used as an ongoing repository of hard data regarding organizational "soft stuff" (its culture). All executives acknowledge the importance

and relevance of culture to the success and uniqueness of their companies, but few have dealt with it purposely to gain a competitive advantage by molding organizational culture consistently and appropriately.

Benefits to the New Leader (and the Organization)

- The new Leader Selection Process is a powerful due-diligence tool to help candidates look past the glitter and appeal of a new job opportunity to see if they really are the right person for what the job requires. Without the kind of comprehensive approach it offers (or even a fast-track variation of it undertaken immediately upon their arrival), new leaders take unnecessarily huge career risks without adequately understanding what it will take to be successful and how to go about doing so in the organizations they are being called on to lead.
- The new Leader Selection Process is a tool for the leader to use to shape him- or herself to fit into a situation in ways that will maximize his or her effectiveness immediately and decrease the likelihood of making a mistake caused by trial and error approaches to understanding the culture.
- The new Leader Selection Process is a tool to increase the rate at which a new leader comes up to speed. With an understanding of the true needs of the situation: the elements to be left alone and those to be addressed, an understanding of the jargon and of the concerns of the existing leadership team immediately upon accepting the position, the new leader is in the position to begin to make meaningful and more accurate decisions almost immediately.
- The new Leader Selection Process is a tool to be used by the leader to achieve organizational alignment. By using the findings of the Mapping Process rather than his or her own perceptions and "gut instincts" alone, the new leader has a resource that can be used with his or her direct reports to determine the extent to which the picture that has been painted is indeed accurate, and once verified, it becomes a tool to be used with the board to help them understand the needs and sensitivities of the situation with precision and clarity.
- The new Leader Selection Process is a tool for understanding organizational needs and establishing priorities that go into the new leader's onboarding plan.

Avoiding Culture Shock

It is hoped that *The Right Leader* will suggest better ways to evaluate the abilities and personalities of candidates for leadership positions, as well as help you develop a clearer understanding of your company's needs. However, these are not our primary concern. Our primary concern is that you come away with an appreciation of the central role that the organizations' culture and the candidate's character play in the success of the hiring process.

If you think these elements of the process are secondary, consider the story of Nike and William Perez:

The Bill Perez and Nike Debacle

Just thirteen months earlier (in December 2004) when William D. Perez was appointed to Nike's top job everyone had reason to believe that only success could be forthcoming for him and for Nike. Nike had plucked Perez from the S.C. Johnson Company, where he had served as CEO of that privately held company, to become Nike's new president and CEO. His background seemed tailor-made for the job, and the Nike official press release gushed optimism and enthusiasm. Phil Knight, Nike's chairman and founder, was particularly ebullient about having Mr. Perez on his team. Speaking on behalf of the board, Mr. Knight said:

> *This begins an exciting new chapter in Nike's ongoing business evolution. Bill is a highly regarded and deeply talented leader with more than 30 years experience as a builder of global brands and businesses. Bill has demonstrated commitment to consumers, new product innovation and development, growth, team building and talent development. He also knows how to operate a highly socially responsible global business, all of which make him the right person to lead Nike Inc.*

In the same release, Mr. Knight went on to say that, "In the near term, I will focus my efforts on ensuring an effective transition and on evolving into my role as an active Chairman."[4]

Just over a year later a somewhat chagrined Phil Knight informed the world that Bill Perez had resigned, stating that "the expectations that Bill and I had when he joined the company a year ago didn't play out as we had hoped." The way Perez put it, "Phil and I weren't entirely aligned on some aspects of how to best lead the company's long-term growth,"[5]

Under the headline "Nike's CEO Gets the Boot," *Business Week* quoted Knight as saying, "Basically the distance between the company Bill managed (previously) . . . and (Nike) . . . was too great. The cultural leap was really too great." The Nike founder also said that, "it wasn't one big clash or disagreement with Perez. Rather it boiled down to 'lots of little incidents over a year. . . . '"[6]

The day following Perez's announcement Knight was quoted in *The New York Times* as saying, "Perez had failed to 'get his arms around this place' and that his tenure was 'a situation where the cultural leap was too great.'"[7]

Although few report a problem of cultural fit as openly as this one, stories in the press like this raise a lot of questions: What was it in the Nike culture that Bill Perez did not fit into? Or what was it about Bill Perez— something about his abilities, his personality, or his behaviors—that did not align with that culture? Most importantly what went wrong with the process that put Perez and Nike together in the first place? What could have been changed in the selection process so that both Nike and Bill Perez could have known *before* making a commitment that Perez was not going to be successful at Nike as everyone expected?

While both Nike and Bill Perez (as CEO at Wrigley), have gone on to continued success, the costs to both were great and, we believe, completely avoidable. It is exactly this kind of situation that the new Leader Selection Process can help you and countless others to keep from happening to your organization, your stakeholders, and your career.

Based on experience with executives in transition and with the new Leader Selection Process, we believe it is the fit between the individual's personality, energy, and character with the cultures of the company that need to be scrutinized with considerably greater diligence and in advance if more leaders are to be successful. This is particularly true because, contrary to some peoples' notion that character is either "good" or "bad," something a person either "has" or "doesn't have," one's character is always its own unique blend of predispositions, attitudes, values, beliefs, and philosophics. It is made up of numerous variables that we all possess to one degree or another. It is how they are blended and expressed in the behaviors of the particular individual that determine their fit with the company culture.

In the Match-Fit Model you will see where a lack of alignment can cause disruption; through reading about the new Leader Selection Process you will learn new ways to assess the candidate's personality, energy, and character as well as the company's cultures so as to ensure a good fit. And it is in this last regard that we hope this book can change how you see, and deal with, your corporate world.

Beyond providing companies and their selected leaders with greater chances for success in the increasingly complex and globalized world in which they must win, our "stretch goal" in writing *The Right Leader* is to open as many eyes as possible to the fact that culture is one of those remaining frontiers; that, by measuring it and understanding it for what it is (and what it is not!), future generations of leaders can begin to find better ways of molding and shaping their organizations to make them more competitive, more cost-effective, and more fun places to work. It is time we stopped regarding culture as "soft stuff" and started understanding what the term really means to organizations and their leaders. It is time to open our eyes to the power that cultures have and how they can either support or undermine the success of their leaders. Ultimately, that is our target.

That said, let me simply conclude with a statement that will make much more sense once you have read the book: "Hit my smoke . . . you're cleared in hot."

Nat Stoddard
New York, NY

1

Introduction

The way up and the way down are one and the same.
—T. S. Eliot

O ver the past decade more and more stories like Nike's have appeared in the business press—stories about companies that chose leaders who had been highly successful in another setting but who did not succeed in the new one, *in spite of* the best intentions of everybody involved. Furthermore countless stories of a similar nature never reach the public eye, as evidenced by the statistics regarding executive turnover and failures.

The intent of this chapter is to put the facts squarely on the table and understand their impact. To do this we will focus on the following key areas:

- The facts about C-Level failures and the resultant turnover rates occurring today
- The costs of executive turnover to corporations
- The costs to the individuals who are involved
- The Traditional Selection Process through which today's leaders are chosen

Much of the data we will present pertains to chief executive officers specifically, because they receive most of the attention and media coverage. Reports and other data sources for executives further down in the organization are simply not publicly available to track. However, it is our assertion that the factors that can be seen clearly in the CEO data also apply, in general, to their direct reports and other senior executives as well.

The Rising Rate of Leadership Failures

From the data that is available, it is fairly evident that during the last half of the 1990s turnover rates of CEOs of major North American corporations was consistently in the 10 to 11 percent range or lower. In the last five years (2003–2007), however, the average turnover rate has jumped to 14 percent—nearly a 50 percent increase.[1]

Looking beyond the big, public corporations, the trend is the same, only worse. According to Challenger, Gray & Christmas the number of CEO departures in the United States for the three-year period from 2005 to 2007 averaged nearly twice that of the preceding three years. The increased departure rates for U.S. CEOs can be clearly seen in Figure 1.1. By mid-year 2008 the turnover rate was again on the increase.[2]

To place today's "churn at the top" into even sharper focus, additional statistics indicate that 64 percent—nearly two-thirds—of U.S. CEOs fail to

FIGURE 1.1 U.S. CEO Departures 2002–2007

Data Source: Challenger, Gray & Christmas, Inc.

achieve the objectives for which they were brought in and are replaced or "retired" within four years of their appointment.[3] Forty percent are gone within eighteen months.[4] Moreover, CEOs are being held more accountable for their results as performance-related terminations have increased by 318 percent in the past ten years.[5]

For those who are promoted from within the organization, the odds of success do not dramatically improve as conventional wisdom would lead us to expect. In fact leaders newly selected from within an organization don't seem to perform any better than those who come from the outside. Data shows that during their first five years in the position outsiders actually outperform inside appointees for those who manage to stay that long.[6]

Also belying conventional wisdom is that fact that prior CEO experience does not apparently help increase the chances of success either. In 2005 the percentage of sitting CEOs who had prior CEO experience when they took their current positions was approximately 37 percent.[7] Yet that same year, 35 percent of the CEOs who left office due to performance issues were from that very same group.[8] If prior experience had any appreciable value, then the failure rate of this group should have been significantly lower than those who had not had any previous CEO experience, but that was not the case.

As a result of all this turnover at the top of the house, by the end of 2006 nearly half of the CEOs of New York Stock Exchange (NYSE) member companies (46 percent) had less than four years of on-the-job experience and a quarter of them (26 percent) had been in the role less than two years.[9] Since 1995 the tenure of sitting CEOs of public U.S. companies has fallen from ten years to seven years by 2001,[10] and to five years by 2007.[11] Alan Murray, editor-in-chief of the *Wall Street Journal Online* concisely summarizes it: "The tenure of CEOs is getting shorter each year."[12]

At this rate America will soon have the most inexperienced cadre of corporate leaders of any developed country, and some boards will even feel as though they are engaged in two cycles of succession planning simultaneously. As the tenure of CEOs drops below the lead times required to conduct a meaningful succession and grooming plan, they will have to start looking for the successor's successor at the same time they are looking for the successor. Clearly, something is terribly wrong.

What's more, the problems of turnover at the top are not limited just to the United States. In 2007 the turnover rate of European CEOs hit a record high of 17.6 percent, significantly higher than the North American rate of 15.2 percent.[13] Tenure (time in the job) is also low globally. According to a survey conducted in March 2008 of 378 market-leading companies from around the world, a staggering 41.5 percent of CEOs have held their positions for three years or less; 17.6 percent were under a year! To top it off the 2008 study reported that high turnover rates permeated the entire C-Suite. Forty-eight percent of CFOs were in their jobs for three or fewer years, and 46.4 percent of COOs.[14]

It can certainly be argued that some amount of change in the executive suite is appropriate and essential to promote innovation. Further, as baby boomer leaders begin to retire, the number of executive replacements should also increase naturally. Regardless, no one has suggested that today's level of churn is healthy, or natural, or in the interest of anyone who has a stake in the process or an interest in the future of the company itself.

The Costs of Leadership Failure

No matter what the cause, the impact of any change in leadership to both the company and the individual are huge. The cost of replacing senior-level executives (excluding CEOs) can run between two and ten times their total compensation, or roughly $2.7 million on average.[15]

At the very top, the costs escalate. When William Perez departed Nike, the company gave him a severance package valued at more than $14 million, including two years' salary of $1.4 million per year and a bonus of at least $1.76 million.[16] Fortunately for Nike shareholders, his package paled in comparison to the severance packages of some of the more public departures of CEOs like Bob Nardelli from Home Depot ($210 million),[17] Hank McKinnell from Pfizer ($123 million), Gary Forsee from Sprint ($40 million), Carly Fiorino from Hewlett Packard (a mere $23 million), and

Richard Grasso's highly controversial package from the New York Stock Exchange ($188 million).[18] While such extravagant severance packages certainly are occasionally provided, our experience with senior-level executives' severance provisions is less sensational than the extremes already mentioned.[19] Paul Hodgson, senior research associate at The Corporate Library, puts the customary severance that most companies pay a departing CEO equal to approximately three years' total compensation and that for other senior executives at two times their total annual compensation, which is more consistent with our experiences.[20] In 2007 the compensation experts at Crenshaw Associates informed us that the average total cash compensation (including bonuses) for CEOs of large-cap corporations (revenues greater than $4.5 billion) was $1,650,000—which, using a three-times multiplier, would put their severance at around $5 million.[21] It has also been our experience that most CEOs of mid-cap or smaller corporations receive lower severance rates—two years is more common at the middle-size companies and one year's total compensation seems to be the rule at smaller firms. Using average total compensation figures for these groups, their severance payments would be closer to $1.7 million and $650,000, respectively.

While not as impressive as the headline "funny money" payments to a handful of executives, severance costs are, nevertheless, a very real, direct cash cost to the company when a CEO failure occurs—and there are more. Other costs may include such expenses as the cost of a retained search to find a replacement or to "benchmark" an internal candidate at 27 to 33 percent of total annual first-year compensation, plus the travel costs to and from interviews for all concerned, as well as for the final candidate's family to visit the new location. Then add to it the possibility of buying out the bonuses, options, and other incentives the new hire would be leaving on the table at his or her current position. As previously noted, severance guarantees made by the candidate's company for purposes of retention must be addressed. Continue by factoring in a six-digit sign-up bonus to help with incidental, up-front expenses, and then add in the cost of both parties' advisory support teams, including contract lawyers, compensation and tax specialists, an assessment team, and increasingly an onboarding adviser. Since it usually takes a newly hired or promoted executive six months to reach breakeven—the point at which new leaders have contributed as much value to their new company as they have taken from it—that initial "sunk cost" needs to be factored in, too.[22]

Now throw in all the "exceptional items" for both the departing CEO and the new replacement: the buyback of the house, outplacement services, partial or full-year bonuses (often paid to the outgoing executive and guaranteed to the incoming one), Special Executive Retirement Plan (SERP) costs, relocation expenses (including gross-ups for tax purposes), special medical and life insurance premiums, reimbursement of club memberships and the loss on the sale of the executive's company car, and on, and on, and on. Having tallied up all these direct costs that are out of pocket and impact the bottom line, take 50 percent, and multiply that amount times three—the approximate cost to replace each of the three executives who will comprise the "involuntary departures" of the 25 percent of executives who will, on average, leave the company after a new CEO is brought in from the outside as his or her "new team" is assembled.[23]

But hold on. We are not through yet. There are other, noncash costs that occur when the CEO fails to deliver the expected results. For public companies, one extremely important indirect, but very real, cost comes from the stock market's reaction to the change. Here is what the research reveals: Researchers at Booz Allen Hamilton recently found that in North America, announcing the replacement of a CEO produces a positive effect (3.8 percentage points better than the average return) when a company has been performing poorly for two years and a negative effect (10.2 percentage points worse than average) when the company has been doing well. More notable than this predictable stock movement is that the "selection of an outsider produces a big downtick in stock price; selection of an insider triggers an uptick."[24]

Depending on the condition of the company when the CEO leaves, the "cure could be worse than the disease" insofar as the stock price is concerned— an outside replacement for a company that is not doing well could pose a double-whammy on the stock's price and market capitalization.

While the stock price will adjust itself over time based on the performance of the company under its new leader, the impact on its volatility can remain a factor for quite some time following a change at the top. In 2003 Rutgers University and the University of Texas, in conjunction with the Federal Reserve Bank, published research reporting that a firm's stock volatility increased with *any* form of leadership turnover, but a forced departure could trigger an increase in volatility of up to 25 percent, which could last for as long as two years following the event.[25]

In short, a company's market capitalization and the stability of its stock are affected when a change is made at the top of a public corporation, and it can take years to fully recover from their effects.

Yet another—and in some ways perhaps the greatest and certainly the most insidious—cost attributable to a failed leadership change comes from its impact on the organization. This is the price of all the opportunities missed because an organization or an operating unit is leaderless, if even for a short while. The loss of momentum and rise of uncertainty that go hand in hand with a change in leadership can, and does, in the estimation of many, cost companies more money, more market share, more loss of reputation, and more customer goodwill than any other single event. Internally, morale suffers, especially among senior managers, who may wonder if theirs will be the next head on the chopping block. A spirit of innovation and willingness to take risks can disappear for a while, too, as employees wait to see what's expected of them in the new regime.[26] These people-related impacts are not the "soft, people-stuff" that they are sometimes labeled. On the contrary, this "people stuff" is as hard and as real as the currency used to measure organizational success and failure.

Just as the volatility of a company's stock does not settle out immediately upon the appointment of a new leader, neither do the problems afflicting the organization. As a matter of fact there is one particularly debilitating effect that turnover at the top can instill: the loss of trust. Organizational trust, once lost, can take years to restore.

During the course of my career I have observed, experienced, and dealt with the effects of turnover at the top too often to ever underestimate the crippling effect it can have on an organization. Here's the rub: With turnover rates what they are today, *every* newly appointed leader risks being tarred with the same brush of skepticism and distrust even though the company may otherwise be relatively stable. People see what they expect to see.

The Bottom-Line Impact

The financial fallout from leadership failures, then, plays out in many directions: There are direct costs related to the individual's compensation (salary and bonuses) and to the cost of maintaining the person in the job (health insurance, travel, office expense, and the like). There are other, much greater costs that result from errors in judgment, bad strategies, poor execution, opportunities foregone, and the disruption to the organization caused by inconsistencies, lack of direction, and worst of all, loss of trust.

Trying to isolate and measure the financial impacts to the organization of all these factors on a meaningful basis is a challenging exercise because there are so many moving parts, some of which are intangible. However, Dr. Bradford Smart, author of *Topgrading*, has given us a framework for estimating the overall financial effects of failure among CEOs based on research findings from work done by Chris Mursau.[27] Through a series of interviews with executives (half of whom were division presidents or higher) about their experiences with twenty-six "mis-hires," the amounts these poorly performing "B" and "C" managers (whose salaries averaged slightly more than $168,000 per year when the research was conducted in 1998) cost their companies during their first eighteen months in the job were identified. We conservatively assumed that the impact of the CEO who failed after eighteen months in the job (which is 40 percent of the cases, as you will recall!) would be, proportionately, no less than that of the lower-level executives as reported by Smart. Clearly, the case can be made as to why these numbers should be *greater* given the impact the CEO has versus a middle-level manager. Our

Table 1.1
Estimated Costs of CEO Failures at 18 Months in Job ($000)

No.	Item	Large-Cap Companies ($4.5B and up)	Mid-Cap Companies ($1B to $4.5B)	Small-Cap Companies ($300M to $1B)
1	Average Annual [a] Cash Comp (2007)	1,650	860	640
2	Cost of Hiring [b]	825	430	320
3	Total Cash Comp [c]	2,475	1,290	960
4	Cost of Maintaining [d] Person in the Job	455	230	170
5	Severance [e]	4,950	1,720	640
6	Mistakes, Failures, [f] Wasted and Missed Business Opportunities	32,645	13,770	7,840
7	Cost of Disruption [g]	16,320	6,890	3,920
8	Total Cost of Failure	57,670	24,330	13,850
9	Value of Contribution [h]	5,170	2,230	1,250
10	Net Cost of Failure	52,500	22,100	12,600

[a] Courtesy of Capital IQ, a division of Standard & Poor's. See https://www.capitaliq.com.

[b] Crenshaw assumes that recruiter's fees (33 percent) and other hiring costs total 50 percent of first year's total compensation.

[c] This is calculated as 1½ times the average annual cash compensation to cover the first 18 months.

[d] Smart, *Topgrading*. The author reports that the percentage of total compensation spent on maintaining a senior executive is 20 percent.

[e] Paul Hodgson at the Corporate Library has collected data that shows severance for executives three times their average annual compensation; this has been reduced to two times average annual compensation at mid-cap firms, and one time at small cap firms based on experience at Crenshaw Associates.

[f] Smart. *Topgrading*. The author determined that these costs represent 80 percent of the total costs of a mis-hire.

[g] Crenshaw Associates assumes that, at the top, disruption is very costly and equal to at least 50 percent of the failures and mistakes (totaled in the preceding line).

[h] Smart, *Topgrading*. The author found that positive contributions made during the first 18 months equal 9 percent of the total costs.

estimates are shown in Table 1.1. Where we made changes to the ratios in Dr. Smart's findings we have provided notes.[28]

As shown in Table 1.1, the cost of having the wrong CEO at the helm, even for just eighteen months, can range between $12.6 million and $52.5

million depending on the size of the corporation. This analysis also reveals two other relevant points:

1. **Smaller companies are hurt significantly more by selecting the wrong CEO.** If we assume that the profit-margin percentages are the same regardless of the size of the company, then the impact of having selected the wrong CEO to lead the business is greater on the small-cap companies than the bigger ones, even though the absolute dollar impact is roughly five times greater for the large-cap firms. Assuming that the profit margin for mid-size and small-cap companies is 6.0 percent as it is for the 487 publicly traded U.S. corporations with revenues in excess of $4.5 billion that constitute the large-cap group, then the estimated direct (cash) costs of CEO failures as a percent of average profits goes from .3 percent for large-cap companies, to 9.6 percent for mid-cap firms, to a whopping 23.2 percent for small-caps.[29] Needless to say, the effect of the wrong leader on a smaller entity can be devastating, as has been seen time and again over the years.

2. **The impact on the U.S. economy is nearly $14 billion per year.** Recognizing that the turnover rate of CEOs has plateaued over the past three years at an average of 1,385 per year, the total cost of CEO failures in terms of cash, inefficiencies, and opportunities foregone is calculated to be $13.8 billion, assuming the failures are distributed on a quid pro quo basis relative to the number of companies in each of the three segments. And this number does *not* include the lost shareholder value caused by the mistakes, failed strategies, organizational upheaval, and increased stock volatility that comes from having selected the wrong leader—all of which add up to a very target-rich environment for anyone looking to find disciplined ways to put an end to such waste.

The Human Cost

The effects of a failed leadership transition are not limited to just the company, its shareholders, and its employees. Its impact on the lives of the people who are affected should not be ignored. While the stakes and costs of failed leadership transitions can have a big impact on corporations, companies do not have feelings; they do not grieve; they do not have to fight the way the affected leader does to continue on. Even though their departure may make them very wealthy overnight (some excessively so!), rarely is that much solace. The loss of status, power, and reputation, not to mention the damage done to their egos and self-esteem, is often so great that some never recover from the experience. Too frequently the battle back to their former "heroic status" demands so much time, courage, and determined fortitude that the former leader does not really make a comeback.[30]

Having now been in the senior executive outplacement business for over seven years, I have seen the impact that career setbacks can have on the self-confidence of even some of the strongest personalities. As one client articulated it to me, "Even though I've been going to my club almost once a week for the past ten years, all of a sudden it feels like I don't belong there—that I'm in arrears in my dues or something. Guys who have been friends for years seem to avoid talking with me and shun my presence. Maybe it's me, but I just don't feel like I'm a full-fledged member anymore."

As devastating as leadership failures can be for the executives involved, theirs is by no means the greatest of the human costs. Hundreds, thousands, and even tens of thousands of other people can be significantly impacted by a single leadership failure and often in proportionately far greater ways. And the failure doesn't have to be of a cataclysmic nature to exact a large toll on others. To return a company to solid footing, jobs are often reduced and people furloughed as a part of needed cost-cutting or organizational restructuring within the firm. In a ripple effect, jobs at suppliers and in community support functions can then also be affected. Those whose jobs remain intact often find their pay reduced through lower year-end profit-sharing bonuses, lower incentive compensation payouts, reduced corporate participation in matching 401K contributions, and fewer overtime opportunities for hourly people. Opportunities for promotion and career advancements can be lost for people who worked hard for them, prompting them to significantly re-think and adjust their career plans. This can frequently lead them to make lifestyle changes, accept higher-risk jobs, relocate, take second jobs, moonlight, delay retirement, or force the unplanned return to the workforce of a non-working spouse—all of which take a huge toll on the individuals and their families.

Consequently, the effect of today's high leadership turnover is borne widely and in very real, very painful ways. Sadly, nobody escapes a failed leadership assignment unscathed. Companies *and* individuals alike pay huge prices whenever a failure occurs. So why are there so many of them nowadays?

The Rules Have Changed and So Has the Game

One of the saddest aspects of these failures is that they may have very little to do with the individuals' competence. During the past ten years the performance climate for business leaders has undergone significant changes in almost every possible dimension. It is no longer good enough to just "beat last year's top- and bottom-line numbers" to declare the year a victory. It's not even good enough to beat the same quarter's numbers every quarter through-out the year. Now, executives must beat those benchmarks plus a whole set of other expectations to be considered as having had a winning year.

The facts are that today's leaders are not only expected to do more with less and faster than ever before, they are now supposed to involve more people, produce more reports, and even provide more input and oversight into other areas as well. As one of my coaching clients recently put it in a moment of frustration, "It's not like I'm hiding anything or doing anything I shouldn't be doing. It's just that there aren't enough hours in the day to read all my e-mails and produce enough PowerPoint presentations to satisfy everyone's desire for more information, more scrutiny, more assurances, more, more, more. It's like the world has forgotten that, inherently, business is risky, and *no* amount of inspection is ever going to change that fact!"

Although reams could be written about the many changes that have impacted the nature of the leadership climate over the past decade, suffice it to say that business leaders today are faced with the challenge of having to manage a greater order of complexity in a more transparent manner and to deliver more finite results in more compressed periods of time than has any previous generation of leaders.

How Much More Perfect Can We Get?

Given this environment, the chances are greater than ever before that even the most highly trained, experienced, and capable leaders will fail to measure up to the expectations held for them at the time they are hired. This is undoubtedly why we have seen so many books and articles on the subject of leadership in the past decade. Trying to refine and improve our insights into what makes a successful leader is an understandable response. However, the lack of impact of these studies on the failure rates indicates that these analyses have probably not helped to any significant degree.

At the same time that our knowledge of what qualities a successful leader should possess has grown, there has also been an increased emphasis in defining the competencies of the candidates. Historically, the hiring process used by most companies has been focused on finding the best leader for the position based on a position description—a profile of what the ideal candidate should "look like" in terms of specific "must possess" and "desirable" experiences, education, and background. More and more frequently a specific set of competencies required of the individual is also a part of the hiring specifica-tions. The underlying belief on which the typical hiring process is built is that, "if you find the right person, he or she will know how to get the job done."

To help ensure they have found the "right" person, companies today put candidates through extensive interviews, in-depth background checks, and even psychological and behavioral assessments, which we will discuss in later chapters. In short, what has happened is that our understanding of what it takes to be a leader has been expanded greatly, and we have employed that knowledge to scrutinize candidates more closely. Even so, failure rates have increased significantly. Something is still chronically wrong.

A More "Holistic" Approach to Hiring

We have done little, however, to change how we view the job the new leader will fill and the context in which that job must be carried out. While the world has changed—the risks and costs and likelihood of leadership failures have changed, and the expectations, timetables, and the complexities of the jobs have changed—beyond looking more closely at the candidate, the Traditional Selection Process has not. As always this process still focuses on selecting the right "peg" with little, if any, effort made to understand the specific shape and nature of the "hole" into which the peg is supposed to fit.

Given the continuing failure rates of scores of bright, motivated, and, yes, competent, leaders, it is time for the paradigm to shift. It is time that companies and candidates put as much of the same critical and data-driven effort into understanding the shape of the hole as they do the shape of the peg, realizing that just because the Bill Perez peg fit well with the S.C. Johnson hole previously, it was not going to automatically fit into the Nike hole no matter how patiently or how hard it was pushed. As we have seen, trying to jam the wrong peg into the wrong hole has costly and painful consequences for one and all.

Find a Need and Meet It

Figure 1.2 depicts what we shall call throughout this book the "Traditional Selection Process" that is typically in use today.[31] It closely resembles the selection process that has been in use since the middle of the twentieth century. During the intervening decades many of the steps that make up the Traditional Selection Process have undergone refinement and change: The types of interviews that are used are vastly different from those used in the past; in addition, three steps have been added (shown in bold). But, of these, only onboarding has significantly changed the original model, and that regrettably occurs *after* the leader has already been selected.

If you look closely at the Traditional Selection Process Gantt Chart (Figure 1.2), something may strike you: Other than the second step, every one in the process, including the new onboarding one, is focused on the individual. The process has been designed to identify the right candidate for the situation. But only one of the eleven steps even attempts to analyze the

FIGURE 1.2 Traditional Selection Process

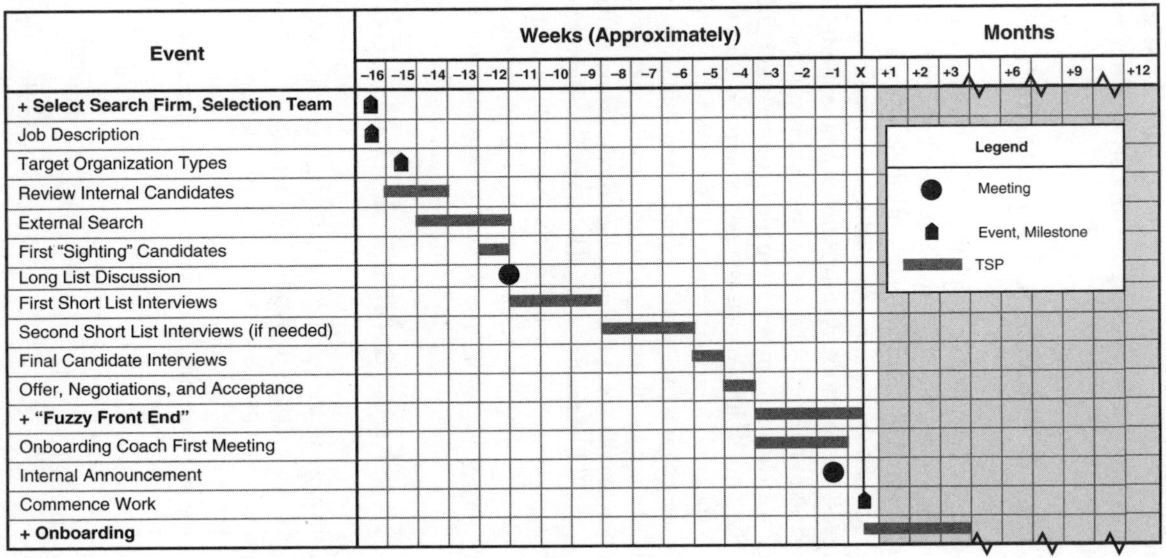

realities of the business situation that will define what the right candidate will have to accomplish.

Through my years as a journeyman CEO, I have seen a number of job specifications for various CEO positions; as the head of a career transition and outplacement company for senior executives, I have seen even more job specs during the past seven years. One of my clearest conclusions is that, if you took the company name off the top of the page, you would not be able to tell one from another. There are several reasons that this is largely true: For one, the people who write the position specifications have rarely ever actually done the job, so how would they know what it takes to do it well? Second, in this politically correct world, there is a tendency to try to put specifications in for everything anyone else has ever included, "just to be on the safe side." A third reason is that the search executives who are involved in the process will often want to help the company by broadening the specs to ensure they can cast a net wide enough to land someone for the job who might not otherwise be considered.

However, the two most compelling reasons the position specs usually look the same for the top jobs are:

1. The people who know the most about what needs to be done by the new leader to deliver the desired results—namely the direct reports of the new leader—are rarely asked. Rarer still are situations in which they are asked for their input in ways that will prompt anything other than a safe, politically correct response. In other words there is very little rigor involved in gathering data from this valuable source of highly relevant information.
2. Mistakenly the deliverables in the specifications are based on the experiences and perceptions of the people writing them and are focused on outcomes, not on hard facts expressed in terms of the specific actions required to produce these outcomes in a particular situation. Both of these points get companies into trouble when hiring new leaders.

A case in point (and just in time), follows.

Real Vs. Perceived Corporate Needs

A few years ago, my company was brought in on a consulting assignment by a NYSE-traded corporation while the search for a new CEO was underway. According to the position specifications developed by the head of HR in collaboration with the executive recruiter, the lead director, and the head of the board's search committee, one of the key attributes that the new CEO would have to possess was "strong experience dealing with sales organizations and their restructuring." The reason for this spec was that the board suspected systemic problems existed in the sales organization.

(continued)

When we looked at the company's sales performance for the previous three years, their concern seemed quite legitimate and their conclusion understandable. Sales had been basically flat for three years while previously the same field sales organization had delivered consistent growth above the industry average. This was no small feat since they were the dominant player in their industry. Clearly something had to be done to get sales growing again. Based on the perception of the board, that would entail restructuring and replacing a lot of people. They wanted to be sure that their new CEO was no stranger to this kind of work.

When we conducted our interviews with the people closest to the work, however, a very different picture began to emerge. As it turned out, the sales force had the enviable reputation of being the best trained and most disciplined of any in the industry, and the company was highly respected for its service delivery. Furthermore, every one of their competitors' top sales executives had, at one time or another, come from my client's company.

At first the pieces did not fit, but as we kept digging, we eventually got to the crux of the problem. In three of the preceding four years the former CEO had insisted on changing the sales compensation plan in an attempt to achieve alignment with that year's management directives! One year, the sales goals were based on obtaining new dealers; the next, they were based on selling new products; in the third, the incentives were intended to stimulate customer retention and increased sales through existing accounts. Since these changes were developed at the initiative of the CEO, it was self-defeating for him to go to the board and admit that, "Oops, I shouldn't have been trying to drive short-term results in a long-lead time business." Neither was the head of HR inclined to point at the numerous changes to the comp plans since he was their architect; he just went along with the board's view of the problem while developing the position specs for the new CEO. As a result the board focused on other reasons for the poor sales performance. Meanwhile, with all the changes thrown at them, the sales team did not know whether they were on foot or on horseback.

Fortunately, as a result of our findings, we were able to eliminate the requirement that the top candidate possess a heavy sales background, allowing another candidate—one who had leadership traits and background experiences that were more aligned with the true needs of the company—to get the nod. Over time, he proved to be the right person to make the changes that were really needed. These included stabilizing the sales compensation plans. By focusing on the real needs instead of the perceived needs, less time was required to reenergize the existing sales team than if restructuring the field sales organization had been pursued. A disaster had been averted.

This is one of many experiences that support our contention that the current hiring process often fails to account for the real needs of the situation. None of the steps incorporate rigorous "fact-finding" or bona fide research to verify what things *really* need to change and which changes should come first. Nor, as in the case with my client described previously, does the Traditional Selection Process identify those things that should be left alone.

Culture—A Matter of Fitting In

Now if you look back at Figure 1.2, there is something else that should be noted—something that is missing entirely. No place in this "peg-oriented" process is there a step to identify anything about the culture of the company overall, or of the culture of the team the new hire is going to lead. Just as importantly, nowhere in this process is there a place to identify anything about the culture of the team on which the new leader is going to be a member—the boss's team.

The Nike story we told earlier helps explain the need to focus on the missing steps in the Traditional Selection Process. As it illustrates, most leaders do not fail because they cannot do the job. They fail because the way they go about it is simply not compatible with the culture of one or more of the prevailing groups they have joined. In other words, leaders do not fail just because of *what* they do; their problems usually stem as much from *how* they do it. Yet nowhere in the Traditional Selection Process is there any step to specify the kind of culture(s) through which the proverbial "right person" is supposed to work effectively. Without that knowledge, how are hirers supposed to know what characteristics to look for that are necessary for someone to fit in here?

The day after William Perez "resigned," the *New York Times* ran a story under the headline, "Another Outsider Falls Casualty to Nike's Insider Culture." It identified several key points about Nike's culture that included: New hires are expected to operate within strict "lines of orthodoxy"; there were unclear lines of authority and responsibility at the top; there were entrenched pockets of political resistance on the team Perez inherited; certain changes were viewed as being "off-limits"; and that outsiders have had difficulty transitioning successfully into the company.[32]

So, if this information about the culture of the Nike organization was available for publication the day *after* Mr. Perez got the boot, wasn't it probably available the day before he left, too? Then, how about the day thirteen months earlier before he *arrived*? Based upon my experiences over these past years, I am quite certain that every bit of this information about the Nike culture that so curtailed Bill Perez's effectiveness was completely available *before* he accepted the offer. But no one seems to make the effort to look for them.

Had Mr. Perez had access to the information about Nike's culture prior to deciding to join them, he would have had two clear-cut options to deal with the situation: He could have elected to *refuse* the position if the problems were more than he wanted to tackle, or he could have elected to *change* the way he went about doing things. When faced with a new set of facts, leaders consistently demonstrate a remarkable ability to adapt to the most demanding of situations and, in effect, modify the shape of their own "peg-ness" to better fit into the "hole" at hand. As we shall see, however, this leadership malleability works only up to a point; it is more likely to affect behaviors associated with style than those connected to the leader's values and basic business beliefs.

The New Leadership Selection Strategy

This is what *The Right Leader* is all about—using the time either before a search begins or concurrent with it to identify and analyze the missing factors that the candidate will have to address: first, the people, processes, structure, strategy, and capital (the true "needs") of the company; and second, the nature of the cultures in which he or she will have to work.

The Leadership Selection Process this book describes is truly revolutionary. It adds entirely new steps to the Traditional Process. It changes the paradigm so that the capabilities of the selected individual not only match the needs of the company, but it also ensures that his or her character fits with the culture of the company. Without increasing the time that selection takes, the Accelerated Leader Selection Process provides the company and the hiree with two vital elements:

1. **A true understanding of what needs to be done to be successful.** What needs to be done should have a big impact on who is selected to do it. Unfortunately, without sufficient rigor, the needs that make it into the hiring specification for most leadership positions tend to be those based on perceptions and not facts. It is time to incorporate those same data-driven principles into the hiring process that have worked to reduce costs and improve quality in other disciplines. Getting to the real needs entails conducting research and building the hiring process on hard data instead of on perceptions, opinions, and politically correct generalizations. The expression, "You can't manage what you can't measure," which serves as the philosophic foundation of Six Sigma, "Lean," and Continuous Improvement processes is just as applicable to the hiring process as to any other area of the business.

2. **A clearer understanding of what it means for an executive to "fit" the organization and the importance of obtaining proper fit.** The second change is the addition of an element that heretofore has been

absent—a methodology that bursts the bubble surrounding the term "culture" and helps to define, describe, measure, and clarify exactly what and how a *particular* culture can affect a *particular* leader's success or failure in a *particular* work situation. It is time that the shape of the "hole"—the cultures of the corporation and of the work teams of which the new "peg" will be a member—are measured and analytically defined. It is time to treat culture like any other factor critical to the company's success—to measure it to manage it.

This is not to say that the current hiring model should be abandoned entirely. On the contrary, all the excellent work that has gone in to refining the existing steps should remain intact. But it is time to incorporate further, purposeful improvements to what is there while adding what is missing from the process into it. Only then will the process be responsive to the realities of today's work environment and reduce the risks and extraordinary costs of failed leadership.

The good news for those who must lead the hiring process and are under the gun to "fill the slot yesterday" is that the work associated with these changes to the hiring process can be, and often *should* be, conducted simultaneously with the existing traditional steps in the selection process so no incremental time is required to complete it. Another piece of good news is that these changes are best performed by independent consultants so the burden of work does not land on some already overworked individual within the company who may be ill-prepared to handle the task. More importantly, though, the work needs to be done by an outsider because nobody who is a part of a given culture can detach themselves from it sufficiently to examine and describe it objectively. That, as we shall see, is a very real part of the nature of cultures. Finally it should be clear that there is a huge cost-benefit justification to implementing these changes instead of the simple rationale that "it's the right thing to do." Even so, for many, many good reasons, selecting the *right* leader *is* the right thing to do.

Takeaways

Here's a quick recap of the current state of the executive selection process:

- The failure rate of CEOs (and other senior leaders) today seems to have plateaued at record highs—more than 50 percent greater than just a few years ago. Performance-related terminations of CEOs are more than three times what they were ten years ago. The costs of a failed leadership assignment are huge and go well beyond the direct cash costs incurred by companies. Even without monetizing the costs of lost market cap and the impact of increased stock volatility, the costs of today's turnover at the top after just eighteen months in the job ranges between $12.6 and $52.5 million depending on the size of the company.

- Smaller companies are hurt more than large ones primarily because they have less room for error due to their size, relative to the direct costs associated with CEO failures.

- In total the cost to the U.S. economy for selecting the wrong leaders is approximately $14 billion per year in cash, inefficiencies, and opportunities foregone.

- Leadership failures have far-reaching implications for many, many people, well beyond those who are directly affected. Sadly, no one escapes a failed leadership transition unscathed.

- The world has changed, and so have the risks, costs, and likelihood of leadership failures. Changes have also occurred in the expectations for deliverables, timetables for achievement, and the complexities associated with virtually every aspect of leaders' jobs. The Traditional Selection Process used for selecting leaders has not, however, changed significantly to keep pace.

- The Traditional Selection Process focuses on the right "peg" with little, if anything, done to rigorously comprehend the specific shape and nature of the "hole" into which the peg is supposed to fit—the true needs of the company and its various cultures into which the right leader will have to fit to deliver the expected results.

- The Traditional Selection Process should not be abandoned entirely, but it is time to make some needed improvements and to incorporate what is missing into it.

PART ONE

The New Paradigm for Leadership Selection

2

Design for a New
Selection Model

There is a time for everything . . . a time to keep and a time to throw away . . .

—Ecclesiastes 3

What's Now Showing Is Probably a Rerun

There are times when the movies can provide us with valuable learning experiences. Unencumbered by the constraints of reality, Hollywood writers can, and often do, manage to reduce the human experience to its basic elements. How often have we seen the following interview depicted in the movies in one form or another over the years:

The scene: a horse corral (or gangland garage or army barracks)
(The scene opens with Character A addressing Character B.)
Character A (A ranch foreman or mob boss or army sergeant):
". . . So your name's Slim (or Mugsy or Murphy).What is it ya do?"
Character B (A cowboy or gangster or private):
"I'm jest a wrangler (or safecracker or demolition specialist)."
Character A:
"And where'd you learn how to do that?"
Character B:
"Rio Lobo (or da South Side or Fort Bragg, sir)."
Character A:
"And how long have you been at it?"
Character B:
"Since I was born (or got outta the pen or volunteered), sir."
Character A:
"And what, exactly, do you want from me?"
Character B:
"I come for some work. I'm sure you could use a good cowpuncher
(or safecracker or demolitions guy) around here from the
looks o' things."
Character A: (After a long gaze, sizing Character B up and down.)
"You look like you can handle the job alright, but you must be crazy
to want it. Get settled in, come back later, and I'll fill you in on
what's going on."
Character B: (Picking up his saddle or violin case or B-4 bag.)
"Thanks, Pardner (or Boss or Sarge). You won't regret this."
Character B exits screen left, passing Character C, who has been sitting on a
hay bale (or car fender or caisson) listening all the while.
Character C (A close but junior comrade to Character A):

"Now, what'd you go and do that for? You ain't never even met that cowboy (or punk or dogface) before. How do you know he's one of us and not some rustler (or cop or wet-behind-the-ears malingerer)?"

Character A (thoughtfully):

"I don't know . . . There's just something about him that tells me he may just be the wrangler (or hitman or soldier) we've been lookin' for."

Fade to black . . .

We can accept even the shorthand format of the above scene because it is a caricature of what we know to be the essence of selecting new team members. Although stripped of all the steps that go into the real-world selection process, these outtakes still resonate with us. As moviegoers we are comfortable because the individual gets to join the team through practices that resemble what we know collectively to be the basics of the current hiring system.

This chapter focuses on the model that the current selection process is based on. In it, we'll take a look at:

- The concepts of match and fit and how they are being used in the selection process
- The influences that character and culture have
- How modifying the model can lead to the creation of a new, more successful selection process

How it Works (or Doesn't)

In reality it is unlikely that even a cowboy (or gangster, or demolitions expert) is going to get hired as the result of such a quick interaction as the movies portray. However, they still affirm that in order for an individual to be chosen for any position, whether in the movies or in reality, two fundamental questions must be answered:

1. Can this person do what needs to be done here?
2. Will this person fit in here?

And while the familiar, celluloid hiring scenes are oversimplified and dramatically abbreviated, they are, unfortunately, not always too far from what actually occurs. Take, for example, a situation I experienced.

A Match Made (Quickly) in Heaven

In November 1999, I had been at the helm of CAMCO, Inc. for five years. The largest manufacturer and marketer of major home appliances in Canada, CAMCO was General Electric's affiliate there. Although GE was our largest shareholder, CAMCO was a public company, and I had gathered a great deal of knowledge and experience in my role as chairman, president, and CEO. My leadership mettle had been well tested, and I was considered a proven CEO.

That December I began to transition out of my responsibilities while remaining the nonexecutive chairman of the company. I had hired and groomed my successor and the five-year commitment I had made to the board would soon be over. My personal plan was to take three months off before beginning a job search in earnest. I could use some R&R. However, to play it safe, I cobbled together an updated résumé, along with a brief cover letter describing my intended plans, and sent them to a handful of executive search professionals I had come to know over the years.

On December 16 I received a call from John Wood in the New York office of the search firm Spencer Stuart. A mutual contact had sent him a copy of my résumé, and he was calling to see if I would come to New York to discuss a situation he had just been retained on. The search was on behalf of World Kitchen, Inc. (WKI), a highly leveraged, $1 billion rollup of three housewares companies owned by the private equity firm of Kohlberg, Kravis, Roberts, & Co. (KKR). They had been looking for a CEO for several months and had seen a number of candidates, but none had clicked. John had just been engaged to see if he and his resources could help find the right person for the position.

Just nine working days later, on January 3, 2000, I signed a term sheet agreeing to become the president and CEO of World Kitchen, a job that in everyone's eyes I was eminently qualified for. During the days between December 16 and January 3, I had met with the key people from KKR and the WKI board. Since the rollup had occurred, literally, only days before, I used the bank plans as my source of due-diligence information. Everyone took time off for Christmas and to ring in the new millennium, yet we still found enough to determine that, not only could I do the job, but that I was the best person they had seen to fit into the World Kitchen environment. From everyone's perspective it was truly a "match made in heaven."

The Basic Script

The selection process that companies have been using during the post-World War II era involves many more steps than those shown in the movies or even at WKI. In some instances, the questions that are asked can become quite specific, and the process can be highly structured. Yet regardless of how simple or elaborate the various steps may be or how much (or little!) time is devoted to each, the two fundamental questions they are all intended to answer are still the same: Can the individual do the job? And will he or she fit in here?

As my experience with WKI suggests, these two elements—the match and the fit—are so basic to the selection process that events can move quite quickly depending on the participants' degree of comfort with them. World Kitchen needed a proven leader with in-depth knowledge of consumer durables manufacturing and marketing to execute the bank plans and to integrate the previously separate businesses. The ownership group needed someone who could deliver the expected results, and all those involved, myself included, felt it was absolutely the right decision for me to join the company. The questions that were central to their selection processes had been answered even though the steps of the process had been significantly condensed.

The Plot Thickens

The script World Kitchen used is the one most contemporary corporations follow to select candidates. We refer to it as the "Traditional Selection Process," and it is illustrated in Figure 1.2 (shown in Chapter 1). This process is intended to get at the answers to the two basic hiring questions as efficiently and as accurately as possible.

Figure 2.1 depicts the underlying construct on which the Traditional Selection Process is built. In this model the candidate can be seen as possessing certain abilities. These include his or her talents, accumulated experiences, knowledge, and skills. The extent to which they align with the perceived needs of the company is often referenced as "the match."[1]

Without getting tied up in a lot of technical, psychological jargon, the outward appearance of the individual—the way he or she behaves and displays his or her abilities—is referred to in the model as "personality." Many people think of the connection between the personality of the candidate and the company as the individual's "fit."

The steps comprising the Traditional Selection Process are all geared toward determining the extent to which a given candidate's abilities match up with the perceived needs of the situation and the extent to which, based on

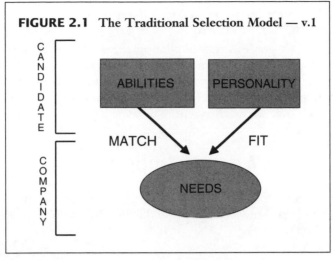

FIGURE 2.1 The Traditional Selection Model — v.1

outward appearances, he or she will fit into the work situation. *If* the perceived needs are indeed what is really needed in a particular situation, then having measurable parameters of ability is a good thing.

Take Me to Your Leader

Of the two—match and fit—the greater emphasis is invariably placed on the match in the Traditional Selection Process. There are several reasons for this:

1. In our results-oriented business world, the ability to deliver the goods and make the numbers is valued much more than the way the results are achieved. The mantra, "Get me someone qualified to do this job!" invariably refers to the candidate's ability, not their personality.

2. Because abilities can usually be expressed in tangible, measurable terms in position descriptions, those involved in facilitating the selection process will stress the importance of these traits to demonstrate accountability. For instance, abilities can be measured when expressed as X number of years of industry experience, the requisite undergraduate degree, a desirable MBA, or the availability to relocate. Either a candidate has these characteristics or they do not. Sticking to the job specs puts the emphasis on the candidate's abilities rather than on the intangibles involved in assessing his or her personality. Because they are measurable, candidates who possess these quantifiable characteristics

are the ones who get presented for consideration before any other aspects are even considered.

3. Success in a previous situation (another measure of ability) is usually looked on as a key barometer of future success in a new one. Even though the statistics regarding CEO failures do not support this contention, the perception of its truth does add fuel to the importance of ability over personality.[2]

When to Improvise

Those limited situations when the importance of someone fitting in may win out over their demonstrated ability to do the job are occasionally found. They include the following:

1. In some positions looking the part is considered as important as doing it. In heavily sales-oriented leadership positions, for instance, an energetic, extroverted persona may be a heavy component of the job. In these situations, specific skills may take a backseat to personality. While seeming to defy both logic and propriety, there are times when form is valued over content or, more accurately, to achieve success, form becomes content. These situations are rare, but they do exist.

2. Occasionally no highly qualified people are available for the job. When nobody is found who has demonstrated the abilities that the hirer thinks are essential to perform the job, some will move fit higher up the selection scale. They figure the proper fit will give the candidate the time they need to learn what they did not know at the start. If all candidates are viewed as equally ill-qualified for a position, the lowest risk candidate would then be the one who seems to at least fit well into the situation. This situation is not uncommon in very hot job markets when demand for qualified executives outstrips the supply—during the halcyon days of the dot-com bubble, for example.

3. The more hierarchical the organization and the more concentrated the power at the top, the more likely the choice of leaders will emphasize the fit than it will the extent to which the individual's capabilities align with the organization's needs (the match).

The Actors Lurking in the Shadows

In the movie scenes at the beginning of this chapter, you may have sensed that there was more to the rancher's (or mobster's or sergeant's) decision to hire the cowboy (or hitman or demolitions specialist) than just the candidate's skills and personality. The hirer's long gaze as he sized up the candidate and his answer to Character C's (his sidekick's) anxious question pertaining to fit ("Now, what'd you go and do that for? You ain't never even met that cowboy [or punk or dogface] before!") suggest that there is more to be considered when hiring someone than just tangible skills or demeanor. As a matter of fact the most significant element of the fit equation is deeper than personality.

In other words, there is more to the selection process than just evaluating ability, personality, and company needs. While doing so will satisfy the main objectives of the Traditional Selection Process, there is more to people than just their abilities and personality. *And* there is more to work than just needs.

Although not depicted earlier in the overview of the Traditional Selection Model (Figure 2.1), there are generally three other elements taken into consideration during executive selection, although not often in any formal way. Figure 2.2 shows these shadowy areas that hirers are aware of but rarely address directly: one is the *energy* of the candidate; another is their *character*; and a third is the organization's *culture*.

Energy. Have you ever gone down to the paddock area at a racetrack when the thoroughbreds are being saddled and readied for the race? If so, you know what the presence of physical energy looks and feels like—there is an electricity in the area that emanates from the horses, each of which is primed to do what it has been bred and trained for.

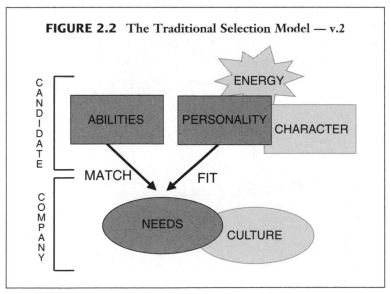

FIGURE 2.2 The Traditional Selection Model — v.2

People, too, have energy that, like racehorses and other creatures, has a large physical component. But human energy goes beyond the purely physical. Human energy includes mental, emotional, and spiritual elements as well. When we think of a candidate as "being high-powered," or "really centered," or "grounded," we are invariably talking about the level of their energy, or its abundance, or its quality.

Top-level jobs are incredibly demanding, and to be successful, leaders need a replenishable source of energy. Jim Loehr and Tony Schwartz, authors of *The Power of Full Engagement,* regard energy as "the fundamental currency of high performance."[3] While closely related to personality in that we can see it (or at least sense it), only energy is manifest in the way people behave; in their eye contact, their presence, their self-confidence, and the degree to which they are engaged. Loehr and Schwarz describe full engagement in the following manner:

> *To be fully engaged, we must be physically energized, emotionally connected, mentally focused, and spiritually aligned with purpose beyond our immediate self-interest. Full engagement begins with feeling eager to get to work in the morning, equally happy to return home in the evening, and capable of setting clear boundaries between the two. It means being able to immerse oneself in the mission you're on whether that is grappling with a creative challenge at work, managing a group on a project, spending time with loved ones, or simply having fun.[4]*

Character. As Jim Collins emphasizes in *Good to Great*, getting the right people on board is critical.[5] Therefore, those who do the selecting need to understand that the organization's most important asset is not people, it is the *right* people. To ensure they get those people, it is vital for executives to confirm that the people they hire have the character as well as innate capabilities (not skills) that fit.

An important part of character is trustworthiness. That quality is in turn a key element in determining whether someone fits well with an organization. In fact, trust and trustworthiness are absolutely central to the fit question. As Stephen R. Covey so clearly asserts in all of his writings about principle-centered leadership: ". . . trust is essential to cooperation and long-term personal and interpersonal growth. . . . When trust is high, communication is easy, instant, and effective."[6]

While trustworthiness is not a part of a candidate's personality, it may play a big part in determining the degree to which he or she belongs in a given situation. Taken to an extreme, however, too much emphasis on trustworthiness can become a very ugly thing. In situations where trustworthiness, allegiance, and loyalty take precedence over competence, nepotism, or favoritism (usually in the form of exclusionary, good-old-folk networks) will prevail over qualifications. Sad, but true.

As we will see later, there are other elements of character (such as beliefs and values) that are also crucial to determining whether or not someone fits in. That is why it is especially unfortunate that very little has been done in the Traditional Selection Process to spend effort in determining much about a candidate's character.

The primary reason is that, in American society (along with many others), discussing or openly exploring character is something to be frowned upon. To even *ask* a question about someone's character can be taken as an insult; as recently as 150 years ago in the United States or in Europe, you could end up losing your life in a duel for "questioning my honor, sir!" Even now in the gang-dominated neighborhoods of L.A. and Detroit, it is still the case that dissing (disrespecting someone's reputation) is grounds for bloodletting. One's character is generally still *not* something to be questioned.

In fact, the taboo on asking legitimate questions about a person's character is so ingrained in our thinking that even reference checks shy away from digging into anything that might suggest a character problem. Add to it today's increased emphasis on preserving personal privacy (fostered by increased laws and regulations), and a real shroud makes getting at the essence of a candidate's character very difficult.

Because one's character is not subject to the same scrutiny as stated abilities or even personality in the Traditional Selection Process, some people who lack the necessary character will misrepresent themselves and their credentials during the interview process in order to get the job. Some will even go so far as to lie about their backgrounds and experiences in order to get ahead. Take, for example, George O'Leary, Notre Dame's football coach for five days, or Gene Shen, a longtime professional recruiter who was named president and CEO of A.T. Kearney. When claims made on their résumés proved false, both had to resign.[7]

While anyone from the HR or executive search ranks who has been trained in various interview techniques can get a fairly accurate bead on a candidate's character, few hiring executives can do little more on this score than trust their own intuition. In reality, corporate America's selection process really is not that far removed from the movie scenes depicted at the beginning of the chapter. I know of situations where qualified candidates have been dinged because someone on the Selection Team "wouldn't want to sit next to him or her on a cross-country flight," and another where a member of the Selection Team dropped a candidate from contention because, "While I like him well enough, I wouldn't want him as my best friend."

In other words, the assessment of a candidate's character too often comes down to a hiring executive's mistaken belief that "You can learn enough about who a person really is in a single round of golf." Or, as the rancher (or mobster or sergeant) in our movie example put it, "I don't know . . . but there's just something about him that tells me he may just be what we're looking for."

While there *is* a place for "gut feel" in almost every decision regarding people, overdependence on it can, and often does, result in disaster. It is through someone's reliance on intuition more than on facts that some executives who do not belong in top leadership jobs usually end up there. Because they presented themselves well, or possessed a charismatic personality and could talk the talk, they wound up being selected for top jobs for which they otherwise had no business even being considered.

Culture. The third shadow that is lurking in the Traditional Selection Model is culture. Although the term "culture" was not in the lexicon of most business executives twenty years ago, everyone knew culture existed and that all organizations possess it. Today most enlightened executives will acknowledge that the culture of their company is the thing that sets it apart from its competitors and is the source of one of its greatest competitive advantages.

We know companies have cultures, and culture is something that needs to be appreciated and respected. We also know that each company's culture is unique. Equally important, we know at the gut level how relevant culture is in determining whether or not someone really fits an organization. Yet few, if any, executives actually know what "culture" is and could define the word "culture" if asked; nor could they describe their culture in any quantifiable terms. The reason is that, up until now, no satisfactory methodology has existed.

We live in an age that has spawned increasingly finite controls on costs, highly granular strategic plans (an oxymoron), Six Sigma, "Lean," and Continuous Improvement processes—all under the mantra that, "If you can't measure it, you can't manage it." That is why it is a bit surprising that something as pervasive and as important as culture would not have come under scrutiny long before this. But it has not. It has been labeled part of that "soft stuff" and avoided like the plague.

Since executives do not know how to define culture, and they cannot measure it, one might conclude then that they do not know what they are talking about. Actually, this is not altogether true.

In 1957 the U.S. Supreme Court rendered an unprecedented opinion about pornography in *Roth v. United States.* In the course of the deliberations, Justice Potter Stewart was quoted as saying, "I don't know what it is, but I do know it when I see it."[8] This is also the way most executives regard culture. They do not know exactly what it *is,* but they do know what it *feels* like. Like Justice Stewart, they know culture as they experience it. They know what it is because they live it. They know the culture of their company because they are in it—well, at least in part of it. As we will see later, however, the way they experience it is rarely the same as the way the rest of the organization does. So the way they know it and the way the rest of the organization knows it are usually quite different. This difference in how people inside a culture perceive it often contributes to the problems in the Traditional Selection Process. Like energy and character, culture lacks a definitive role in the existing process for selecting leaders. It is time to give them a real place.

Introducing the Match-Fit Model

One way to bring energy, character, and culture out of the shadows of the Traditional Selection Process is to create a new selection model. Figure 2.3 depicts the one Crenshaw Associates has developed, which we have dubbed the "Match-Fit Model."

Up until our firm began developing this model, the terms "match" and "fit" had often been used interchangeably. There was no real distinction between them as they were commonly used, except that the connotation of "fit" tended to imply that the person's style (or personality) was similar to that of others in the company and thus she or he would probably "get along well here."

The significance of the Match-Fit Model is that:

- It defines a model—a conceptual construct—where previously there were only vague and disjointed notions of undefined concepts; only an informal set of shadowy notions.

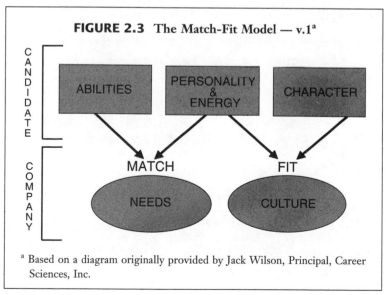

FIGURE 2.3 The Match-Fit Model — v.1[a]

[a] Based on a diagram originally provided by Jack Wilson, Principal, Career Sciences, Inc.

- This model permits analysis and redesign of the selection process.
- Terms are clarified and now take on specific meaning.

In the Match-Fit Model, "match" is a function of how well the candidate's abilities, personality (behaviors), and energy relate to the needs of the company. And the crucial "fit" of the new leader now comes down to a blend of personality (often referred to in this context as "style"), energy, and character relative to the culture of the company.

Shaping the Match-Fit Model

As we started working with this model and learning how to use it to improve the basis on which leaders can be selected for any position (not just those at the very top), we began to observe aspects of it that needed to be fleshed out. Almost at once we decided to take a closer look at what is meant by "needs." The modification that resulted appears in Version 2 of the Match-Fit Model (Figure 2.4).

This refinement reflects the realization that there are two distinct types of needs with which leaders must be able to deal: Some are executional needs. These are tactical in nature—they must be accomplished for the company to succeed.[9]

The other kind of needs is directional. Directional needs, as the term implies, are those that chart the strategic course for the company to achieve long-term success. Directional needs include such capabilities as defining a vision for the organization, determining its mission, developing new

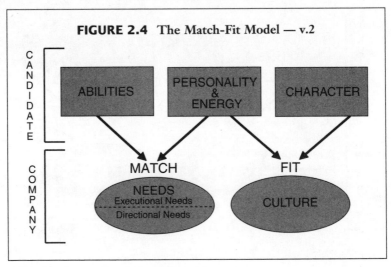

FIGURE 2.4 The Match-Fit Model — v.2

strategies, driving the creation of annual operating plans, and overseeing their successful execution. Together the mix of executional needs and directional needs will drive the job specs for the position being filled. To be meaningful, however, they must be based on facts and not on perceptions.

One of the problems with the Traditional Selection Process is that needs have not historically been well defined. Needs—both executional and directional—must involve action to achieve the desired outcomes. Directional needs, in particular, should be defined in terms of specific, tangible, time-phased deliverables, not just generalized descriptors that portray desired outcomes like, "the candidate must be able to create a strategic vision for the company and energize people around it." When the true needs of the company are defined on the basis of facts (who, why, when, what, where), their type and nature significantly alter the defination of what it takes to make the right match for the situation. They can then be used to define the real competencies and experiences candidates must possess.

Multi-Cultures Do Not Make You Multicultural

Eventually a second change to the Match-Fit Model was needed in the area of culture. Many years of working with executives in transition—onboarding them, coaching them to grow in their current assignments, and guiding them through outplacement—has exposed us to a range of stories about careers and corporate experiences. From these it has become clear that success is determined not only by a proper fit with the culture of the overall organization, but by the fit with the team he or she leads personally, as well as with the team on which he or she is a member—the boss's team.

These two key subcultures are depicted in Version 3 of the Match-Fit Model shown in Figure 2.5. They are paramount to the concept of fit; lack of compatibility with either of these two teams—the leader's team and the boss's team—will usually spell disaster for senior-level executives more so than a lack of fit with the organization at large.[10]

My experience at World Kitchen illustrates how these important subcultures can make a difference. Remember that wonderful match made (quickly) in heaven I described earlier? Well, it probably would have been wonderful if not for one cultural conflict I encountered. Although I fit the culture of the company and that of the leadership team I assembled, I simply did not fit into the culture of the private-equity ownership group of which I was also expected to be a part. The five preceding years as chairman of a public company had confirmed my strong sense of independence, reinforced my self-defined position as a "planned-growth guy," and put my horizon for measuring meaningful results farther out than the monthly-quarterly focus of the financially driven private equity owners. We just did not share enough of the same principles about how to run a business to make things workable in the long run. While there were other contributing factors, I had to face the fact that at this stage of my career I was just not interested in becoming that kind of "private-equity guy." It's not that it's bad, but it just wasn't for me. A year to the day after joining WKI I was gone—to the relief of both the KKR owners *and* me.

For the expat executive, the issue of culture has yet another dimension. Besides dealing with the cultures of the organization and its two important subgroups, the expat must relate to the culture of the country (society) in which his or her business unit operates and from which it draws its people. Clearly, this culture can have a huge impact on the leader's fit with a particular assignment. In today's world of global businesses, this factor is as important to the American CEO based in Holland as it is to the Japanese group executive responsible for the U.S. operations headquartered in New York City. With so many global touch points for business leaders today, a sensitive working knowledge of differences among cultures is essential. Even with the United States, an executive moving from one region to another (such as Boston to Savannah, or even Atlanta) may encounter important cultural shifts.

Looking Back, Looking Ahead

So, the final version of the Match-Fit Model that we will be using to develop the Leader Selection Process of the future is Version 3, as shown in Figure 2.5.

It recognizes that the paradigm underlying the selection process in use today is both flawed and incomplete. As a result the Traditional Selection

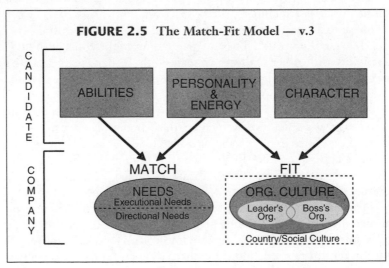

FIGURE 2.5 The Match-Fit Model — v.3

Copyright © 2009 Crenshaw Associates

Process cannot, and does not, work in today's globalized business world. It places too much emphasis on the candidate's abilities and to a lesser degree, their personality and energy, and not anywhere near enough on his or her character. It focuses too heavily on the company's *perceived* needs and not enough on the short- and long-range actions that the new leader must take. More significant, it fails to recognize the enormous importance of the various cultures at play in any hiring situation.

In the chapters that follow in Part One, we will look at each of the key elements of the Match-Fit Model v.3 to understand what makes it up and how it impacts the more comprehensive Leader Selection Process of the future. Three of the most important concerns we will address pertain to the elements the candidates bring to the process. In the paradigm we have created, these are lumped into three buckets: the candidates' abilities (Chapter 3), their personality and energy (Chapter 4), and their character (Chapter 5). Each of these buckets consists of qualities that go into the makeup of all human beings. What we have to determine is how those qualities are currently being identified and assessed and how they might be described differently. We can then take a look at those attributes of companies that affect the new selection process—their executional and directional needs (Chapter 6) and the company cultures (Chapter 7). Once we have identified some new ways to determine the true nature of the forces affecting what it takes to be the *right* leader for a given position, we will be better prepared to design a more effective selection process in Part Two—a selection process that uses familiar elements in some exciting new ways.

Takeaways

The following are some of the key points that were hopefully made clear during this chapter introducing you to the Match-Fit Model:

- The Traditional Selection Process is based on an old paradigm, depicted here as the Traditional Selection Model.
- Statistics and experience suggest that other factors need to be considered when selecting leaders than just those represented in the traditional model. It no longer does an adequate job of supporting a selection process that works.
- In the existing model, a candidate's abilities usually receive more attention and weight than his or her personality.
- The traditional model does not directly take the energy or the character of the candidate or the culture(s) of the organization into consideration.
- In reality, there are two different types of company needs that can significantly alter the profile of a leader whose abilities and personality

and energy best matches up with them—executional needs (such as operating processes, discipline, delivering timely results, restructuring, cost-containment, and the like) and directional needs (including visioning, mission creation, strategies, organization development, and more).

- Historically, needs are usually expressed in job specifications as they are perceived to exist rather than based on current research or hard data. They are also usually expressed in terms of outcomes rather than actions required.

- There are many cultures in any work setting: The culture of the larger society and the culture of the organization, along with the subcultures of the team the leader leads and that of the team on which the leader must play a role as a member must be considered.

- The Match-Fit Model provides a construct where previously there was only an informal set of vague, often interchangeable terms and undefined concepts.

- The Match-Fit Model redefines the factors that determine what makes a good match (abilities and personality) and the extent to which a person (their personality and character) really fits into a given situation.

- The Match-Fit Model not only permits analysis and redesign of the Traditional Selection Process, but it calls for it.

- In the following chapters of Part One, we will look at each of the five elements that make up the Match-Fit Model. This overview, although broad, will provide sufficient understanding to put new insights to use to start formulating in Part Two a selection process that works better than the one in use today.

3

The Abilities Bucket

Able was I ere I saw Elba

—well-known palindrome

T his quotation, which some link to Napoleon, is reportedly the longest palindrome in the English language. For our purposes, however, its value lies in its implicit truth about abilities: Abilities are an enduring part of each individual who possesses them, and they are transportable from place to place. (Well, maybe not a place as forsaken as Elba!)

In terms of the three attribute buckets that candidates bring to the selection process—abilities, personality and energy, and character—the assessment of abilities is by far the best-developed and refined element of the Traditional Selection Process. In fact the assessment of abilities relative to a job spec is what the Traditional Selection Process is all about. There are, nevertheless, some new insights that are proving useful in selecting leaders whose abilities truly match the needs of the organization.

In this chapter we are going to look at the role abilities play in selecting the right leader by examining:

- The importance of abilities
- Interviewing executives
- Reference checking
- Specialized tools for assessing abilities

The Importance of A·BIL·I·TIES [ə bil'ə tēs]

Webster's defines ability as: "1. a) being able; power to do (something physical or mental) 2. a) skill, expertness, or talent."[1] When used in reference to selecting a candidate, the term usually takes into account all those learned and inherent skills, knowledge, aptitudes, talents, and intellectual capabilities that allow an individual to accomplish certain executive functions at appropriate levels of expertise to achieve certain predetermined outcomes.

A belief that what the individual was capable of doing elsewhere can be replicated satisfactorily in a new situation rests at the heart of the Traditional Selection Process. This is why most companies place so much emphasis, time, and scrutiny on fully understanding a candidate's capabilities—the more they know about a candidate's abilities the better prepared they believe they will be to answer the two basic questions raised in the previous chapter:

1. Can this person do what needs to be done here?
2. Will this person fit in here?

For this reason, interviews are heavily oriented toward gaining an appreciation of the candidate's true abilities and whether or not he or she can actually do the work that needs to be done. To see just how important abilities are in the Traditional Selection Process one only needs to look at the tool most candidates use to "get an interview" with a company—the résumé.

Résumés emphasize abilities. In fact, abilities are what résumés are designed to describe. Other than a few lines about the candidate's aspirations and an occasional reference to some outside activities (family, sports, charity work, and the like), the most effective, time-tested résumés portray their authors with the broadest and deepest set of capabilities space permits. As chairman of a firm that has prepared literally thousands of résumés for senior executives over the past twenty-five years, I can assure you that *no* relevant accomplishment that serves to demonstrate a key leadership ability is over-looked! As much as possible, metrics are incorporated to tell the proficiency of the story—how big, how fast, and exactly under what circumstances were results achieved. If the résumé is an advertisement for an individual to get an interview, then the feature-benefit story used to excite the reader to action is strictly one about abilities.

This emphasis on the strength of certain necessary abilities makes sense. While the key to success is not nearly as simple as anyone would like it to be— simply a strong alignment between a leader's abilities and the needs of the situation—it is safe to say that someone who possesses only a few of the key abilities needed for the job has a much lower chance of succeeding. When looking at a candidate's abilities, it boils down to the question, "Can we expect this person to be able to do what is needed here at the required level of competency?"

Interviewing Executives

Although the specific ways in which most companies go about assessing the abilities of senior executives varies greatly, clearly the primary tools used to make the determination regarding external candidates are interviews and reference checks. Interviews are used for internal candidates, too.

While the interview is the most important way to get a true appreciation for an internal or external candidate's abilities, interviews can vary greatly from place to place and from person to person, depending upon:

- The culture of the organization
- The way in which the Traditional Selection Process has evolved within that particular organization
- The degree of training and experience possessed by the interviewer

In Part Two of this book, we will emphasize the importance of interviewer training in the new Leader Selection Process. This is especially needed since many of the interviewers are themselves senior executives with little or no training in interviewing techniques. For now, however, we will look at types of interviewers and interviewing techniques to see how they affect the selection of senior candidates.

In addition, we need to remember that neither the interviewer nor the interview can be effective without the most important piece in the process—a thorough and detailed description of the job that needs to be done. That comes first.

The Job Description

The first thing the hirers do in the Traditional Selection Process when setting out to select a senior executive is to get together and write down the requirements of the job. The job description, also called the position description, search specification, candidate profile, or job/position spec (specification), should, according to the creators of the *Harvard Essentials Guide: Hiring and Keeping the Best People*, include the following:

- The primary responsibilities and tasks involved in the job
- The background characteristics needed to perform the job
- The personal characteristics required
- The key features of your organization's culture
- The boss's managerial style and its implications for an effective working relationship[2]

While we agree with these premises, our experience is that far too often these essential elements are based on *perceptions* rather than *facts* and are expressed in terms of *outcomes* rather than specific, needs-related *actions*. We find this to be true particularly with top-level jobs. Without knowing the specific executional and directional needs that the new leader must address, there is no way to specify what actions must be taken. Without knowing what actions are required, there is no way to know what behaviors the individual must be capable of and therefore what previous experiences and competencies he or she must possess. Without this specificity the interviewing process gets off-track right from the start. The intent of this book is to give readers the knowledge and the methodology to factually examine both their needs and their cultures in such a way as to avoid this missing element in the Traditional Selection Process—fact gathering.

Interviewer Styles

In *Competence at Work*, Lyle and Signe Spencer provide clues as to why some interviewing techniques fail. (These are techniques that senior executives, untrained in interviewing other senior executives, frequently use.) Interviewing style is often a contributing factor to the problem of selecting the right leader under the Traditional Selection Process. The Spencers categorize traditional interviewers into five types. Without training, many senior executives may find themselves in one (or more) of these categories:

Fact-Finding Interviewer: This type of interviewer is focused on the specifics of the candidate's background—their college grade point average, the number of direct reports they have, and the like. When fact-finders focus more on the data than the reasons for it, they fail to learn much about the candidate's actual competencies.

Therapeutic Interviewer: Asking about the candidate's feelings, according to the Spencers, may be irrelevant. Some candidates do not like certain tasks, but still do them well. Competencies, as we shall see, are about achievements and skills, not about attitudes and feelings. Nevertheless, some interviewers think that an appreciation of a candidate's motives is a valuable insight into who they are and whether or not they will "fit in here." To an extent, this may be true but this information is better ascertained through a disciplined assessment of the candidate's behaviors, tracking back to their associated feelings and thoughts rather than trying to get at them directly.

Theoretical Interviewer: An interviewer who asks about beliefs and values can have results that are similar to one who focuses on feelings. Neither provides information about actual behaviors, and so the interviewer fails to learn what the candidate is actually capable of. Instead the interviewer gets a picture of what the candidate *might* look like—or looks like in his or her own mind's eye—neither of which may be close to his or her *actual* behaviors in the workplace.

Hypothetical Interviewer: This type of interviewer—who places the focus on what the candidate *would* do—suffers from the same weaknesses as the two preceding ones. Because the candidates' answers are pure speculation and disconnected from past and present reality, this type of interviewer may enjoy the mental gymnastics but fails to learn much of anything related to the important attributes of success.

Sales-Oriented Interviewer: When sales-oriented hirers conduct interviews they frequently try to interpret the information the candidate provides for them. Leading questions like, "Don't you think that this approach might work?" only put words in the candidates' mouths; they do not clarify what the candidates have done or could do to meet the company's needs.[3]

As we shall see in a little bit, there is a sixth type of interviewer that we recommend to all those who participate in the interviewing of candidates for leadership positions—the one called the Behavioral-Based Interviewer.

Types of Interviews

Just as there are a variety of interviewer types so too are there a number of different ways interviews are constructed. Although most of those used with senior executives being interviewed for leadership positions are structured, the one that is unstructured is perhaps the best known or most familiar technique—the traditional, "Tell me about yourself" approach.

The Traditional or "Tell Me About Yourself" Interview

This approach has been around for as long as there have been interviews and is undoubtedly the least regarded form in the eyes of professional interviewers. Interviewers ask the standard, favorite questions about "biggest achievement," "strengths and weaknesses," "toughest day," and the like. These traditional questions allow the candidate to highlight whatever he or she wants to highlight and avoid areas that need to be addressed. They also provide the least amount of connectivity to the needs of the position and the competencies required for success in it. Moreover, almost everybody knows what these questions are and has rehearsed their answers. John Lucht's primer on *Rites of Passage at $100,000 to $1million+* devotes twenty-eight pages to helping candidates prepare for such interviews.[4]

Structured vs. Unstructured Interviews

It is relatively rare for interviews involving C-Suite positions to be of the structured variety. However, Dr. Bradford Smart has developed an interviewing technique described in his book *Topgrading* that is a part of a highly structured and well-conceived process for assessing talent.[5] The interviews are conducted by a pair of interviewers who follow a specific sequence and often use specific phraseology during a four-hour session. While it may be quite an effective interviewing technique judging by the positive results and testimonies of his quoted clients, its suitability for use in the executive suite may not be appropriate because of its length and its structure, especially if the executives under consideration have never had exposure to it previously. Nevertheless its rigor is noteworthy.

Of the unstructured variety of interviews, several are known by multiple names. Often an interviewer will incorporate questions from one or more types into an interview, so rarely is there ever an unstructured interview made up of all one type of questions. For this reason it is better to look at unstructured interviews in terms of their types of questions rather than as types of interviews.

Motivational Interview Questions

These questions focus on the goals and motives of candidates as they relate to the job and the company.[6] The problem is that what people want to be and what they hope to achieve do not necessarily relate to what they are actually capable of doing or have done in the past. Being motivated to do a job is certainly important, but other aspects of the Ability Bucket—knowledge, skills, talents, aptitudes, and intellectual skills—certainly cannot be done without.

Situational Interview Questions

These ask candidates to describe how they would deal with different hypothetical situations that relate to the job. While more predictive than motivational questions, their shortcoming is that what people *say* they will do and what they actually *do* are often two very different things, making their answers meaningless.[7]

Brainteaser Interview Questions

Pioneered at Microsoft, this approach has been used in many technology companies for some time. Interviewers ask off-the-wall questions to see how the candidate analyzes problems, deals with stress, and reacts to unanticipated challenges: ("If you could remove any one of the fifty states, which one would it be and why? How would you weigh an airplane without using a scale?"). It also provides insight into the individual's intelligence and creativity. When the candidate does not have a great deal of experience, this kind of question may give them a chance to demonstrate capabilities that have not yet been tested.[8] This is not, however, the case at the senior levels. Like the traditional questions, brainteasers may provide some insight but do not have a lot to do with the usual challenges of leadership. They may also raise significant questions in the mind of your candidate regarding your commitment to the interview process or your ideas of proper decorum. He or she may just get up and walk out.

Stress Interview Questions

Originally designed as a very structured process involving a succession of interviewers (one at a time or en masse) whose mission was to keep the candidate off balance to see how well he or she handled stress, this technique is now employed infrequently. Individual questions, however, are interjected by some interviewers to see their effect (such as, How do you think this interview is going? I don't think we're getting to the heart of the matter [*big sigh*], Do you want to try again?).[9] Personally I am opposed to any such interview practice because it is fundamentally disingenuous, and it destroys the trust that can be built during the interview process that is so essential to the future relationship the chosen leader will have with the company. I wish I could say that these stress-creating methods no longer exist, but that is not the case. We recently had a transition client who was on the very short list for a CEO position for a company she really liked. After the final day of meetings with the private equity owners she went to bed feeling very confident and looking forward to the next day's breakfast meeting that she had been told, "You'll thoroughly enjoy." She fully expected an offer to be presented. At breakfast, the person she met, grim-faced, told her they had decided *not* to make her the offer because after she left, the concern was raised that she might not have enough energy to handle the rigors of the job. Fortunately our client stayed engaged and centered in her own self and was able to ask mature, unemotional questions and probe the issue. Before long the matter "went away," the offer appeared on the table, and our client realized that it had all been a ploy to see how she would react. She took the job having gained some insight into the trustworthiness of her PE owners.

Behavioral-Based Interviews

Also known as Behavioral Event Interviews (BEI), competency interviews, and Competency-Based Behavioral Interviews (CBBI), this technique is by far the most preferred approach to interviewing, judging by the extent to which it is used by executive recruiters and others trained in assessing executives' abilities.[10] We will generally refer to them as behavioral-based interviews (BBI), throughout the book unless we are referring to other authors' work where we will use their nomenclature. Regardless of what they are called, interviews of this type are reportedly five times more effective at predicting a person's potential behavior than traditional interviews.[11]

The premise underlying behavioral-based interviews is that, with few exceptions:

- The best predictor of future performance (in other words, future behavior) is past/behavior.
- The more recent the performance or behavior, the more likely it is to be repeated.[12]

Behavioral-based interviews can actually be implemented as structured or unstructured interviews depending upon the extent to which the questions are proscriptively followed. If done well, however, even a structured approach can (and should) feel to the candidate as though it is an unstructured conversation and not a mechanical inquisition of some sort.

Simply put, behavioral-based interviewing is a technique to get a very detailed behavioral description of how a person goes about doing their work. The goal is for the interviewer to understand what specific behaviors, thoughts, and actions the candidate has exhibited in actual situations.[13] It became known as "competency interviewing" or "competency-based behavioral interviewing" when the notion of corporate core competencies introduced in 1994 by Gary Hamel was adopted in the HR arena to refer to the unique skills required for success a particular role.[14]

Behavioral-Event Questions

According to the Spencers the central objective of the behavioral-based interviews (which they prefer to call Behavioral-Event Interviews) is for the interviewee to describe, in detail, four to six complete stories of critical incidents that are related to key aspects (competencies) of the job. They describe the five key questions to be asked this way:

1. "What was the situation? What events led up to it?"
2. "Who was involved?"
3. "What did you (the candidate) think, feel, or want to do in the situation?"
4. "What did you actually *do* or say?"
5. "What was the outcome? What happened?"[15]

Criteria for Interviews

When interviewing senior-level executives, the framework for exploring competencies that one of the prominent executive recruitment firms uses is reportedly based on vignettes about:

- Knowledge, experience, and results
- Performance competencies
- Personal competencies

The results from behavioral-based interviews that probe these areas will provide them with important insights into not only the candidate's skills, but also into areas such as setting strategy, leading teams, interpersonal acumen, and so forth.

EQ and BEI/CBBI

The concept of emotional intelligence (referred to as "EQ" for "Emotional Quotient") came on the corporate interviewing scene in 1995 with the publication of Daniel Goleman's popular book by that name.[16] The value of the concept to the selection process has since lost some of its initial luster.

Nevertheless, author Adele Lynn has adapted the concepts of EQ to the behavioral–based interview technique, which she prefers to call the "Competency Based Behavioral Interview" (CBBI). By using the "drill down" approach of BBI/CBBI, interviewers can gain great insight into those competencies related to emotional intelligence, not just knowledge and skills. This is an important concept because later on in this book we are going to recommend that the same approach be adopted to examine character in a modified approach we call the Character Interview. Lynn describes the five key areas of EQ as follows:

1. *Self-awareness and self-control comprise one's ability to fully understand oneself and to use the information to manage emotions productively. This area includes the competencies of accurately understanding one's emotions and the impact emotions have on performance, accurate assessment of strengths and weakness, understanding one's impact on others, and self-management or self-control, including managing anger, disappointment, or failure (resulting in resilience) and managing fear (resulting in courage).*
2. *Empathy is the ability to understand the perspective of others. This area includes the competencies of listening to others, understanding others' points of view, understanding how one's words and actions affect others, and wanting to be of service to others.*
3. *Social Expertness is the ability to build genuine relationships and bonds and express caring, concern, and conflict in healthy ways. This area includes the competencies of building relationships, organizational savvy, collaboration, and conflict resolution.*
4. *Personal Influence is the ability to positively lead and inspire others as well as oneself. This area includes the competencies of leading others, creating a positive work climate, and getting results from others. It also includes self-confidence, initiative and motivation, optimism, and flexibility.*
5. *Mastery of purpose and vision is the ability to bring authenticity to one's life and to live out one's intentions and values. This area includes the competencies of understanding one's purpose, taking actions toward one's purpose, and being authentic.*[17]

The "Director's Cut" Version of an Earlier Rerun

Chapter 2 began with an example of a scene from one or more movies that depict the essence of the interview process as we all know it. If, as in the director's cut versions of Hollywood films (which are always longer and filled with more detail), we were to rerun the opening scene with the ranch foreman now having been trained as a behavioral-based interviewer, it would probably go like this (we will spare you with the gangland and war movie versions this time!):

The scene: a horse corral
(The scene opens with Character A addressing Character B.)
Character A (A ranch foreman):
"So your name's Slim. What is it you do?"
Character B (a cowboy):
"I'm jest a wrangler."
Character A:
"And where'd you learn how to do that?"
Character B:
"Rio Lobo."
Character A:
"So, you ever rope and brand doggies before?"
Character B:
"Yep."
Character A:
"Where was that and when—how'd you come to be doing that anyway?"
Character B:
"It was on my pa's spread, which was kinda small. Ever since I could sit a saddle he had me cuttin' and ropin' but it wasn't 'til I was twelve that he let me near a hot iron."
Character A:
"Tell me about it—who all was involved?"
Character B:
(Pulls the piece of hay he's been chewing on from his mouth and launches into a long story recounting his first roping and branding experience with his father and their neighbor (a well-known cowpuncher known as "Charlie Red Scarf") holding the calf while he nearly fainted seeing the branding iron leave its mark.)
Character A:
"How do you feel about that experience today as opposed to back then?"
Character B:
"Back then I thought I might have hurt the calf but my kin assured me I hadn't. Their back-slappin' and smiles made me feel like I was growed up. Felt purty good. Nowadays I do it so automatic I don't give it a thought."
Character A:
"What do you actually do now that you've done it so often it's automatic?"

Character B:
"Well, I hold the iron in the fire with my right hand and pump the bellows till it's about the color of old Charlie's scarf, then I . . ." (a lengthy story of exactly how he brands his calves ensues).

Character A:
"And what's the outcome of all this? You ever make a mistake?"

Character B:
(Tells tales of getting kicked and knocked down with the iron in his hand, shows some scars and tells about lessons he's learned.)

Character A:
"And what, exactly, do you want from me?"

Character B:
"I come for some work. I'm sure you could use a good cowpuncher around here from the looks o' things."

Character A: (After a long gaze, sizing Character B up and down.)
"You look like you can handle the job alright, but you must be crazy to want it. Get settled in and come back later, and I'll fill you in on what's going on."

Character B: (picking up his saddle)
"Thanks, pardner. You won't regret this."

Character B exits screen left, passing Character C who has been sitting on a hay bale listening all the while.

Character C: (A close but junior comrade to Character A.)
"Now, what'd you go and do that for? You ain't never even met that cowboy before. How do you know he's one of us and not some rustler?"

Character A: (thoughtfully)
"Oh, hell, Sam . . . Didn't you hear him? He's Charlie Mullins's neighbor, so he learned from one of the best, and he sure knows how to handle a branding iron—you can't make up those kinds of stories.
He's just what we've been lookin' for."

Fade to black . . .

Reference Checks

As indicated in *Hiring and Keeping the Best People*, the purpose of a reference check is to:

> *Verify claims made by the candidate during the interview process and fill in information gaps. They can also provide valuable outside perspectives on the candidate and his or her potential fit with the position. Check references when you are near the end of your recruiting process and close*

to making a decision. But be sure to obtain permission from the candidates first to avoid affecting someone's current employment—for example, the applicant's company may have no idea that he or she is interviewing for a job elsewhere.[18]

At the senior levels reference checks test the objectivity of the Selection Team: Have we become enamored with the idea of this candidate and lost touch with his or her reality? Have we failed in any way to see and accept this person for who they really are?

Just like interviewing, reference-checking can be done around a competency-based framework where you continue to "drill down" with follow-on questions until you hit rock bottom. To do this effectively, you must allow the reference to talk. Checklists can be used to check facts (employment dates, job titles, reporting relationships, and the like), but what you really want for senior-level reference checks are conversations.

The same 360-degree approach that works well when gathering assessment data on internal candidates also works well with references. An executive recruiter friend says that his firm tries to get the names of two direct reports, two peers, and a current and former boss, although they will never contact them without the approval of the candidate first.

Check Those in Authority

In addition to checking references by placing phone calls to people who can verify aspects of candidates' work behaviors, there are also public records that can and should be investigated before finalizing a decision on a leader. They are,

- Criminal record checks
- Social security verification
- Credit reports[19]
- Internet information and blogs related to the candidate's current or former employers

Obviously, the value of all this information is only as good as the source and sometimes, particularly when doing senior-level reference checks, some people may be difficult (or reluctant) to be reached. Or they may hesitate to talk openly for fear of saying something that might create a legal problem for them. In those situations here are two approaches we have found work quite well:

1. *"Call me back if the candidate was outstanding."* Dr. Pierre Mornell, author of *Hiring Smart!*, suggests a way to get though to someone quickly: Call during lunchtime when they are not there so that you can leave a voice mail message. In the message state the name of the person you are

checking and your purpose. Close by saying, "Call me back if the candidate was outstanding." Mornell says the speed of the response and the attitude and willingness are often incredible.[20]

2. *"How can a good boss help continue his or her development?"* Alan Renne with Russell Reynolds will often use this question at an end of a reference check if the source has not been particularly forthcoming about the client's strengths and weak spots. By putting a positive twist on it, people who inherently want to be of help to others will frequently start to speak more candidly about development needs and areas for future improvement.[21]

Specialized Tools for Assessing Abilities

It is worth noting that even though the Chinese first started using standardized selection testing to appoint civil servants as far back as 1115 BCE,[22] modern American businesses still do not readily use tests (also referred to as "assessment instruments") with much regularity to shed light on abilities. At senior levels they are used only rarely. One reason is that there simply are not many tests available that add to what an experienced interviewer can obtain from a well-conducted interview process. Of the three candidate buckets, the Traditional Selection Process is quite well suited to get at the abilities of candidates so there is not a great deal of incremental improvement to be gained in this area. There are, however, a few testing instruments that may be of help in certain rare situations. Again, the use of these tools is *not* recommended for inclusion in most screening processes for senior executives. Only when an exceptional situation arises will it prove helpful to know that the following resources exist. (Other testing instruments can be found in Appendix A, which is included as a reference tool for hirers.)

Intelligence Quotient (IQ) Testing

One type of instrument that may be valuable in certain instances is the IQ test. One reason IQ tests are not used very often is that they are shrouded in an historical cloud regarding both their validity (do they really measure what they say they do, and are the results free from cultural, educational, or other biases that could make them prejudiced?) and their relevance (beyond a certain level, is a higher IQ really an essential requirement to do the work involved in a particular senior-level position?).[23]

Testing for intelligence has decided legal implications. When using this tool it is important that these tests be given with the candidate's full support, by a qualified administrator, and to all candidates equally. Nevertheless, the use of intelligence testing should not be ruled out as a means of gaining insight into this aspect of the candidate's abilities for situations where it is a demonstrated requirement for success.

Aptitude Testing

Another component of the Abilities Bucket that may, in rare instances, be worthwhile to examine through the use of an objective testing instrument is aptitude. One test to consider in this area is the Johnson O'Connor Aptitude Test.

Following the research Johnson O'Connor conducted at GE in 1922, he established the Human Engineering Laboratory which has since identified seventeen aptitudes that are measured in a six-hour battery of tests. These can be taken in eleven U.S. cities and have already been given to over a half-million respondents. The aptitudes that are examined by the Johnson O'Connor Aptitude Test are as follows.[24]

Personality	Tweezers Dexterity	Number Memory
Graphoria	Observation	Numerical Reasoning
Ideaphoria	Design Memory	Silograms
Structural Visualization	Tonal Memory	Artistic Judgment
Inductive Reasoning	Pitch Discrimination	Color Discrimination
Analytical Reasoning	Rhythm Memory	

Depending on how someone scores on these various aptitudes, the feedback report provides insights into the types of work and the types of industries where he or she may find a natural place for themselves. While the Johnson O'Connor Aptitude Test is more frequently used with lower-level positions and people at earlier stages of their careers, there *may* be some instances where candidates under consideration for a senior position warrant this kind of testing. It may apply especially if the company is in an industry requiring a high degree of left-brain (creative) or other unique aptitudes.[25] If the test is used, it should be used with all candidates under consideration.

Talents and Inherent Strengths Testing

Closely associated with aptitudes, talents are another trait found in the Abilities Bucket. One test for talents is the *StrengthsFinder*® *Profile*, in which candidates can learn about their talents and share the results with the hirers.[26] The assessment is conducted online through the use of the *StrengthsFinder*® *Profile*. This instrument is described in *NOW Understand Your Strengths* by Marcus Buckingham.[27] It is based on interviews conducted by the Gallup Organization with over 2 million participants, more than a quarter of whom were managers. It is designed to help individuals identify the most prevalent of thirty-four talent themes that can be developed into strengths when combined with pertinent knowledge (facts and experiences) and skills (the steps of an activity).

Although tests like the *StrengthsFinder* and the Johnson O'Connor Aptitude Test were originally created for individuals to use for their own purposes, they could be adapted by companies interested in gaining insights into prospects' abilities—*assuming* they have adopted a partnership approach with candidates as described further on in this book. (See Chapter 9.)

In the Leader Selection Process of the future (which is based on a more collaborative approach than the Traditional Selection Process), such instruments could be used to help answer any questions that might exist about the aptitudes and talents of senior-level candidates to ensure that the match is right.

Shifting the Paradigm

Just as abilities are important in the Traditional Selection Process, they also play an important role in the new process to be built around the Match-Fit Model. However, one weakness the Match-Fit Model reveals is that the selection process in use today depends *too* heavily on the candidate's abilities. Regardless of the type of interview and regardless of the techniques used by the interviewer (such as clarifying questions, use of silence, expanding responses, mirroring feedback, confirming feelings, summarizing key ideas, or following a structured, behavioral, competency-based interview track),[28] the purpose of the interview is usually focused on determining *what* a person is capable of doing, and to a lesser degree, on *who* this person really is. This, as pointed out in the previous chapter, is one of the deficiencies of the Traditional Selection Process: it overemphasizes finding the individual whose abilities best match the needs of the company, rather than one who also *fits* the situation.

As we move toward developing a more successful Leader Selection Process, we will want to lessen the relative emphasis placed on abilities in favor of some of the other factors in the Match-Fit Model. After all, if you were to look critically at the final slate of candidates for any top executive position presented by any reputable executive search firm, without much doubt every one of the finalists has the ability to do the job. Success in the job does not come just from having the right abilities; personality and energy and character must also come into play.

Interviewing's Never-Never Land

Regardless of the type of interviewer you are and what type of structured or unstructured approach you use, when it comes to certain questions, an interviewer must know where *not* to tread. To raise any of these issues would be in violation of the candidate's civil or personal rights. If for any reason, you chose not to offer the position to the candidate of whom these questions had been asked, then you could be the target of a lawsuit—one that you probably would not win. At a minimum, the following are questions that should *never* be asked in any employment conversation:

How old are you?
When did you graduate?
What is your sexual orientation?
What is your race or nationality?
Where were you born?
How much do you weigh?
Are you pregnant or plan to become so?
Do you have any disability or health problem?
Are you married, divorced, separated, widowed, or single?
Do you have a family (or what are the ages of your children)?
Who lives in your household (disabled or dependent parents, relatives)?
What is your spouse's occupation?
What church, if any, do you attend (or what is your religion)?
Would your religion prevent you from working on weekends?
Have you ever taken a leave of absence from a job?
Have you ever been arrested?[29]

Takeaways

Before putting the lid on the abilities bucket, here is a summary of the key points about abilities:

- Abilities include skills, knowledge, aptitudes, talents, and intellect.
- Understanding a candidate's true abilities is an important part of the process in both the Traditional Selection Process and any future one. It is particularly important that hirers understand candidates' true abilities (competencies) relative to the requirements of the job.
- All the work that has gone into assessing the abilities of senior candidates should continue in the future. This aspect of the Traditional Selection Process is well refined and should not be lost.
- The interview is the primary tool hirers use to obtain information about all candidates' abilities.

- Interviewers of senior executives are themselves senior executives, few of whom have proficiency at highly effective interviewing techniques. Interview training is strongly recommended for *all* hirers to ensure the best possible data is gathered about candidates' abilities.

- There are two major types of interviews: structured and unstructured. The traditional, "Tell me about Yourself" interview is the most common example of an unstructured interview.

- Structured interview questions include motivational questions, situational questions, brainteaser questions, and the stress interview. The Topgrading interview process developed by Dr. Bradford Smart is a highly structured one.

- Behavioral-based interviews (also known as Behavior-Event Interviews [BEIs], Competency-Based Interviews, and Competency-Based Behavioral Interviews [CBBIs]) are viewed by most professional interviewers as the most effective way to clearly ascertain whether or not the candidate possesses the ability to do what is required in the job.

- Behavioral-based interviews can also be used to explore the behaviors and situations in which candidates have utilized aspects of their Emotional Intelligence (EQ) as well.

- Reference checks are another important tool used by hirers to confirm the candidates' abilities.

- There are testing instruments that can provide additional information about the intelligence, aptitudes, and talents of senior leaders if needed.

4

The Personality and Energy Bucket

Leadership is a performing art.
—Meg Armstrong, Executive Coach

The primary value of the Match-Fit Model is that it will change the approach used to select business leaders, enabling companies to build a better selection process—better because it reduces the risks (and costs) of the leadership failures that are occurring with increasing frequency. Based on the Match-Fit Model, the new Leader Selection Process will assist hirers in selecting senior leaders who are more successful in their new organizations.

In the Match-Fit Model, the Personality and Energy Bucket plays a central role. Of the three buckets of individual attributes—abilities, personality and energy, and character—the Personality and Energy Bucket is the only one that affects both the match and the fit of the individual to the organization. In order to understand why, we need to examine three aspects of personality and then one regarding the matter of energy. The aspects of personality to be considered here are as follows.

- The role of personality in executive success and failure
- Its importance in the Match-Fit Model
- Ways to get beyond just the behavioral aspects of personality

In describing personality attributes, business people often refer to a leader's style rather than his or her personality. While the term "style" may encompass the abilities and character that influence an executive's behavior, his or her personality is the more important contributor to style. One only needs to look at the reasons executives fail to appreciate how important the implications of personality are.

Personality Traits That Spell Success (or Failure)

Two books were published in 2003 that dealt exclusively with the causes of leadership failure. That year Sydney Finklestein, a professor of business at the Tuck School, wrote a well-researched book entitled *Why Smart Executives Fail*. In it he identified seven habits of spectacularly unsuccessful executives. These seven habits include:

1. *Seeing themselves and their companies as dominating their environments.*
2. *Identifying so completely with the company that there is no clear boundary between their personal interests and their corporation's interests.*

3. *Thinking they have all the answers.*
4. *Ruthlessly eliminating anyone who is not 100 percent behind them.*
5. *Being consummate spokespersons, obsessed with the company's image.*
6. *Underestimating obstacles.*
7. *Stubbornly relying on what worked for them in the past.[1]*

Regardless of the events surrounding an executive's failure, the point the book makes is that executives fail because, for a variety of reasons, they behave inappropriately when events occur. These behaviors are due in part to the makeup of their personalities. Of the seven causes of failure identified by Sydney Finkelstein, five relate to how the executives see themselves and their thought processes, perceptions, and predispositions.

Also in 2003 consultants David Dotlich and Peter Cairo came out with a book concisely entitled *Why CEOs Fail.* In it they elaborated on eleven derailers that are identified in a psychometric test called the Hogan Challenge Report. We often use this test when coaching a client who has recently moved from being a functional head into general management. It helps him or her see how—when under increased stress or when they are relaxed and their guards are down—certain behaviors will tend to come out that can work against them.

What Dotlich and Cairo discuss are behaviors emanating from the dark side of personality that will derail an otherwise successful executive. The eleven personality traits Dotlich and Cairo describe are:

Arrogance	Mischievousness
Melodrama	Eccentricity
Volatility	Passive resistance
Excessive caution	Perfectionism
Habitual distrust	Eagerness to please[2]
Aloofness	

The point of both books is the same: The root causes of failure have little to do with missing forecasts, or having the wrong strategy, or lacking a compelling vision for the company. The reasons executives fail are that they react inappropriately when they find they are missing their forecasts, or their strategies are not working, or they have not yet been able to determine the future direction for their companies. Rarely is it the event(s) that causes leaders to fail as much as it is the way they deal with the event. After all, most executives under consideration for a given senior position have the ability to *do* the job; they possess the necessary skills, knowledge, experiences, aptitudes, and talents at the necessary levels of proficiency to do what is required to be successful. Their failure to apply those abilities in a winning fashion is a function of *how* they go about doing their jobs, which is dictated by their personalities and their characters (see Chapter 5). Thus, the importance of fully understanding one's personality must be given greater importance and consideration in the selection process of the future.

In 2005 a study by Leadership IQ summarized the current situation. It reported that 46 percent of (all) newly hired employees will fail within eighteen months, while only 19 percent will achieve unequivocal success. But contrary to popular belief, technical skills are not the primary reason that new hires fail; instead, poor interpersonal skills dominate the list, flaws that many of their managers admit were overlooked during the interview process. "The typical interview process fixates on ensuring that new hires are technically competent," explains Mark Murphy, CEO of Leadership IQ. "But coachability, emotional intelligence, motivation, and temperament are much more predictive of a new hire's success or failure. Do technical skills really matter if the employee isn't open to improving, alienates their coworkers, lacks drive. and has the wrong personality for the job?"[3] The same can be said for senior executives as well.

Leaders are not immune to personality problems, and these can be especially damaging since personality is the outward expression of how leaders deal with the needs they were hired to address. The significance of personality is further heightened since it also affects the way the leader interacts with the powerful cultures at play (see Chapter 7).

Actions Really Do Speak Louder Than Words

As noted when we began this discussion of personality, the Personality and Energy Bucket is defined largely by behaviors. According to the American Psychological Association's (APA) Web site, *Psychology Matters*, the term "personality" refers to the "unique psychological qualities of an individual that influence a variety of characteristic behavior patterns (both overt and covert) across different situations and over time."[4]

Webster provides several definitions of the term that are also helpful here:

> **per·son·al·i·ty** *3. a) habitual patterns and qualities of behavior of any individual as expressed by physical and mental activities and attitudes 4. a)the sum of such qualities as impressing or likely to impress others.*[5]

However, there is more—a lot more—to personality than just observable behaviors, regardless of whether you look at it from the technical perspective of the APA or from that of the layman. Both acknowledge that there is more to personality than meets the eye (in other words, more than just the observable behaviors). These include unique psychological qualities, attitudes, mental activities, or even thoughts. The mental activities referred to in the Webster's definition that fit into the Match-Fit Model's Personality and Energy Bucket include such qualities as motivation, prejudices, perception, emotions, cognitive capabilities, and memory; habits, style, and even speech impediments and physical handicaps are among the physical manifestations, as is, of course, energy.[6] Because those who are responsible for selecting leaders rarely get to see candidates perform in the role in advance of making a selection, understanding the candidates' personalities is of value to the extent that they are predictive of the leaders' behaviors under various circumstances that may impact their success in their new positions.

To get a solid reading of which of these qualities a candidate possesses, it is vital to consider ways to determine how they affect a leader's behavior other than through an exclusive reliance on job interviews. This is especially true since, as the Webster's definition points out, there is a natural tendency for people (even skilled interviewers) to be drawn to the impressive qualities of others. Hence relying on interviewers' impressions as the sole source of information about a candidate's personality skews any evaluation in favor of the candidate who possesses the qualities likely to impress. A candidate who *appears* to possess the abilities and character to do what is needed in ways that will be accepted by the organization's culture will have the upper hand over someone who is less impressive but may, in actuality, be better equipped to succeed. This is where psychological testing or assessment can prove very helpful.

The Importance of Personality in the Match-Fit Model

Figure 4.1 contrasts the model on which the Traditional Selection Process is based with the Match-Fit Model, which will be used as the basis for creating the Leader Selection Process of the future. Both of these models were presented in Chapter 2 and are repeated here for ease in referring to them.

As pointed out in the preceding chapter, there is no significant difference in the role of abilities between the two match-fit models. However, the new model implies that the relative importance of one's abilities is reduced in favor of other factors. One of these factors is personality. In the new model, the importance of personality is increased because a candidate's personality is recognized as having an impact on both the candidate's match as well as his or her fit with the organization. The importance that personality will thereby

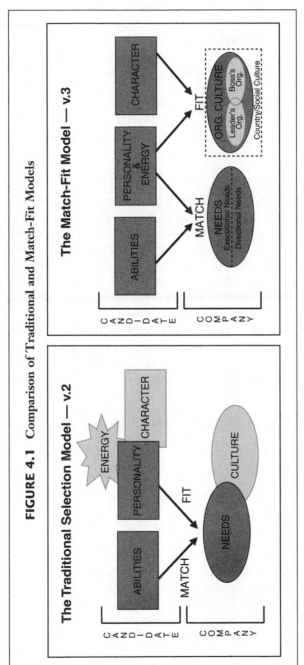

FIGURE 4.1 Comparison of Traditional and Match-Fit Models

assume is the reason to take a closer look at a candidate's personality and style during the selection process.

In the traditional model, personality is viewed as being aligned solely with the question of the candidate's potential fit with the existing organization. As a result, in the current selection process a candidate's manner of interacting with those doing the interviewing will often serve as the entire basis for assessing fit. If, collectively, the hirers who interview the candidate like his or her presentation, then the candidate is proclaimed to be "one of us" and rarely is any more time or thought spent on determining whether or not that feeling of fit was anything more than a fleeting affinity or something more concrete.

On rare instances when one or more of the interviewers may come away with negative "vibes" about a favored candidate, some additional, and often behind-the-scenes, background checks might be conducted. In such instances, however, the intention of the additional checking and/or interviews is more often to find reasons to dispel the concerns than to determine objectively whether or not the candidate may actually fit into the organization. After all filling the position quickly with someone who possesses the right abilities is usually the driving objective of the Traditional Selection Process. If personality affects both match and fit, however, this will clearly not suffice.

Nor will the popular practice of just asking a candidate to describe him- or herself as a particular type of leader, such as a general (decisive, bold, directive, lead from the front), a coach (develops the game plan, calls plays, does a lot of training), a parent (grows people, nurtures, supports initiatives, motivates), or a teacher (instructs, communicates, is theory-based).[7] Not even a stress interview can get to the crux of style, let alone the deeper issue of personality, to the extent that some of the testing instruments or a trained psychologist can.

When It Comes to People, What You See Is Not Always What You Get

There are many ways hirers can gain deeper and more meaningful insights into the personality of an executive job candidate and learn more about his or her behaviors, style, attitudes, motivators, and derailers. Personality tests have been around since 1919, when the U.S. Army began using the Woodward Personal Data Sheet as a way to prescreen soldiers who might be susceptible to shell shock under fire. Over the years various theories and different types of tests related to personality have come along. They include the Rorschach inkblot test in 1921, the TAT (Thematic Apperception Test, introduced in the 1930s by the forerunner agency of the CIA to identify personalities that might be susceptible to being turned by enemy agents), and the Minnesota Multiphasic Personality Inventory that was published in 1942 as a way to assess psychopathology in clinical settings.[8]

From the work we do with our outplacement candidates who are transitioning into new jobs, it is our clear impression that companies have increased their use of personality and behavioral assessments to help select senior executives during the past decade. The new Leader Selection Process advises using assessments of candidates for senior positions. In our experience there are instruments designed for this purpose that can provide critical insights into the makeup of potential company leaders *before* they are selected and before their *real* personality tendencies—both the good and the bad— become topics of conversation at every coffeepot in the company. In our discussion of the new Leader Selection Process (Chapter 9), we will detail some of the tests that have been successful for us and how to use them to find the right leader for your organization.

People With That "Special Something"—Energy

The title "The Personality and Energy Bucket" was chosen for this chapter to reflect the fact that, although energy is technically characterized as an aspect of personality by many, it occupies a unique place in the selection of executives. It is a very interesting and important part of a person's appearance, the way they are perceived by others, and how they relate to them. When we evaluate salespeople we sometimes refer to how "hungry" they are; when we talk about musicians and other artists we speak of their "passion" for their art; in the case of politicians, we rate their "charisma." All of these catchwords are shorthand terms for energy.

Business leaders, too, can be very hungry and are usually quite passionate about their work. (Why else would they devote such long hours to it?) And many have charisma. It is this energy that attracts us to them.

For example, Bill Swanson, former CEO of Raytheon, is reputed to have "a knack for making complex ideas easy to grasp. . . . His imperative is to have fun at work." According to psychologist Daniel Goleman, Swanson's personality is an asset because, "Research shows that when people are in a good mood at work, it builds emotional capital and enhances productivity."[9] At the same time, the display of too much energy in some situations can create just as detrimental an image as too little can in another.

Moreover the importance of a leader's energy level goes beyond just their individual persona. According to authors Jim Loehr and Tony Schwartz, "Leaders are the stewards of organizational energy. . . ." Loehr and Schwartz maintain that if an executive has the capacity to manage energy skillfully (both their own and the organization's), they will be capable of what the authors call "full engagement." An executive who is fully engaged is "able to immerse themselves in the mission they are on."[10]

Not only must leaders possess the right levels of energy, but they must be able to manage it skillfully to succeed. As part of the new Leader Selection Process, we advocate that hirers take a close look at candidates' energy manifestations and use behavior-based interviews to understand how they purposefully manage, channel, and replenish their energy levels (see Chapter 9).

Closely allied with the leader's energy is his or her motivation. It is important that there be alignment between what needs to get done and what motivates the candidate. If the job they are interviewing for "turns them on," it is likely their energy levels will be higher.

Selecting the leader with the right motivation and energy levels to handle the rigors of the job is especially critical, as the complexity of most top jobs has increased significantly over the past decades. In 2003 the Center for Creative Leadership found that the more stress an organization is under, the more its leader's soft skills are important. Leaders cited the usefulness of these skills in meeting the following challenges:

- Motivating staff in the face of uncertainty
- Communicating clearly about organization changes
- Working in cross-functional leadership roles
- Developing and retaining staff needed to accomplish more with less[11]

The importance of possessing the right mix of varied personality traits and the energy to sustain the rigors faced by senior executives on a daily basis is clearly seen in this quote from executive coach Meg Armstrong:

> *Leadership is a performing art, and you are always on—from the moment you leave home until you return. This means that leaders are on stage wherever they are—in front of the security analysts or standing in line at a fast food place with their kids. Or communicating with large audiences of their employees or shareholders. And everything counts—choice of words, facial expressions, appearance, posture, tone of voice, everything. A demeanor of confidence and competence is one of the most potent ways leaders create a robust and positive atmosphere in an organization. But good as most leaders are at communicating, far too many forget they are communicating all the time, which requires constant attention to each performance skill and deliberate practice— just like a top athlete or musician.[12]*

Takeaways

The following is a summary of the role personality and energy play in the selection process:

- Recent studies show that executives usually fail because of bad behaviors stemming largely from bad attitudes toward themselves or others rather than from bad judgments, bad strategies, bad plans, or the lack of necessary skill sets.
- Because it is largely through his or her behavior (leadership style) that an executive manifests his or her personality, this factor plays a key role in the Match-Fit Model.
- To the extent that style is a manifestation of personality, it affects both the match and the fit of the individual.
- Personality is more than style and behaviors, however. While these are large components of one's personality, other factors like mental activities and attitudes that go into creating habitual patterns must also be considered.
- By using standard personality and behavior tests or through insights gained by trained therapists, interviewers can gain more insight into the makeup of a candidate's personality than through the traditional interview process most hirers rely on today.
- A leader's energy is a very important aspect of who they are; it affects both how they are perceived as well as their ability to endure and persevere against the stress and strain of their responsibilities and the work environment. Their energy level can set the tone for the entire organization.

5

The Character Bucket

Ability may get you to the top, but it takes character to keep you there.

—Stevie Wonder

In the Traditional Selection Process, character is a shadowy concept—an aspect of the candidate the importance of which is recognized but rarely focused on. This is especially ironic considering its critical role in the candidate's success. It is typically glossed over—often regarded as that inner something that people either possess ("good character") or do not ("bad character"). Consequently its place has not previously been defined nor has the Traditional Selection Process provided any clear steps for addressing it.

As a youngster, I can remember my mother telling me over and over again, "Son, there are some things like politics, sex, and religion that people just don't discuss in 'polite society.'" Well, without knowing it, my dear mom was not far from hitting the bull's-eye of the character problem in the Traditional Selection Process. Businesspeople are usually respectful, polite people, and interviews are intended to seem courteous and friendly. Like politics, sex, and religion, character has historically been treated as a topic that just is not discussed in polite interviews.

This atmosphere of collegiality is especially true at higher organizational levels where the subtleties of *how* things are said are often as important as *what* is said. Unfortunately some of the very topics that are skirted are central to what goes into the candidate's Character Bucket.

As we shall see in this chapter, character is at the core of one's humanity. It is far from a simple "good-bad," "has it-lacks it" binary consideration in any selection process that works. A candidate's Character Bucket contains a complex mix of inner qualities—values, beliefs, philosophies, aspirations, principles, priorities, standards, ethics, morals, and even virtues. Only some of these elements of character are relevant in the selection process (*highly* relevant) while others are less relevant; and others are not only irrelevant, they are even illegal to discuss. As pointed out in Chapter 3, questions about a candidate's personal choices regarding political affiliations, sexual orientation, and religious beliefs, for instance, are so inappropriate in the selection process that they are prohibited under a host of state and federal discrimination laws along with matters of race, gender, age, pregnancy, or certain physical or mental disabilities.[1] Yet avoiding steps to explore candidates' *relevant*, leadership-related inner qualities—particularly their values and their business philosophies— is something that *must* change if turnover at the top is going to be reduced. In the Match-Fit Model the character of the candidate comes under as bright a spotlight as is shone on a candidate's abilities, personality and energy because understanding character is a necessary ingredient for any true assessment of fit.

So even though some aspects of a candidate's Character Bucket are not germane to the selection process (while others are flat off-limits), these difficulties should no longer be used as reasons *not* to take a rigorous look at those aspects of character that *are* highly relevant to selecting the right leader. Hirers must stop throwing the baby out with the bathwater—this baby is too precious to the future success of your organization!

In this chapter we will go about examining them by:

- Looking at what is meant by "character" and what its constituent elements are
- Seeing how character is acquired and developed
- Discussing why character is so important when selecting key executives

What *Is* Character?

Have you ever wondered what an Egyptian hieroglyph (a character), a cipher in the Chinese alphabet (a character), an astrological symbol (a character), a person in a drama or novel (a character), a single piece of type for printing (a character), and one's reputation for moral excellence (character) all have in common that they should bear the same name? All these seemingly diverse entities share three elements:

1. They are all created by being scratched out or engraved.
2. They all are unique entities unto themselves—there is no other one like them.
3. They all represent something of meaning or worth.

The challenge in assessing a person's character—what that individual stands for that has been scratched out of his or her human clay by a lifetime of experiences, hardships, and teachings—can be met if you know what you are looking for. But because each character is unique and ultimately so significant in determining readiness for a top leadership position, it warrants the time and effort of everyone involved in the selection process to do it thoroughly.

Various definitions of character can be found in different sources, but certain common threads tie them together. Webster's tells us that it is "one of the attributes or features that make up and distinguish an individual . . . moral excellence and firmness."[2] The U.S. Air Force Academy's definition is similar but has a slightly different emphasis: "The sum of those qualities of moral excellence that stimulates a person to do the right thing, which is manifested through right and proper actions despite internal or external pressures to the contrary."[3]

According to Wikipedia character is "a variety of attributes including the existence, or lack, of virtues such as integrity, courage, fortitude, honesty, or loyalty, or of good behaviors or habits."[4]

Gene Klann, working at the Center for Creative Leadership, puts the emphasis on the behavioral aspects of character in his book *Building Character*:

> *Leadership character is all about behavior. . . . Leadership character is defined as behaviors that have a positive influence on others. It's how leaders behave (based on what inner qualities they may possess or thoughts they may cherish) that determines their reputation and good name.*[5]

The Educational Psychology Interactive Web site contains an essay by Reginald Ferguson entitled, "Character Is Who You Are," in which he supports Klann's emphasis on behavior but incorporates the importance of values in defining character:

> *In general, character . . . is considered to be observable in one's conduct. Thus, character is different from values in that values are orientations or dispositions, whereas character involves action or activation of knowledge and values.*[6]

Regardless of where the emphasis is placed, all definitions of character identify two basic components that go into it—the laudable *behavior* of the individual *and* the *inner qualities* that prompt the individual to choose those laudable behaviors over others in particular circumstances.

In the Match-Fit Model, both the behaviors and the inner qualities are extremely important. Given the nature of selection, however, our new process will focus more on understanding the *qualities* that drive behaviors than on the behaviors themselves only because when selecting new leaders, opportunities to create or replicate behaviors that reveal character are limited. As Larry Bossidy and Ram Charan point out in *Execution*, "Traditional interviews aren't useful for spotting the qualities of leaders who execute."[7] Since we cannot observe the candidate's character in action, we must at least determine that the underlying qualities of leadership are there to be drawn upon when needed. We should also try to find out if the behaviors based upon those values have occurred in previous situations. Later we will talk about the Character Interview, which is a way to ask the candidate about his or her specific values and beliefs using the behavioral-based interview technique described in Chapter 3.

The Winning Combination

The specific inner qualities that make a leader of strong moral character vary from society to society and even within the institutions and organizations of each society. Generally these inner qualities fall into two broad compartments of the Character Bucket: values and beliefs (sometimes called philosophies).

The Value of Values

Values have been around as long as civilization and are found in every culture. They are attitudes (principles, priorities, or standards) about the worth of people, concepts, or things. Values have a huge influence on behavior because they require people to weigh the relative importance of one behavior over another in specific situations and then to choose one accordingly.

Closely related to values are ethics and virtues. Ethics are values that pertain to matters or moral worth.[8] Virtues are values taken to the ultimate level of all excellence. They are the conceptual ideal of the various principles that are held by individuals and valued by others.[9]

The primary virtues valued by the cultures of two different societies (Greek and Roman), four different religious and philosophic traditions (Jewish, Christian, Islamic, and Buddhist), and those from the ancient Chinese principles of morality are illustrated in Appendix B.

Also included in this appendix, under the column labeled "Psychological Qualities," is a list of traits and virtues published in *Character Strengths and Virtues*.[10] These are the traits found in modern Western civilizations that are deemed to constitute a healthy and stable individual. They were developed by a unique branch of psychology that recently emerged in the United States to study the positive elements of the human psyche, just as many earlier psychologists studied the negative aspects (abnormalities, psychological disorders, mental illness, and the like).

The implication for hirers of the table in Appendix B is that by using these virtues as a gauge, it is apparent that values vary greatly from culture to culture—not a little, but a lot. As we shall see shortly, the values of individuals are formed by the disparate cultures and powerful subcultures within them. Nevertheless many scholars of the nature of leadership would assert that some key value sets are shared by successful leaders regardless of culture and certainly within certain specific cultural units.

Universal Character Traits of Successful Leaders

Depending upon the source, the essential leadership virtues (referred to variously as "principles," "attributes," "values," or "traits") that need to be possessed by leaders in order to be successful range from as few as two to as many as ten depending upon the source. In the *Power Principle*, Blaine Lee describes ten basic principles that he believes allow leaders to garner the power necessary to lead. Lee's ten principles are as follows:[11]

Persuasion	Kindness
Patience	Knowledge
Gentleness	Discipline
Teachability	Consistency
Acceptance	Integrity

As a result of work done at the Center for Creative Leadership, Gene Klann focuses on just five key attributes that he feels are essential to the character of any leader:[12]

Courage	Self-Control
Caring	Communication
Optimism	

Rushworth Kidder has also identified five key values that leaders possess. His were developed from hundreds of tests administered by scores of different facilitators in countries around the world. His list includes the following:[13]

Honesty	Respect
Responsibility	Fairness
Compassion	

Interestingly, Kidder's list does not include courage, although it is obviously a key aspect of his book *Moral Courage: Taking Action When Your Values Are Put to the Test*. That is because Kidder views courage as an action based upon principle. Besides agreeing with him that courage only exists when action occurs, I would also maintain that integrity must also be manifested by action (in other words, if one's *deeds* align with his or her words).

In *Good to Great*, his best-selling study of corporations that have consistently outperformed their competitors, Jim Collins identifies two traits that are shared by all "Level 5" leaders—leaders who are able to achieve and sustain successful companies.[14]

Personal Humility	Professional Will

Combining these four sources creates a list of twenty-two separate qualities, values, or virtues that may be considered key Universal Character Traits of Successful Leaders. Two of them—courage and integrity—can be

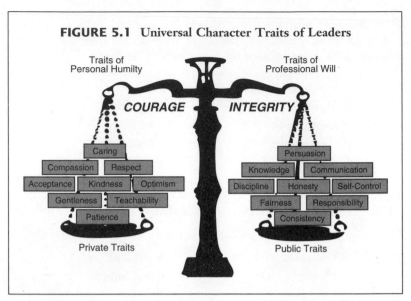

FIGURE 5.1 Universal Character Traits of Leaders

eliminated, however, because they describe *behaviors* prompted by inner qualities, not the inner qualities themselves. Two other traits (Collins's traits of personal humility and professional will) are such broad categories that we can use them as category headings into which the remaining eighteen traits can be divided.

Figure 5.1 illustrates how these eighteen Universal Character Traits of Successful Leaders can be viewed in relation to the two key categories Collins provides.

The value of this figure is that it allows us to make a few relevant points about executives' inner qualities as they relate to the Match-Fit Model—points that will ultimately have a bearing on the future process for selecting the right leader on the basis of fit:

- There are a number of very private character traits pertaining to personal humility, and there are other, more public traits associated with professional will.

- As the scale suggests, a successful leader not only needs to possess many of these various traits, but must also keep them in balance. Too much emphasis on the traits that constitute humility at the expense of those of professional resolve will yield disaster, not greatness. The opposite of this is all too frequently seen in the executive ranks where some leaders have an overly developed set of public traits and not enough counterbalance on the private ones. The unfortunate result is empty, unfulfilled leaders who miss out on many meaningful personal relationships. These leaders become so connected to their work they lose their sense of personal self. Obviously, then, maintaining a balance between these universal public and private virtues is absolutely essential for the well-being of both the individual and the company.

- "Courage" and "integrity" are words used by observers to identify whether a leader is, indeed, true not only to his or her *stated* principles (public virtues) but also to those unstated ones (private virtues). These terms are also the basis on which the most successful leaders I have known measure their own personal success (as opposed to the more conventional scorecards of personal wealth, market cap creation, achievements, honors, and the like). The Level 5 leaders who truly possess the traits associated with personal humility appear to be as interested in *how* they deliver results as in the results themselves.

The Mirror Image

Now here is an important consideration to keep in mind about the Universal Character Traits of Successful Leaders—they are not absolutes. As we shall see in Chapter 7, work is done by companies, and, like all other organizations of people, companies possess cultures. Among other things, companies possess values held collectively by the people who make up the organization. For leadership to exist, the values (and beliefs) of the leader must approximate those of the organization; without that alignment people will not trust the leader, and, as has been proven time and again, an organization will not follow a leader they do not trust. No followers means no leader, plain and simple. The point is, while the values the leaders must possess are universal in nature, the *relative emphasis* the individual gives them must closely align with those of the cultures in which the leader will be enmeshed.

Consequently, as we will discuss later, it is not enough just to identify the character traits possessed by a candidate to determine if he or she is right for a given job. To select the candidate who fits best in a particular organization, you must first know the values and beliefs that exist in the organization's cultures and then select a capable, personable, high-energy person whose values are closely aligned to them on a relative basis. Ultimately this is what "fit" is all about.

In a culture that sanctions the belief that you do not become team captain by crying in the locker room and where the discussion of personal values and beliefs in polite society is not encouraged, it is hardly any wonder that some of the most important traits of successful leaders are rarely identified during the selection process. If we consider the material produced by executives seeking to become candidates for a top position, it is not surprising that you have probably never seen a cover letter reading:

> *You'll find me to be a shy, patient, and gentle person who cares greatly for the people with whom I work. I am compassionate and kind and have little interest working with people who do not respect and openly appreciate one another.*

Or one that reads:

> *I am disappointed I didn't realize sooner that the majority owners did not, in fact, value employees as they claimed and are prone to manipulate their HR policies to suit their own financial interests. Such practices gall me and if I had recognized them sooner, I would have left sooner.*

In the interviews that serve as the mainstay of today's Traditional Selection Process, interviewers are eager to garner examples of where, in other work situations, a candidate's integrity came into play. They also look for ways the laudable public virtues of professional will have been demonstrated. Anecdotal evidence along these lines can provide important insights into a candidate's character. But most of the time such insights are obtained opportunistically—even haphazardly—and not as the result of a concerted, focused, and purposeful methodology. When it comes to evaluating something as important as character, a more rigorous approach to learning about the candidates' values is essential to reduce the risks and costs of making the wrong choice.

Beliefs Are to Be Believed

The second element in the Character Bucket of the Match-Fit Model is beliefs. When someone has a particular belief, they accept it as fact.[15] Like values, beliefs can have varying degrees of effect on behavior depending upon how strongly they are held.

While beliefs are equally important as values to grasp when selecting a new leader, they are often more difficult to get at. The reason is that they are frequently related to personal matters—issues that the law may prevent us from exploring and, frankly, hirers have no need knowing about to select the right leader. At the same time there *are* some beliefs—beliefs and philosophies about business practices, priorities and methodologies—that are highly relevant to the process of selecting the right leader and are fair game for an interviewer.

An Unexpected Character Interview

Perhaps the best interview I ever had for a job occurred in December, 1988 when I was a candidate for the position as president and chief operating officer of GardenWay, Incorporated. GardenWay was then the $200 million, privately-held parent of Troy-Bilt and Bolens Outdoor Power Equipment. I had flown to Albany the night before I was to meet the CEO and majority owner Jairo Estrada. He was going to drive me to the Troy plant where I was scheduled to meet with the head of HR and then tour the facilities. Mr. Estrada and I were supposed to have no more than an hour together during our first meeting.

Around 8:00 A.M. I went to the hotel gift shop to pick up a local paper to see what I could learn about the community. As I crossed the lobby, Mr. Estrada came through the front door—an hour ahead of our appointment. As it turned out his Sunday routine was to have breakfast in the hotel's restaurant and read the *New York Times*. I recognized him from pictures I had seen and, to avoid an awkward situation later, I introduced myself. He graciously invited me to join him for a cup of coffee over breakfast.

Four hours later I left the booth in the coffee shop and made a dash to catch my plane back to Baltimore. He and I had abandoned the day's plan in favor of allowing a long and comfortable conversation to unfold—one covering a host of topics about each other's views, aspirations, beliefs, philosophies, life experiences, backgrounds, families, hopes, and dreams. We talked about the business, its roots and its resources; its challenges and its changes; its people and its problems. Eventually we talked about the things that could possibly be if the company were to be molded and shaped differently going forward.

The time we spent drinking coffee and talking in the booth at the restaurant was a true conversation, too, not a one-sided, fact-finding inquest by one party or the other. I learned as much about him as he did about me. As he opened up, I became increasingly willing to talk candidly also. When I arrived home later that afternoon, I told my wife, "I've never met another business executive whose views and philosophies about business and people are so closely aligned with mine. There is no question about our ability to work together."

And work together we did. Over the course of the next four-and-a-half years the company was transformed from what was fundamentally a single-product, single-channel business to a new products company and the brand leader at the high end of the outdoor power equipment market. When I left GardenWay, the company was

(continued)

50 percent bigger than it was when we first sat and talked about the important things that dealt with fit. Furthermore, during that same time frame, the company's return on sales had increased threefold, and the book value of the company had gone from $10.50 per share to over $52.00 per share.

To this day I can't help but wonder what would have happened if Mr. Estrada and I had stuck to the original agenda that was so clearly the product of a Traditional Selection Process. Had we missed out on that in-depth exchange of personal values and relevant beliefs about business, about the situation at hand, and about ourselves, would we ever have made that all important human connection that led to such an exciting and fulfilling chapter in each of our lives? The insights into my character that Mr. Estrada gained gave him sufficient comfort after checking references and observing me for himself to let go of the reins and allow me to do what I was qualified to do. For me, our discussion provided a high degree of trust knowing that he held the same fundamental beliefs that I did. I also came away feeling that I would be able to work successfully within the GardenWay culture. Not only did our coffee-shop conversation lead to an exciting and fulfilling time for us, but so it was for the outstanding leadership team who delivered (and exceeded!) the results we had hoped to realize.

Of course, at the conclusion of our in-depth interview (which I have come to call the Character Interview) neither of us could be sure that what we heard from the other was actually a reflection of his character. At that point we had not seen evidence (tangible behaviors) that what each of us said was actually in line with what we did. But, hearing it was a whole lot better than having to intuit it. We now had a starting point from which we could test our own observations. We were also able to assess the input of other people who had seen if, in practice, the two of us had consistently behaved with courage and integrity. If Mr. Estrada had been familiar with behavioral-based interviewing techniques, he could have asked me for more specific examples from my past to serve as evidence that what I said about myself was, in fact, how I behaved (see Chapter 9).

The time we invested getting inside each others' head that morning substantially increased the likelihood that a successful working relationship would occur. Our meeting had created a basis to trust one another right from the start. That trust emanated from the way we shared aspects of our inner qualities—things that most people keep guarded and out of sight from others. We both believed in open and direct communication. By practicing that shared value we experienced the other as being trustworthy—a person of character.

How Character Is Fed

My story illustrates why any new process for selecting leaders must include better ways of understanding character. To develop such techniques, we need to know where character comes from and why selecting leaders with the right character traits for a given culture is so incredibly important to the organization. The following fable may provide some clues:

The Fable of the Wise Old Indian and the Young Brave

There once was a young Indian Brave who desperately wanted to become a highly respected leader of his tribe when he grew up. He dreamed of becoming a skilled hunter and of being first into battle. He wanted the younger boys to look up to him and the older men to listen when he spoke at tribal meetings. He hoped that the young woman whom he cared for would someday become his wife. Everyday he tried to live up to these virtues and the others of his tribe.

But it was not easy. At times he found himself so frightened by the prospect of war that he feared that he would flee the fray. He enjoyed hunting but was often so impatient that he scared away his quarry. He was also prone to exaggeration to the point that some of his stories were complete fabrications for which he felt guilty. Upon occasion he would bully the smaller boys for no good reason and he was ashamed that he coveted his best friend's girl. Some days he did not even care about his tribal teachings and just wanted to do what was easy and self-serving.

Becoming troubled with these inner thoughts and feelings, he decided to talk with someone whom he thought might be able to help him with his conflicts. He sought out one of the oldest members of his tribe who was looked upon by everyone as very wise. When the younger man had shared his aspirations and his conflicted thoughts, he was both amazed and relieved to hear the old man say that he fully understood what the younger man was wrestling with and that he too felt such inner conflicts. "As a matter of fact," the wise old Indian said, "even to this day it's as if there is a battle going on inside of me between two powerful dogs—one good dog and one evil dog—fighting over which way I will choose to go on almost every decision I have to make."

The young Brave was relieved to learn that he was not alone in being conflicted about the vital decisions he struggled with, but he couldn't help but ask the old man, "But how do you know which dog will win?" The wise old Indian smiled and said, "Oh, that's easy. It all depends on which dog you feed."

When it comes to the development of character, it is just as the wise old Indian said to the young Brave: "It all depends on which dog you feed." Many people believe that the basic shape of character is formed early in life. But the feeding of character is not a onetime event; it is a regular, repetitive occurrence that can happen in a variety of places: family upbringing, youth peer groups, and life's continuing experiences.

Where Character Is Formed

Historically the character of children was formed primarily in the family of origin. From conversations around the dinner table, to family gatherings, to assigning chores and helping with early work experiences, parents have always played the dominant role in shaping their children's values and beliefs. The key universal characteristics of leaders were often taught at home. They might also have been reinforced in schools and other institutions with stories about private values like patience, gentleness, kindness, caring, and respect.

That picture began to change with the Industrial Revolution. Given the slow decay of the traditional family structure with a simultaneous decline in regular religious involvement, schools and educational institutions of all sorts were forced into a bigger role in shaping character. Their role was well described a few decades ago by Dr. Martin Luther King, Jr., in *The Purpose of Education:*

> *The function of education, therefore, is to teach one to think intensively and to think critically. The education which stops with efficiency may prove the greatest menace to society. The most dangerous criminal may be the man gifted with reason but with no morals . . . we must remember that intelligence is not enough. Intelligence plus character — that is the goal of education.*[16]

Some schools, like many parents and religious institutions, have continued to do an excellent job of forming the character of many young people. When traditional sources have faltered, other institutions, associations, and organizations have come forward to help fill the void. Two excellent examples of such organizations are the Boy Scouts (BSA) and Girl Scouts of America (GSUSA). The BSA and GSUSA have done an admirable job in teaching values to hundreds of millions of young men and women since they were each founded nearly 100 years ago. If you ask anyone who was a scout to repeat the boy or girl scout law, even decades after having left scouting, you will almost always have it repeated back to you verbatim (or at least a close facsimile):

The Boy Scout Law: A Scout is trustworthy, loyal, helpful, friendly, courteous, kind, obedient, cheerful, thrifty, brave, clean, and reverent.[17]

The Girl Scout Law: I will do my best to be honest and fair, friendly, and helpful, considerate and caring, courageous and strong, and responsible for what I say and do, and to respect myself and others, respect authority, use resources wisely, make the world a better place, and be a sister to every Girl Scout.[18]

Interestingly, if you compare the values expressed in these two sets of scouts' laws with the eighteen Universal Character Traits of Successful Leaders defined in Figure 5.1, you will note many similarities. That may indeed say something about the fundamental values of leadership *and* about the importance of teaching leadership values to youngsters at an early age.

Although many of the traditional sources and other institutions, organizations, and associations have done an excellent job of preparing young people for roles as future leaders, others have not. When they fail to feed the character development needs of young people, peer groups—which now include both real and virtual ones on the Internet—will intercede, as will the perceptions of heroes and celebrities. Those foundations of character that are relegated to youth peer groups, television, the Internet, or other media put a formative individual's character at great risk. The food for the evil dog from these sources is often so great that that the good dog within does not have much of a chance.

How Character Can Change

While much of who we are is determined at a fairly early age, significant changes to one's character *can* occur later as the result of life experiences. For generations we have been told, "Experience is the best teacher." And it is true that various experiences can alter the values and beliefs we learned as children. The experiences that can have a significant effect on an individual's character most often come from hardship, either of a business nature (litigation, loss of a job, personality conflicts, and more) or from personal hardships (death of a loved one, significant illness, bankruptcy, divorce, recovery from drug or alcohol addiction, and the like). As Gene Klann points out, such experiences:

> *. . . can cause leaders to look inside themselves, asking questions, the answers to which can result in huge learnings, and behavioral adjustments. Hardships can reveal a leader's behavioral blind spots,*

inconsistencies, weaknesses, personal limitations, and ineffective or bad behavior . . . [and] how [their] lives may be out of balance.[19]

Besides business and personal hardships, character changes can also occur as the result of religious or spiritual experiences, which can be of a sudden, burning-bush variety or of a more gradual type that result from a course of study or by practicing certain dietary, physical, or mental disciplines.

A third way that experience can change a person's character is through coaching. Coaching is all about behavior change—be it by modifying the client's behavior (as with remedial coaching) or by enhancing it (as with developmental coaching). With the help of a coach, an individual can examine long-held values and beliefs for their current relevance and future applicability. For many individuals, this reappraisal may require the help of a trained psychotherapist. Behaviors that have deep-seated psychological roots are best treated through an appropriate form of therapy rather than by a coach, even one with training in clinical psychology.

Whether it is the result of early childhood education or subsequent hardships, through spiritual awakenings, or through purposeful development, character is, indeed, "scratched out" from the stuff of our life's experiences. Such learning experiences usually result in a heightened level of maturity and an increased sensitivity to others and to the value of personal relationships. Because the values and beliefs that constitute the universal leadership traits of personal humility and professional resolve can be learned, then anyone should have the potential of becoming a highly effective (Level 5) leader simply by feeding the right dog.[20] But, being the right leader for a particular situation takes more in the way of character than just possessing a handful of key universal traits. The values and beliefs of the right leader must align closely with those of the organization the leader is called upon to lead.

It's All About Trust, Satisfaction, and Retention

Warren Bennis has been quoted as stating, "Managers do things right. Leaders do the right things."[21] Gene Klann takes the distinction between managers and leaders further:

> *Management deals with such tasks as planning, designing, directing, controlling, and coordinating execution. By contrast, leadership is about motivating, inspiring, encouraging, and influencing people. We lead people and manage things.*[22]

Having the right leaders in a business context is of particular importance because leadership is the ultimate advantage. When it is present, it makes all other advantages possible.[23]

For leaders to lead, they must have followers; however, people will not follow someone they do not trust. Plain and simple—no trust, no leadership. And here is the key: trust is created when people hold common values.[24] So for a new leader to be the *right* leader in a given situation, that person must possess not only the right blend of universal leadership traits, but she or he must also share the specific values of the organization they are charged with leading. Peter F. Drucker puts it this way:

> *Organizations, like people, have values. To be effective in an organization, a person's values must be compatible with the organization's values. They do not need to be same, but they do need to be close enough to coexist.*[25]

In a *Harvard Business Review* article entitled, "The Enemies of Trust," Robert Galford, the managing director of the Center for Executive Development, and Anne Seibold Drapeau wrote:

> *The building blocks of trust are unsurprising: they're old-fashioned managerial virtues . . . in our experience, building a trustworthy (and trusting) organization requires close attention to those virtues. But it also requires a defensive game: You need to protect trustworthiness from its enemies, both big and small, because trust takes years to build and can suffer serious damage in just a moment.*[26]

The reason it is so important to explore the contents of the Character Bucket of any candidate for a top leadership position is that leaders cannot lead if followers will not follow; and followers will not follow unless the leader's values are closely aligned with theirs. Unfortunately the emphasis of most selection processes in use today rests on the collective perception of the prospective leader's *personality* rather than on their *character*. Because trust does not come from a particular technique but from the character of the leader, leadership style and personality have little to do with creating followership.[27]

While the Traditional Selection Model on which today's selection processes are built does little to determine the values of the candidate, it does even less to empirically ascertain the prevailing values of the organization. Even in companies that have robust values statements, they are rarely used in the selection process to explore the alignment of the candidate's values for all the reasons previously delineated; questioning candidates along these lines just isn't done on a sufficiently purposeful and regular basis today.

Given the fact that leadership is all about character and how well the leader's values approximate those of the organization, another key inference is clear—leaders who have been successful in one situation (where their values were closely aligned with those of that organization) will not *necessarily* succeed in another if their values are not sufficiently aligned with those of the new organization. The data presented in Chapter 1 corroborates this point. This notion, then, points out the fallacy of hiring the "best athlete" for a senior executive slot. Besides possessing many of the Universal Leadership Traits shown in Figure 5.1, the other situation-specific values and the relative weighting ascribed to each one are of equal, or possibly greater, importance. Someone who was successful in other situations—a star player by all rights—just may not fit a new situation where his or her values, business beliefs, and philosophies are not in sync with the rest of the organization's.

Consider the following examples of situations where some of my clients have learned about the importance of having shared values with the organization they joined:

Joseph P.: After a long and successful career in finance with the largest family-owned company of its type where he built a reputation with Wall Street for the number of major acquisitions he led, Joe left to join a very prestigious private equity group in New York City as their CFO.

Joe's Values, Beliefs, Philosophies	Company's Values, Beliefs, Philosophies
Respectfulness; fairness	Dominance; do the deal at any (Human) cost
Team Play; collegial	Individualism; self first
Hard work	Hard work
Deliver on commitments; his word is his bond	The end justifies the means
Honesty; genuineness	Flamboyance; appearances
Discipline; precision	Speed; creative solutions

Outcome: Joe stayed for less than a year before becoming CFO of a family-owned regional player in the same related business as his former company. Joe is "deliriously happy" with his new job in southern Florida.

Sharon O.: After making partner in a major accounting firm in record time, she moved quickly through a series of corporate and subsidiary finance jobs for a well-known, consumer package goods firm before being recruited into the CFO slot for XYZ, a global entertainment conglomerate.

Sharon's Values	Company's Values
Structured; process oriented	Creative; shoot from the hip
Optimistic realism	Overly optimistic
Self-control responsibility	Impetuous; grandiose
Accountability	Blaming

Outcome: During her first two years, Sharon discovered and took $1+ billion in write-downs for overvalued acquisitions made earlier. She also discovered accounting irregularities in subsidiaries that led to two restatements. Sharon was able to successfully lead the company through a Securities and Exchange Commission (SEC) investigation, describing this period as "the most miserable three years of my life." Today, her career, tainted simply by her association with the problems at XYZ (even though she only reported them and had nothing to do with their creation), is CFO at a small not-for-profit organization near her home, has taken up golf and ballroom dancing, and once again cannot wait to get to work.

Richard K. (Dick): He started with a small specialty natural resources company right after engineering school where he was recognized for his operating savvy and strategic vision. He became president seven years later and ran the company successfully for ten more years. During that time it was acquired by a global industry leader headquartered in Europe. Three years after the acquisition Dick was promoted to senior vice president with group responsibility for three operating companies in the Southwest. This was the job his current boss previously held. Two of the major units were losing money in their low-margin, long lead-time business.

Dick's Values	Boss's Values
Respectful; caring	Upwardly sensitive; downwardly indifferent
Gentle; thoughtful	Rough; reactive
Optimistic	Pessimistic
Persuasive	Dictatorial
Fair; rewards merit	Political; rewards loyalty
Teachable; innovation	Knows-it-all; by-the-book

Outcome: After two years in the job Dick is highly regarded by the people who work for him, and all three units are showing profit improvement with a growing order book and above-average margins. But Dick is highly frustrated with his boss and feels estranged and undervalued by the company at large. In a company that already lacks talented leaders, Dick is ripe for the picking.

The way trust is built makes the Character Bucket important in other ways. As pointed out in Galford and Drapeau's article about "The Enemies of Trust," "trust takes years to build"—years![28] Since building trust is essential to creating followership as well as to job effectiveness, personal satisfaction, and retention, as the previous cases indicate, the new leader must have the time that is needed—something leaders rarely get these days. Today's turnover statistics indicate that the situation is worsening. However, if hirers focus on how well the values and beliefs of the selected leader fit with those of the organization, they will at least ensure that the new leader has as much going for him or her as possible when they start, and their character will then buy them time.

Looking for Alignment Today and Tomorrow

Finally, the leader's character must be appraised in terms of the leadership challenge going forward. In *The Birth of the Chaordic Age*, author Dee Hock, founder of VISA, paints a picture of the future as follows:

> *Poised on the knife's edge between socioenvironmental disaster and a livable future, one question cuts to the core of our future: Will the result be chaos and the even more repressive and dictatorial regimes so often arising from chaordic conditions? Or will we emerge from the eggshell of our Industrial Age institutions into a new world of profound, constructive organizational change? The answer lies in the very concept of organization and in the beliefs and values of individuals.*[29]

As the future becomes the present, leaders' values will increasingly be challenged by the need to rediscover and reinvent the very nature of the companies for which they are responsible. There will be changes that demand changes in the values shared by the organization and by the leader.

Obviously, as the saying goes, you cannot give away what you do not have. If, for instance, a business unit needs to become a more collegial, open, and results-driven team capable of managing rapid growth and change in order to compete successfully in their changing markets, how can a leader who values discipline, dutifulness, frugality, perseverance, and sternness, and who believes that a strong, authoritative figure is the best spearhead for leading change, ever manage to get the organization to its intended destination? Is it possible? Yes. But is it probable in the short time frames with which leaders are often expected to accomplish such changes? No. Even a leader who has overseen other significant changes elsewhere may not be the right person for the needed change because their particular combination of values and beliefs do not adequately align with those of the current or the future values and beliefs required of the culture once the organizational metamorphosis is complete. So, leaders must be selected not only for their current values and beliefs but, in part, for their potential to evolve new character traits going forward.

Exploring a candidate's business-related character traits is so important to reaching the right selection decision that candidates who balk or who are insulted if their character is questioned should be thanked for their interest and dropped from the prospect list. The rationale for such straightforward (although seemingly rigid) action is simple:

- Candidates who do not have anything to keep in the shadows will help you illuminate whatever you need to know about them.
- Those who object to talking about their character out of fear of what you may learn probably have something to hide. This is especially important given heightened governance strictures.
- If, on the other hand, they do not want to look openly at their character traits because they fear what *they* may find, you can disqualify them for lacking sufficient self-awareness or moral courage.

Regardless of the reason, dropping a candidate from contention for resisting a character assessment is as hard and fast a guideline as I can provide for reducing the risks of selecting the wrong leader. The matter of character is just too important to be optional. Candidates cannot waive it, and hirers cannot duck, diminish, or delegate it. Sydney Finkelstein, author of *Why Smart Executives Fail* underscores the importance of understanding a leader's character this way: "Perhaps the single most important indicator of potential executive failure is the one that is hardest to precisely define—the question of character.[30] From our perspective, it is the alignment between the leaders' character and the cultures they must direct and through which they must deliver results that is the ultimate key to every leader's success.

While the exploration of a prospect's character must become a non-elective, purposeful step in the Leader Selection Processes of the future, evaluating a candidate's character is not as easy as determining their abilities and personality. For one thing, as noted previously, the degree of openness and transparency required to do so is beyond the comfort zone of many executives. Executives who can be piercingly direct on almost any business topic often flounder when asked to talk about their values, beliefs, philosophies, and aspirations. Besides feeling uncomfortable and somewhat unnatural in our culture, the examination carries very high stakes for the candidate. Since the outcome could have a significant impact on his or her income and career goals, a degree of reticence is understandable—who wouldn't prefer to avoid it rather than run the risk of revealing something that may drop them out of contention?

Besides, it is a two-way street. It is often just as uncomfortable for the hiring executive as it is for the candidate. Probing the business-related aspects of another senior executive's character just is not something most executives are accustomed to doing. When, for instance, an executive or a board member of a company interviews a potential CEO who is from a competitive company or has a celebrity cachet, it just does not *feel* appropriate. And what senior HR leader wants to ask penetrating, personal, and even potentially off-putting questions when the person across the table may become their boss after the interview is over? But let me repeat: While it is clearly difficult to undertake a diligent examination of a candidate's character, it is just too important to skip or gloss over.

The importance of principle-centered leadership is evident in the research of Booz Allen Hamilton, which has found that:

> *An organization's corporate values are never as strained as when a company is in the midst of a major transformation. Yet it is just at that juncture in an organization's evolution that positive corporate values are most needed.*[31]

The constituents of character—values, beliefs, and the behaviors of courage and integrity that are aligned with them—will make the difference in the nature of our institutions and organizations of the future. Continued use of an antiquated selection process that does not adequately explore these vital elements of character will only further disadvantage companies that are slow to change. The selection of tomorrow's right leaders begins today.

Takeaways

In considering how character can be factored into the Leader Selection Process of the future, the following points need to be considered:

- Avoiding questions that challenge candidates to reveal their innermost qualities is one strategy that must change if turnover at the top is going to be reduced.
- A list of twenty-two qualities, values, or virtues has been compiled from several noted sources in the field. The authors have reduced the list to

eighteen key Universal Character Traits of Successful Leaders, which in Figure 5.1 are divided into two groups of nine traits each under the headings of Traits of Personal Humility and Traits of Public Resolve.

- The specific inner qualities that make a leader of strong moral character can vary from society to society and even within the institutions and organizations of the same society. The relative weighting of the Universal Character Traits of Successful Leaders will vary greatly from one situation to another.

- Character develops at an early age through repetitive "feedings" from one's family, religious institutions, teachers, peer groups, and the media (books, TV, and the Internet especially).

- Hardships—either business-related or of a personal nature—will also form character. Religious experiences and work done with coaches and therapists can form character as well.

- The reason it is so important to explore the Character Bucket of any candidate for a top leadership position is that leaders cannot lead if followers will not follow, and followers will not follow unless the leader's values are closely aligned with theirs.

- Besides the trust necessary to create followership, job satisfaction and retention are improved by the alignment of the individual's values, beliefs, and philosophies with those of the organization.

- Leaders who have been successful in one situation (where their values were closely aligned with those of that organization) will not *necessarily* be successful in a new situation if their values are not sufficiently aligned with those of the new organization.

- When selecting a new leader, the character of each final candidate must be appraised in terms of the leadership challenge going forward, as well as today's.

6

The Company's Needs

Out of need springs desire, and out of desire springs the energy and the will to win.

—Denis Waitley

I n this chapter we are going to look at the deficiencies that currently exist in understanding company needs and the problems that arise in selecting the right leaders as a result. We will do this by:

- Examining the problem that exists today
- Defining the different types of needs companies have
- Exploring how a different way of defining what really needs to be done will benefit the Leader Selection Process of the future

What's Wrong With This Picture?

About the same time our firm began considering how the Match-Fit Model might affect the selection process, several statistical surveys were published that supported a need for change. One of these was Booz Allen Hamilton's 2004 CEO Succession Study. Like most other surveys from that year, it showed a definite increase in both the rate and the number of CEO dismissals versus prior years'. Its title, "The World's Most Prominent Temp Workers," caught our eye in particular because it not only indicated that more and more CEOs were losing their jobs, but at a faster and faster rate.

This report went further than the others, moreover, in stating that "underperformance—not ethics, not illegality, not power struggles—is the primary reason CEO's get fired."[1] This revelation raised questions about whether the dismissed executives really had the proper skills, experiences, knowledge, and capabilities to do their jobs.

In the Traditional Selection Process (Figure 1.2, Chapter 1), one of the earliest steps involves the development of the job description. As discussed in Chapter 3, this document is regarded by most experienced recruiters as being critical to the entire process, since it is designed to describe the capabilities the selected leader must possess to deliver the expected results successfully.

This tool—the job spec—has been around for a long time. It has been scrutinized, refined, tailored, and institutionalized in various forms in virtually every company on the planet. Because the HR community and the search firms who rely on job descriptions have a long history of working with these documents, we found it highly unlikely that the people who have a significant hand in developing the job spec would then abandon it and pursue candidates who do not meet the desired parameters. That is hardly the case. While it might have happened in some rare instances, our sense is that almost every finalist for a senior executive position has the ability to do the job as the job description specifies.

If it is true, then, that chosen executives generally *do* match the specs in most instances (which most certainly is the case), our early exploration of the Match-Fit Model began to raise a question that there might be a problem with the specs themselves. As we continued researching, we came across other surveys that supported our contention that some new executives were trying to fix the wrong things. In one, 1,087 directors were asked about what caused them to lose faith in their company's leader and decide to sack him or her. Three of the key reasons given were as follows:

1. The CEO mismanaged change (31 percent).
2. The CEO tolerated low performers for too long (29 percent).
3. The CEO denied reality (23 percent).[2]

As with the underperformance issue, we could not help but wonder why these CEOs did such a poor job of managing needed changes, tolerated low performers, and denied reality. Was it because they were bad managers or maybe they were blind to the performance issues of their direct reports? Perhaps they were generally inclined toward denial and escapism. If so, how did they ever get the job in the first place? And if not—if they were otherwise sound managers with a good sense of people and grounded on the fundamental realities of running a business—then perhaps they had simply addressed the wrong changes.

Coincidentally we came upon another research study that indicated that poor performance might be attributed to a disconnect between the needs of the company as perceived by the boss and those perceived by the new leader. Interestingly this study dealt specifically with the reasons that *new* leaders failed. This source ranked the failure "to meet the most important objective" expected of them second in the top four causes of executive departures.[3]

Once again, these results prompted us to wonder why these presumably talented executives, who had recently been subjected to a rigorous and well-established process that reputedly examined and scrutinized their ability and competency to address the needs of the company, would fail to meet the most important objective they were hired to achieve. Something couldn't be right. Either the process did not work because people were routinely selected who could not do the job, or perhaps, the needs the selected people were supposed to address were not the ones that, if addressed, would yield the results that were expected.

My own experiences making changes at the top led me to suspect that the problems lay more in how companies went about stipulating their needs— those things that the new, right leader was expected to address, resolve, and change—than in the ability of the selected leader to do the job. The result would be that the jobs that candidates had been selected to do and the jobs they found to exist once they arrived in their new position were not the same. The culprit then would be that something was missing in the way the needs were determined in the first place, and this oversight was contributing to the rising failure rates of CEOs.

Over the course of the ensuing months, we compiled a list of explanations for why executives failed. They were derived from applying the foregoing analysis to in-depth debriefings and listening to the stories of transition clients. In addition, executive recruiters and clients who were looking for some help with their searches in a range of industries provided opportunities to analyze countless job specifications.

Ultimately, we identified three reasons (other than lack of competence) that new executives might be failing to deliver what was expected of them:

1. The needs that were described to them during the interview process and on which the selection criteria and job descriptions were based were *not* what they really needed to address. As one highly capable executive told me about a situation he inherited when he took on responsibilities in a new division of his company:

   > *What I was told about the situation and what I found when I got into it were two entirely different things. The picture that was described to me was true enough, but it was just the tip of the iceberg. There were systemic people, process, and quality issues that had to be corrected before I could even begin to address the things I was expected to resolve. And no matter how many times I tried to get top management to understand the true reality of the situation, they were not willing to adjust the delivery dates that had been set by my predecessor (who had gone on to become the head of another larger division and a very influential member of the CEO's operating committee).*

2. Comments like that one triggered a second hypothesis: Otherwise highly competent leaders fail in their jobs when their perceptions about what needs to be done differ from those of their bosses (or boards). It is one thing for a new leader to come into a job and not know what needs to be done. It is something else to know what needs to be done but not to be able to persuade those who hired you to accept that the needs *they* think are important are not what really need to be done.

3. A third explanation for the failure of new leaders results from the ways the specs they originally received described the company's needs. Usually, we noted, position descriptions describe *outcomes* rather than *actions*. Often

they say something like, "the right leader will reverse the market share loss trend and return the company to profitability," or "the selected candidate will lead the international expansion of the company's brands." While both statements are very clear expressions of what the new hire is expected to accomplish, neither gives the slightest hint of what kind of specific, sequential actions are required to deliver those outcomes. Nor do they give any indication of the status and the reliability of the planning that has already gone into achieving these objectives, the extent to which resources necessary to achieve them are available, or even if these goals are really worth the price of achieving them in the first place.

Descriptions vs. Definitions

Eventually we concluded that the main reason so many new leaders fail to deliver what is expected of them is that the majority of the people who write the job specs have rarely ever done the job and do not really know what is involved in getting an entire organization redirected and moving in the proper direction. Candidates who accept positions where their deliverables are described in terms of outcomes usually do so believing that what they have done elsewhere to achieve similar results will work for them again in the current situation. Or their recent successes have given rise to the belief of extreme self-confidence that says, "I can do it. I'm a winner." Unfortunately, a lot of very talented winners have found themselves in situations that, as one former CEO in outplacement put it, "If I had realized what was going to be involved in the assignment, I never would have taken the job. It didn't play to my strengths nor, frankly, to my interests. There are a lot of people who are better qualified than I am to do what needed to be done in that situation."

So, even though the document designed to determine which candidate will represent the optimal match between their abilities and style (personality) and the perceived needs of a situation is the most precise and refined area of the Traditional Selection Process, there is still substantial room for improvement in defining the specific needs to be met in most situations.

Different Strokes for Different Folks

From the many transitions our firm has helped orchestrate, it is clear that the types of needs that companies face are as unique as the organizations themselves. In building the Match-Fit Model, however, we were able to organize them into two broad categories: executional needs and directional needs. We have found that it is valuable to differentiate between the two when selecting new leaders, because different skill sets and experiences are needed to accomplish each. Moreover, while all leaders must be able to do both—execute *and* provide direction—the emphasis in any given situation will be greater on one or the other, thereby defining the mix of abilities the right leader must possess.

Executional Needs

In their best-selling book *Execution*, Larry Bossidy and Ram Charan have done an excellent job of spelling out exactly what the term "execution" encompasses in stating:

> *But don't confuse execution with tactics. Execution is a systematic process of rigorously discussing how's and what's, questioning, tenaciously following through, and ensuring accountability. . . . In its most fundamental sense, execution is a systematic way of exposing reality and acting on it. . . . The heart of execution lies in three core processes: the people process, the strategy process, and the operating process. . . .* [4]

Executional needs, then, are all those aspects of how the company does what it does that must be fixed, changed, or stopped in order for things to get done faster, better, and more efficiently. Executional needs are also the *what's*—what must be accomplished and what the expected near-term deliverables are.

In order to be able to execute well, key processes regarding people, strategy, and operations must be in place. More often than not, the new leader will be charged with a task of fixing some aspect(s) of one or more of these. If, for instance, the people process is not providing enough talent to the leadership pipeline, then it must be fixed to execute the strategies and operate the company in the longer term.[5] The same is true with a strategic planning process or the operations process—if they are broken, then the new leader must fix them—pronto.

However, it is not sufficient to hire someone under a broad "fix-it" mandate because the skills required to fix one process one way may be different from those required to fix it another way. If hirers do not really know, factually, what needs to be fixed, as well as something about how the company at large prefers to fix problems (its values), they are setting their new leader up for potential failure.

In our experience, the determination of what needs to be done is best undertaken *before* the leader selection process is completed and *by someone besides the hiring executive* or the incumbent. Advance preparation is necessary because certain executional needs must be met immediately upon the arrival of the new leader, and other changes made to improve the organization's ability to execute in the future.

At the same time that the state of the executional processes is being examined, the specific projects, programs, and initiatives that are underway or on hold until the new leader arrives should also be identified and prioritized. Depending upon the nature of what appears on this list, the background experience of the new right leader may be viewed differently (or at least more deeply) before determining that a "match" exists. It is one thing to say in a position description, "the new right leader will reestablish operating credibility with the board, with investors, and with the street by achieving this year's quarterly and annual forecast." It is something entirely different (and far more helpful!) to be able to say, "The new right leader will reestablish operating credibility with the board, with investors, and with the street by ensuring that the attached list of critical programs, projects, and initiatives is implemented subject to his or her final discretion to thereby achieve this year's quarterly and annual forecasts."

In addition, experience indicates that those who are assigned to do the hiring usually do not *know* what needs to be done. At best they may *think* they understand the needs and how to fix them based on their own experiences and limited insights, but such thinking is often defective. Too often newly appointed leaders fail to achieve the goals expected of them because the needs that hiring executives have presented to them are not the actual needs.

The only accurate picture of the needs is one that has been researched by an impartial observer. While the hiring executives believe that their perceptions of the needs are correct, they seldom have obtained any current facts or data beyond a handful of casual conversations to support their views. In fairness to them, neither the HR head nor the executive recruiter on the selection team has ever done the job, even though they have known many people who have. If a CEO is being hired the director who chairs the search committee has rarely done this job in *this* company. And, while the executive who formerly held the job may have the best insights into what needs to be done, even his or her views may already be dated (or off the mark in the first place).

Unfortunately the complex, competing, and often overwhelming tasks associated with top-level transitions not only interfere with the new leader's chance of emptying the swamp, but even add to what is clogging the drain. To avoid these counterproductive situations, hirers must accept responsibility to know *factually* what the executional needs of the organization are *before* the new leader is selected. Doing so will greatly improve the likelihood that the person who is selected will be the right leader *and* the likelihood that the executional swamp will, indeed, get drained.[6]

Directional Needs

Directional needs pertain to those needs affecting the direction in which the company is heading. Directional needs include such things as the vision, mission, and the degree to which strategies and strategic plans support the achievement of long-term goals tied to the overall mission statement. Directional needs even include the annual operating plan—the current year of the strategic plan broken down into managerial budgets, resource allocations, and metrics-based performance targets. The *manner* in which these operational and strategic plans are achieved is an element of execution, while their *content* is directional in nature.

As with executional needs, hirers should be careful to avoid assuming anything about the true state of directional issues without first testing the truth of those perceptions. It is easy to look at a business that is struggling and assume that it needs a leader with strong directional skills to create a new, more effective plan for growth. While lack of direction may seem to be the problem, there may be any number of executional issues that are interfering with an existing growth strategy that may otherwise be quite attainable, timely, and well conceived. In that instance, the right leader might actually be someone whose strengths lie more in the executional realm than in the directional. Assume nothing. Just as in every other discipline, measure, test, and base your choices on hard data and objective, factual information, and not just appearances.

Equally important, however, we have found that the research into directional needs may be placed on a lower priority basis to executional needs. At first, this may seem illogical. Metaphorically, you may ask what difference it makes how well you can cut trees if you are in the wrong forest. However, as we looked at the realities and completed our first few evaluations of corporate needs, it became evident that putting executional needs ahead of directional needs in terms of importance for newly selected leaders is appropriate for several reasons:

- Except maybe in true startup situations, all stakeholders have performance expectations for the new leader. Research shows that a CEO can endure only five quarters of underperformance before losing the board's support.[7] If the new leader does not deliver results quickly, he or she will not be around long enough to make a significant change in the directional needs.
- Without execution, momentum is lost, which exacerbates whatever other problems are plaguing the company. As Bossidy and Charan put it, "Without execution, the breakthrough thinking breaks down, learning has no value, people don't meet their stretch goals, and the revolution stops dead in its tracks."[8]
- Executional needs relating to deficiencies with people, strategy, or operational processes can significantly impact directional needs that relate to vision, mission, and strategic intent. Even if the company needs to reinvent itself for future success and rechart its future course, it will not be able to do so without those three key executional processes in place and fully functional. Therefore, addressing executional needs *before* directional ones is not only expedient, but sequentially essential.

- Information about executional needs is more readily available and actionable than longer-term directional issues and concerns. Although a former leader was not able to deliver the expected results, the other senior executives are likely capable of, and concerned about, correcting the executional problems. They are in their positions because most of them have earned the right to be, and almost all of them care greatly about the future well-being of the organization. They have committed their time and their careers to the success of their function, and they usually know it better than anyone else in the organization. In most cases their view of which specific projects, programs, and initiatives are critical to the achievement of the shorter term objectives is a far better and more credible source than any other.

- Ownership of major directional initiatives by the person who is responsible for their implementation is extremely important to their success. The new leader must be passionate about the direction in which he or she is leading the organization once they take over. This passion usually comes from the painstaking process of listening to customers, employees, and suppliers, and then wrestling through alternative approaches and possibilities with fellow executives while incubating a strategic plan. For this reason we feel it is often more desirable to provide the new leader with a detailed road map for the first few miles of the journey (the executional needs) but leave the remaining sections of the map (the directional needs) less specific, vague, or even blank for him or her to determine for themselves.

To some degree, all senior executives are expected to be visionaries and strategic thinkers. But let's face it: Some people are better at dealing with these kinds of directional issues than they are at handling executional matters, and vice versa. So knowing the relative weight of the executional versus directional needs can help lead to the selection of someone whose ability to handle that mix of needs is more synchronous, someone whose strengths align with the true needs of the situation.

First Steps in Measuring the Shape of the Hole

If the leader is the peg, then the hole into which the right leader should fit is defined, in part, by the executional and directional actions that are needed to be accomplished. The right leader is one who, at least in part, possesses the abilities, personality, and energy that best match what needs to be done on both executional and directional levels. The Traditional Selection Process has proven itself over time as relatively good at assessing the abilities of senior executives and determining their style-related attributes. And it generally does identify candidates with sufficient energy to match the rigors of the job. One of the ways the Traditional Selection Process needs improvement, however, is in doing a better job of factually defining the organization's executional needs and specifying them in terms of the actions required of the new leader. To a lesser degree, directional needs need to be so defined, too. Even if these data are not available at the outset, so long as it is gathered *before* the selection process is over they can dramatically alter how the hirers look at the relative strengths of the final candidates in terms of their match.

The easiest way to define needs is in terms of actions and outcomes— what does the organization need the new leader to accomplish and how do they anticipate he or she will do this? Once the actions that will satisfy the needs are defined and recorded, they provide the blueprint for identifying the abilities (and to some extent, the personality) the successful candidate must possess. Knowing what abilities are required will then define the interviewing and assessment tools to use in selecting the right leader.

Moreover, consider the value that having such action-oriented job specs can add to the ability of a newly selected leader to execute the things most needed by the company beginning on day one. It takes a lot of the guesswork out of answering the question, "So what is it going to take to achieve this year's operating plan?" The new leader now has accurate information to use in determining not only which initiatives, plans, or programs need support, but also exactly what actions are needed where. No longer does he or she have to rely on one single solution applied across the entire span of their control. Instead, the leader can mobilize the team to address exactly what needs to be fixed exactly where it needs fixing.

As we shall see in Part Two, the research to determine what really needs to be done can best be accomplished by someone from the outside who is not otherwise connected to the company asking questions of the Executive Leadership Team that will report to the new leader. The person who does this research must be able to guarantee that everything said will be anonymous and shared only as part of an overall summary and only to the new leader, the new leader's boss, and/or the board of directors. Questions that assess the company's readiness to address its directional and executional needs are particularly relevant and should be asked of a broader sample to obtain quantifiable responses too. This information becomes an extremely powerful tool for the new leader to use in determining not only which initiative, plan, or programs need support, but also the actions that will improve their likelihood of success.

Knowing what really needs to be done to achieve the desired goals will,

- Allow hirers to focus more specifically on the final candidate's real qualifications to do the job.

- Reduce the risk of failure by providing the new leader with a current, fact-based set of things that must be done—things to initiate, things to continue, things to stop.
- Allow the new leader to do what is expected of him or her more quickly and with greater confidence—to start to lead sooner and more boldly.
- Buy time for the new leader to become acclimated to the new situation, to the new people, and to the new responsibilities, while still making progress on those key actions that are so critical to success.

Regardless of how you get at the true executional and directional needs that must be addressed—whether it is through formal questions or protocol-based interviews with senior management, and regardless of whether it involves collaborating on a detailed analysis of individual departments and geographies—in order to help select the leader whose abilities best match the needs at hand (and to improve the likelihood of success of a new leader), specific actions rather than general outcomes *must* be identified.

Ideally it would be optimal if this information were available at the start of the selection process. But having the necessary lead time to complete this work is rare. Nevertheless once the need to make a change at the top is known, work can begin on identifying the true needs of the company and the key actions that must occur in the short term in order for the new leader to know what needs to be done and to initiate the correct actions to do it.

If these action-oriented needs cannot be incorporated into the initial draft of the job spec, they certainly can be incorporated into updated revisions to it and used in interviews with final candidates. In addition they can become a powerful tool to help the new leader determine not only which initiatives, plans, and programs need support, but also what actions will improve their chances for success once they begin their new job.

Takeaways

The following are some highlights of how a proper understanding of the real corporate needs impact the selection process:

- The focus of the Traditional Selection Process is on the abilities of the candidates to do the perceived job. In this respect, the process is effective and well defined. However, unless the needs are also defined accurately, capable executives may end up trying to fix the wrong things.
- One of the places where the Traditional Selection Process needs improvement is in factually defining the organization's executional and directional needs. They must be defined in terms of actions rather than outcomes.

- Candidates who accept positions where their deliverables are described in terms of outcomes usually do so believing that what they have done elsewhere to achieve similar results will work for them again in the current situation. Rarely is this the case.
- Of the two broad categories of needs—executional and directional—focusing on the executional ones ahead of directional ones first will help the new leader build momentum and fix elements of needed infrastructure essential to longer-term success.
- Whenever possible, research of the executional and directional needs should be carried out *before* the selection process gets underway, so the specific actions required of the new leader can be incorporated into the job specification. Quite often, however, that timing is not realistic, in which case the research can be conducted while the initial phases of the selection process are underway, and the data incorporated into the specs before final candidates are screened.

7

Corporate Culture

People who think culture is a just bunch of bacteria in yogurt set a tone that strips value from a company.

—John Rogers,
Goldman Sachs Management Committee

Jack Goes to Prep School

When my son Jack turned 14, we began looking at private schools in our area. In the process I learned something about the nature of culture. While touring the St. James School, I was intrigued by several of its customs: As at many prep schools, students were required to wear a sport coat and a tie on campus. Unlike other schools we had visited, however, we noticed that no student passed by another anywhere in the academic or dormitory areas without an acknowledgment; moreover, every student would jump to his feet whenever an adult entered a room—even in the middle of a classroom lecture or an exam.

Following a fairly intensive interview process, Jack decided to go to St. James. A few weeks after classes began, I drove out to the school to see how things were going. I found Jack leaving the gym, dressed in a sport coat and tie and looking much older and more mature than I had ever seen him. We shook hands and then hugged warmly. A few months earlier the hug would have been accompanied by a fatherly kiss on the cheek, but now Jack's attire and body language prohibited it.

The day was unseasonably warm and humid, and Jack was still sweating from his soccer practice despite a shower. But he explained that he could not remove his blazer because, "That's the dress code everyone goes by here, no matter what the temperature."

Then as we crossed the quad, I noticed how he greeted all the other boys, many of them by name. A little while later as we sat in his dorm room talking, one of his advisers stuck his head in the door to say "hello," and Jack sprang to his feet with such speed that he startled me.

When we were alone later, I couldn't help asking him, "What gives with the coat and tie on such a hot day? The numerous greetings to schoolmates? And this 'hopping to' when an adult enters the room? You certainly never did these things at home!" "Oh, Dad," he said with a slightly patronizing tone, "it's just the way we do things here at St. James." "Okay, son, that's fair enough," I acknowledged. "But how do you *know* that that's the way you're supposed to behave after being here for only a few short weeks?" "That's simple," he replied. "The first night I was here the headmaster called us to the chapel and explained, 'Gentleman, this is how we do things at St. James.'" Jack went on to recall how the headmaster not only described the way

(*continued*)

students were expected to behave, but also the reasons why they were expected to behave in those ways. The implications of *not* adopting "the way we do things here at St. James" could range from simple peer disapproval to expulsion depending on the infraction, he added.

In the business community, we have not generally emphasized the purposeful management of culture the way the headmaster at St. James did. Not all CEOs are as clear about what their constituents' behaviors should be, and few take the time to teach their culture to new members. Furthermore, as we have already noted, the Traditional Selection Process in use today emphasizes the prospective leader's ability to address perceived needs rather than how that leader might fit in to the company's culture.

In this chapter we will look at these conditions and their significance in the following sequence:

- Understanding organizational culture and its importance to business leaders
- Examining myths associated with the concept of culture in business
- Relating how the proper alignment of a leader's character to the culture of an organization contributes to business success

The Meaning of Culture

My son's exclamation, "It's just the way we do things here at St. James," paints as clear a picture of the power culture has over behavior as can be found. For that is exactly what cultures do—they tell us how to behave. When you are a part of a culture, you know the right way to do things, and when you are not, finding the "right" way can be *very* perplexing.

On my way home from my son's school, I reflected on the visit with my son. Four other important points struck me about the culture I had encountered there:

1. Clearly, the headmaster knew exactly what he (and the administration, and faculty) wanted the culture at St. James to be. Besides knowing what their culture is, they worked at cultivating it—not leaving the transmission of that culture to a new generation to chance.
2. It became evident that cultural designs for living (guidelines for how to properly behave) could easily be taught to new and willing members of the organization. That was evident from the speed with which my son had picked up on the right way to act as a St. James student.

3. I also realized that the rigorous interview process at the school not only determined if candidates were able to handle the schoolwork and contribute something back to the student community (their abilities, personality and energy), but also determined whether their values and beliefs (their character) would predispose them to accept the school's culture. The school had selected my son not only because he *matched* the profile of a good student, but because he would *fit* their culture as well.

4. Seemingly, everyone at the school held the values that made up a large part of the St. James culture. On that sweltering Indian summer's day, I do not recall seeing a single student, faculty member, or school administrator with his jacket slung over his shoulder. As a matter of fact, it seemed as if there were a spirit of camaraderie emanating from the fact that *everybody* was in the same boat and silently suffering from the same shared discomfort—and even enjoying a common badge of honor, a sense of belonging, as a result of it.

While there are many definitions, they all agree that cultures provide normative guidelines for the behavior of those who are a part of the group. Also, most agree that the shared sense of belonging that comes from adhering to those norms provides the group with stability. My favorite definition came originally from Clyde Kluckhohn:

Cultures are the historically created designs for living, explicit and implicit, rational, irrational, and non-rational, which exist at any given time as potential guides to the behaviors of their members.[1]

Looking back at the story of Jack going to prep school, we can see examples of Kluckhohn's definition in action:

- **"explicit guideline"**: The stipulated rules that all students wear a sport coat and tie regardless of the temperature.
- **"implicit guideline"**: The shared knowledge that an affectionate paternal kiss was no longer appropriate under new circumstances.
- **"rational guideline"**: Greeting cohorts while passing one another makes sense, since it helps newcomers feel welcome and encourages all students to get to know one another.
- **"irrational guideline"**: While explicit, wearing a blue blazer and tie after practice on a sweltering day just doesn't make sense to me.
- **"nonrational guideline"**: As far as I can discern, having students jump to their feet is just one of those things that was selected as a mark of respect for adults. Like driving on the right-hand side of the road versus the left, it is more a product of convention than of reason.

Culture Is Not Something You Get at the Met

One business leader who clearly understood the importance of culture to his organization was Melvin Goodes. Goodes was the CEO of Warner-Lambert from 1991 to 1999. During his time as chief executive Warner-Lambert's market value went from $9 billion to almost $60 billion. Unlike so many of his counterparts from that era who used the term "culture" without really understanding it, Goodes knew what he was talking about and used that knowledge to deliver an exceptional track record of success. He described culture as, " . . . the coding of values and deeply held beliefs that mold an organization's decision patterns, guide its actions, and drive individual behavior."[2]

As Goodes's definition indicates, values are the bedrock of any corporate culture. They determine the basic concepts and beliefs of the organization. As such they form the heart of the corporate culture. Values define what "success" means in concrete terms for employees—"if you do this, you too will be a success"—and establish standards of achievement within the organization.[3]

Although many organizations have a formal, written statement of values that appears in policy manuals, on Web sites, and in other official documents, the ones that matter the most are those that are strongly understood and felt by the organization, regardless of whether they are written down or are unwritten. They are the norms that have developed over time and that require a degree of emotional intelligence to identify. Leaders who are effective are those who understand these unwritten values as well as the written ones. As a result they are able to behave in a manner consistent with them. As Robert Goffee and Gareth Jones remarked in "What Holds the Modern Company Together?" "networks can function well if you are an insider—you know the right people, hear the right gossip. Those on the outside often feel lost in the organization, mistreated by it, or simply unable to affect processes or products in any real way."[4]

In addition to values and beliefs, heroes, rites, and rituals contribute to the creation of cultures. And in order to survive, cultures develop informal, but powerful, communications networks. Knowing what is being said is as important as knowing what to say. And knowing how to say it, to whom, and when is every bit as important.[5]

Terrance Deal and Allan Kennedy do an excellent job of pulling together all the elements that make up corporate culture and their importance to an organization in the following statement:

> *Companies that have cultivated their individual identities by shaping values, making heroes, spelling out rites and rituals, and acknowledging a cultural network have an edge. These corporations have values and*

beliefs to pass along—not just products. They have stories to tell—not just profits to make. They have heroes whom managers and workers can emulate—not just faceless bureaucrats. In short, they are human institutions that provide practical meaning for people, both on and off the job.[6]

Culture goes even deeper than this, moreover. In an aptly titled classic on the subject *Organizational Culture and Leadership,* Dr. Edgar Schein, the former chairman of the organizational studies group at MIT's Sloan School of Business, identifies three fundamental characteristics of culture. They are as follows:

1. Artifacts (everything that can be seen, touched, or heard about a culture)
2. The espoused beliefs, values, rules, and behavioral norms held by the group
3. The "tacit, taken-for-granted, basic underlying assumptions" of the organization[7]

My earlier description of my son's first weeks at a new school focuses only on one element of Schein's taxonomy: artifacts. The behaviors I described were all *artifacts*—observable evidence—of the school's underlying values, beliefs, and assumptions. However, when the headmaster spoke to the new students and explained the reasons for the behaviors he was instilling the *values* of the school (the second element). His remarks even touched on the most *basic assumptions* (element three) of the school's culture. (Conform to the rules or run the risk of ostracism; honor your "uniform" or lose the respect of your peers; older means wiser, which is what we revere so stand up when an adult enters the room, and so on.)

Besides the key elements of culture, another dimension that is important to consider is how they are described and compared. As Deal and Kennedy point out, "A strong culture is a powerful lever for guiding behavior; it helps employees do their jobs a little better."[8] Note that this quote talks about how *strong* cultures help employees. It does not refer to cultures as being good or bad, but to their relative intensity—strong versus weak. The implication is that cultures should not be judged but measured. In their article "Leading by Leveraging Culture" Jennifer Chatman and Sandra Cha explain:

> *Strong cultures are based on two characteristics, high levels of agreement among employees about what's valued and high levels of intensity about these values. If both are high, a strong culture exists; and if both are low, the culture is not strong at all. Some organizations are characterized by high levels of intensity but low levels of agreement, or what would be called, "warring factions."*[9]

The value in assessing cultures in terms of their strength or weakness is evident. Consider some of the better-known corporations viewed as having their own unique cultures—companies like Disney, Ritz-Carlton, Nordstrom's, Wal-Mart, Procter & Gamble, and IBM. The cultures of these companies are different—*very* different from each other. But who's to say that one is good and another is not? Or that one is better than another?

Jim Collins and Jerry Portas reinforce this point about the relative strengths of corporate culture in *Built to Last*, when they state:

> *There is no "right" set of core values for being a visionary company. Indeed, two companies can have radically different ideologies, yet both be visionary. Core values in a visionary company don't even have to be "enlightened" or "humanistic," although they often are. The crucial variable is not the content of the company's etiology, but how deeply it believes its etiology and how consistently it lives, breathes, and expresses it in all that it does. Visionary companies do not ask, "What should we value?" They ask, "What do we actually value deep down to our toes?"*[10]

When a company is just starting up, the values and beliefs of its founder are reflected in the values and beliefs of the rest of the organization: the founder hires people whose attitudes and values reflect his or her own and weeds out those whose do not.[11] As time passes some founders pay less attention to developing their company's culture, and it just evolves, while others continue to purposefully and diligently shape the kind of company they want.

As companies continue in their evolution, new leaders come to power and become responsible for shaping the culture. Those organizations with the strongest cultures are those whose continuing generations of leaders have worked diligently at shaping and reshaping their cultures, and it is safe to say that such companies have served as the sustaining forces in America's economic heritage.

Global Cultures

Besides the organization's culture and, as we shall see, its numerous subcultures, a newly selected leader may also have to contend with the culture of the society, country, or region in which the company operates. As national and corporate cultures become increasingly heterogeneous, the challenge of achieving cultural fit is increased. Hirers will need to be increasingly sensitive to differences among customs, norms, and guidelines of behavior. The accountability of leaders from a global fit perspective must increasingly become a factor in the Leader Selection Process of the future.

During the late 1980s through the 1990s the globalization of several companies I worked for was a concern. With changes in technology (cell phones, e-mails, and videoconferences) came the capability to interface with colleagues and cohorts in a variety of ways on a real-time basis around the globe. With the creation of these new global teams came the beginnings of new subcultures. At first our only concern was with explicit guidelines around questions like what language to use, what time zone defines "time," or what Internet protocol to use. More implicit guidelines followed. Some were rational, some irrational, and some nonrational, like decisions about who speaks first during the videoconference discussion, or that putting e-mail messages in bold is comparable to yelling at someone, or whether sending blind copies is or is not an acceptable form of communication. Around the various technology-enabled interfaces, subcultures formed. At the same time some elements of existing cultures became more deeply entrenched. Subtle cultural differences that had never been an issue or a source of irritation or an affront had to be managed. Even clear-cut virtues like courtesy and honesty, to cite just two, began to take on new meanings at points where cultures came in contact with one another.

The added burden of the globalized corporation for leaders comes from the fact that many of the people with whom they deal are not members of the same cultures and do not know the proper conventions and shorthand ways of communication. The old country ways of doing things are the standard fallback position . . . or are they? As an American woman you may greet a close female work associate who is Japanese one way in Japan but in an entirely different way at a sporting event in the States . . . or do you? But what do you do if she receives a promotion to a higher grade level than you, then how do you greet her here and there? Would it matter if your company were an American Internet company or a Japanese automobile manufacturer? What if you run into her in Saudi Arabia?

The point is that societal, country, and even regional cultures can play a very big role in determining the proper behavior of leaders. While in some instances they can, as in the case of global subcultures, play a facilitating role for those operating within them, they can also add considerable complexity to the job as well. Fortunately there are a myriad of sources—internal and external consultants, governmental agencies, books, and Internet sites—that can provide helpful guidelines for specific situations. For hirers the key is that the portion of the job that requires cross-cultural connections is stipulated and explored in as much detail as any other actionable area of a new leader's selection regimen.

Debunking the Myths of Culture

When selecting leaders, culture is clearly a very important consideration. Yet it was not until after *In Search of Excellence* hit the best-seller list in 1982 that many companies even began to develop value statements.[12] Moreover, there are not many that take their own statements to heart and fewer still that have moved further toward purposefully managing their cultures to gain competitive advantage by practicing them. Steps to purposefully manage and shape culture have not advanced very far in the past twenty-five years. Nor is the importance of culture sufficiently detailed in business school curricula to change matters much on that front either. Consequently, while the term is a part of every business leader's executive lexicon, culture remains a largely untapped tool for transformation, labeled as "that soft stuff" and clouded by myths.

Because culture has stayed on the back burner of most company agendas, there still exist today a number of misunderstandings about the subject. If pain is the touchstone of growth (as the old spiritual axiom goes), then we may get past the pain caused by the outrageous number of failed leadership changes in business today, by growing out of these old ideas.

Some more accurate ways of looking at the old myths attached to the concept of culture are shown in Table 7.1.

Now let's examine some of the truths behind these myths in more detail:

Myth 1: Culture is that "soft stuff"—it does not directly affect business results or shareholder returns. Since Peters and Waterman first labeled culture the "softest" stuff around (a reference they later contradicted), numerous studies have documented the fact that culture has a direct impact on company performance.[13] To my way of thinking, that puts it in the hardest-stuff-around category.

Whether the objective is to deliver exceptional bottom-line performance, to facilitate the long-term accomplishment of strategies, or to prevent the catastrophic financial consequences of a failed acquisition or merger, culture unquestionably plays a very *hard* role in determining corporate performance. Take, for example, the role values play in the Toyota production system. While a number of companies have tried to emulate Toyota's success, they have not been able to because, as Gurneck Baines notes in *Meaning Inc.*, "they focused on Toyota's visible activities and structures rather than the unwritten values around quality [a big part of the Toyota culture] that underpinned these activities and structures."[14]

An area that clearly reflects the power organizational culture can have on performance is mergers and acquisitions. In *Liberating the Corporate Soul*, Richard Barrett cites a survey of more than 300 big mergers conducted by Mercer Management Consulting. It found that "the main reasons for merger disappointment are the lack of an integration strategy and the failure to appreciate the difficulties of blending together two different corporate cultures."[15] As a result in the three years following these transactions 57 percent of the merged firms lagged behind their industries in terms of total returns to shareholders.

Table 7.1
Debunking the Myths of Culture

	The Myth	The Reality
Myth 1	Culture is that "soft stuff" — It does not directly affect business results or shareholder returns.	Companies with strong cultures produce higher immediate returns and are more likely to deliver on their strategic objectives.
Myth 2	Corporate cultures are what they are and cannot be appreciably shaped or changed.	Cultures are "living things" that will grow on their own or can be shaped by proper nurturing, renewal, and discipline.
Myth 3	Cultural changes require a strong-willed leader who is willing to "shake things up."	Enduring cultural changes are achieved from the bottom up and require the leaders to have a deep and sensitive understanding of the ways people interact with it.
Myth 4	Culture must be experienced to be understood — It cannot be easily described, measured, or taught.	Tools to measure, describe, and teach culture now exist and like any other business attribute, process, or asset, if you do not measure it you cannot manage it.
Myth 5	Organizations only have one dominant culture — It is pretty much the same everywhere you go in the company.	An organization may have many different cultures or subcultures, or even no discernable dominant culture at the corporate level.
Myth 6	When selecting new leaders, cultural considerations need not be central to the process and are not all that essential for success.	Senior leaders do not fail because they cannot do the job — they fail because they do not fit the culture(s), which makes cultural considerations paramount to the selection process.

In a similar vein Thomas Zweifel, a professor of leadership in international and public affairs at Columbia University, writes, "Statistics tell us that more than half of attempted mergers and acquisitions fail; the number might even be higher with cross-border alliances." He then cites the research of Larraine Segil, involving 200 companies in 60 industries that found that "75%

[sic] of companies surveyed believed that alliance failure was caused by incompatibility of country or corporate cultures."[16]

Whether it is the postacquisition integration of companies or by the day-to-day operations of business units large or small, the strength of the culture will have a direct impact on the performance of the unit, as seen in this telling description:

> *Strong cultures enhance organizational performance in two ways. First, they improve performance by energizing employees— appealing to their higher ideals and values and rallying them around a set of meaningful, unified goals. Such ideals excite employee commitment and effort because they are inherently engaging and fill voids in identity and meaning. Second, strong cultures boost performance by shaping and coordinating employees' behavior. Stated values and norms focus employees' attention on organizational priorities that then guide their behavior and decision making. They do so without impinging, as formal control systems do, on the autonomy necessary for excellent performance under changing conditions.*[17]

Culture, then, is just as "hard" a concept as, say, EBITDA (Earnings Before Interest, Taxes, Depreciation, and Amortization) or EVA (Economic Value Added) or Net Present Value. The only difference is that culture, if managed properly, can lead to the *creation* of the thing those other concepts only *measure*—tangible shareholder returns.

Myth 2: Corporate cultures are what they are and cannot be appreciably shaped or changed. Corporate cultures generally begin with the founders' values and beliefs, which then become very deep-rooted over time. Like brands, cultures change slowly and awkwardly. Cultural change, in the sense of changing the basic, underlying assumptions is "difficult, time-consuming and highly anxiety-provoking—a point especially relevant for the leader who sets out to change the culture of the organization."[18] Cultural changes require patience and consistency of direction. Nevertheless, culture *does* respond to the influence of its leaders, just as plants do to the presence or absence of light, food, and water.

In 1982 Schein identified several ways in which leaders can affect the cultures of even large, multinational corporations.[19] These techniques can be summarized as follows:

1. *Cultures respond to what leaders pay attention to, measure, and control.* What, for instance, do you think young managers will emphasize once they see that a slick presentation will get them recognized? Consider, in contrast, where GE's prescribed presentation layout (single page per item, four blocks, horizontal format) focuses *their* employees' attention. The culture of the former organization values form, the latter values substance.

2. *Culture responds to how leaders react to critical incidents and organizational crises.* Consider the profound effect that Jim Burke, former chairman and CEO of Johnson & Johnson, had on the culture of J&J when, in 1982, he stood up for product integrity and voluntarily pulled 31 million bottles of Tylenol off retail shelves simply at the prospect that one additional bottle might have been tampered with.[20] Because crises are highly observable events while day-to-day, business-as-normal activities are not, crises give organizations a chance to see the true character of their leaders in action. And it gives their leaders a chance to shape the culture by how they behave when in the spotlight. As P&G chief A.G. Lafley discovered while leading the company's Asian operations (through a major earthquake in Japan and an economic collapse), "you learn ten times more in a crisis than during normal times."[21]

3. *Culture responds to the deliberate role-modeling, teaching, and coaching of its leaders.* "Walking the talk" is the most critical way leaders can shape their company's culture. Just as my son Jack and I learned from his first day at the St. James School, not only can cultural norms (artifacts) be taught, so can deeper-seated values, beliefs, and assumptions. It takes a leader, however, to teach them and the leader-teacher must know exactly what it is he or she intends to teach.

4. *Cultures are influenced by the allocation of rewards and status.* This fact has been known and utilized by many companies now for years. The GE "9-block" evaluation system (a variation of which is described in *Execution* by Bossidy and Charan)[22] is one way to formally incorporate both the assessment of an individual's alignment with corporate values as well as of his or her achievement of performance objectives into an annual merit review process.

Chatman and Cha's article makes this point: "Leveraging culture is but one of a number of key leadership tools . . . that by actively managing culture, an organization will be more likely to deliver on strategic objectives over the long run."[23] Culture *can* be actively leveraged to yield improved hard performance. What's more, as Chatman and Cha conclude, "It is a leader's primary role to develop and maintain an effective culture."[24]

Myth 3: Cultural changes require a strong-willed leader who is willing to "shake things up." What is key in debunking this particular myth about culture is realizing that the sheer will of a leader cannot effectively impose cultural change on an organization that already possesses an established culture. It is just not going to happen. As a matter of fact, established cultures crave leaders they can trust, not "celebrity CEOs" or a flamboyant change agent whose ego and self-orientation causes people to wonder what their real motives are. This point is made patently clear in the following paragraph taken from the National Defense University's essay on "Strategic Leadership and Decision Making":

> . . . *many of the problems confronting leaders can be traced to their inability to analyze and evaluate organizational cultures. Many leaders, when trying to implement new strategies or a strategic plan leading to a new vision, will discover that their strategies will fail if they are inconsistent with the organization's culture. A CEO, political appointee, or flag officer who comes into an organization prepared to "shake the place up" and institute sweeping changes often experiences resistance to changes and failure. Difficulties with organizational transformations arise from failures to analyze an organization's existing culture.*[25]

A corollary of this principle is that it is the champions—the leaders whom the existing culture is willing to follow—who can bring about cultural change, not the tyrants and bullies.

Jack Welch, the CEO of General Electric when it was the largest corporation in the world, had the image of a leader whose will to "shake the place up" effectively prevailed over the culture of a huge organization. However, a review of the facts does not support that picture.

First Welch selected key initiatives used to drive desired changes wisely (including Work Out, Speed, Boundarylessness, Six Sigma, and eventually, pocket-sized GE values cards that tied everything together). These change initiatives were purposeful, sequential, and always well explained. People may not have liked the fact that GE was going to be either number one or number two in every business it participated in, but they surely understood the plan and behaved accordingly.

To ensure that his initiatives were fully communicated and produced the desired behavioral changes, Welch leveraged a very broad and deep options plan that kept those people who needed to share the desired values and deliver results focused on the success of the company. He not only tied the changes to executive merit reviews, but made sure they were discussed regularly at business reviews and when doing succession planning. He tracked progress at his quarterly corporate officers' meetings and checked that external audiences like analysts and the press wrote about them and understood their importance. Everywhere he went (and he went everywhere) he talked the talk and, yes, he walked it too. As the key to ensuring no one missed out on the important details of these assumption-changing initiatives, he saw to it that the underlying principles of all change-related activities were an integral part of the curricula of the programs taught at the GE Crotonville facility where he and his direct reports regularly appeared to help reinforce the messages of change.

So, was Jack Welch a "strong-willed" leader? Yes, he most certainly was. Did he "shake up GE" as its CEO? Absolutely. But my contention is that he did not change the culture by forcing his will on it; he did it by becoming a master at creating and leveraging the structures, infrastructures, processes, and procedures available to him on a global basis in order to change the most basic assumptions of "who are we," "what we stand for," and "what we believe in" throughout the worldwide culture of GE.

Myth 4: Culture must be experienced to be understood; it cannot be easily described, measured, or taught. As you study the hero-founders of so many enduring and successful companies—the Tom Watsons, the Henry Fords, the Levi Strausses, the Sam Waltons—you will observe that each had a value-set that he infused into the DNA of his company. These individuals repeatedly described it to their teams, modeled it in their actions, and recruited, selected, and promoted those whose values were in sync with that culture. In other words they consciously taught it. When culture can be measured and therefore described, it can be taught.

Although a relatively new phenomenon, more precise ways of measuring and describing corporate culture have started to be developed. Booz Allen Hamilton has come up with a three-step approach. It provides for:

1. The assessment of current corporate values
2. The development of target corporate values
3. Designing the change program designed to "align a company's values and business goals"

Regarding the rigor used to measure values, Booz Allen Hamilton stresses that "it is important to measure corporate values improvement with the same discipline that one would insist on when measuring increases in productivity or revenue."[26]

Richard Barrett has also developed an assessment tool to measure a corporation's culture in terms of its degree of evolution. He has a seven-tier hierarchy he calls the "Seven Levels of Corporate Consciousness."[27] While not as specific as I feel is necessary for a new senior leader who is transitioning into a key top job, Barrett's approach does provide a means of looking at the compatibility of an individual's values with those of the corporation.

Part Two of this book will describe the methodology Crenshaw Associates has pioneered that we call "Mapping the Corporate Lay of the Land," (or "Mapping" for short). It is one of four separate elements of pre-hire research that we advocate adding to the new Leader Selection Process. The composite work of which Mapping is a part we call "Forward Assessment Consulting." Through the Mapping process leaders can identify both executional and directional needs (see Chapter 10) and the key attributes of culture—artifacts, values, and beliefs.[28]

All these data-driven approaches—Booz Allen Hamilton's, Richard Barrett's, and Crenshaw's Mapping the Corporate Lay of the Land—demonstrate that culture *can* be measured and described in a business context. In different ways, they all provide a foundation for creating a more precise, standardized set of tools to define corporate cultures. Once the tool is implemented, any business can transmit its culture to newcomers just as the headmaster at the St. James School did and just as some company founders have done in the early stages of their companies' lives. A business can use them to select a leader who fits the culture and can implement the changes needed for success.[29]

Myth 5: Organizations only have one dominant culture; it is pretty much the same everywhere you go in the company. One of the first studies to discredit this myth compared various military units during World War II, concluding, "Subcultures within organizations can be widely diverse and even give rise to countercultures."[30] As Schein discovered, when a company starts out, the values of the company are a reflection of those of the founders.[31] As companies grow, however, the direct influence that leaders have is reduced simply because they cannot be in all the places necessary to have direct impact as often as required. Somewhere along the line they stop hiring people who share their personal values and start hiring people who can simply do the work—hence the heavy emphasis on abilities and virtually none on character in the Traditional Selection Process. As companies grow and/or as business units take root farther away from the center or headquarters, subcultures evolve.

Corporate self-knowledge of "who we are" and "why we are the way we are" gets diluted the farther away from the center one gets, often leaving managers of subsidiaries, divisions, and branches to improvise.[32] Culture spreads like the ripples emanating from a pebble dropped in a pool—the farther away from the epicenter you go, the weaker the impact, which makes the study of cultures all the more difficult:

> One additional aspect complicates the study of culture: the group of cultural unit which "owns" the culture. An organization may have many different cultures or subcultures, or even non-discernible dominant culture at the organization level. Recognizing the cultural unit is essential to identifying and understanding the culture.[33]

To be successful, newly appointed leaders must understand and embrace a minimum of three separate cultural units they must operate in and through which they must bring about change. One cultural unit is the organization at large. The second is the team of direct reports that the leader leads. The third we call the "boss's team." Although in the case of the CEO it may be the subculture of the board at large that constitutes his or her boss's team.

Regardless of the makeup of these cultural units, they each have a very powerful effect on the acceptance and success of the new leader. I cannot recount the number of times I have seen newly selected leaders, who were otherwise very competent, fail to understand the values and beliefs of the team they inherited. Committed to bringing about change, they moved too quickly, failing to respect historical conventions, and thereby alienated themselves from the trust of the team. If a new leader lasts eighteen months under these circumstances, it is a surprise. Sometimes it is a lot less, as was the case of Bill, a friend of mine.

Bill's Subculture Chasm

At age 35, Bill was a very fast-track marketing executive. After earning his MBA from a prestigious Eastern school, he went to work for a well-known Midwestern consumer durables manufacturer where he built a well-deserved reputation as a "creative products innovator." Moving through the chairs there quickly, he left after five years to join a large, West Coast sporting goods manufacturer with several excellent brand names. His marketing talents and leadership skills were recognized through a series of successful new product launches, and he was soon recruited to become the head of marketing for a rapidly growing video-gaming company in Silicon Valley. As in his other previous assignments, Bill was well regarded in this role by his peers, and Bill's team was seen as highly energized and packed with talent, many of whom he had attracted to the company himself.

As they say, however, all good things must come to an end. The company was acquired by a larger industry player, which led to a series of painful downsizings in pursuit of "synergies." Before long Bill's job had changed so significantly that he, too, decided to make a change. Because of his demonstrated abilities, winning personality, and contagious energy, he quickly had two very attractive options to consider. He was getting close to a decision on one of them when a recruiter friend called to say that he had the ideal next career step for Bill—one where he would "fit perfectly." As it turned out, a former colleague of Bill's, whom he respected a great deal, was now the head of a large conglomerate and was looking for someone to head up the marketing function of one of their large business units located in western Pennsylvania. The job would surely lead to the division presidency in a few years.

Bill found this very appealing. Bill flew to the parent company's headquarters in Boston and met with his old friend at length and then interviewed with his top executives there, all of whom were very

(continued)

impressive people. Bill felt very much "at ease" with these people who clearly shared Bill's business philosophies and values. The division president to whom Bill would report flew in to meet him, and they spent a considerable amount of time together becoming acquainted and talking about the situation at length. Without any question, the challenges that existed in the job they had in mind for him played to Bill's strengths, and the idea of "reigning in the cowboys in the field" was as intriguing to him as the business itself. From his prior work experiences he could clearly picture what was needed. The division's marketing was in total disarray; systems and measurement tools of the kind that Bill was intimately familiar were virtually nonexistent, but the business was growing by leaps and bounds.

Before concluding the second round of interviews at the headquarters, Bill met with an industrial psychologist who was quite familiar with the work setting at the Pennsylvania site where Bill would be located. He expressed some reservations about Bill's sophisticated style and pointed out some significant differences between the cultures of his previous employers with those at the intended location. Ultimately, the psychologist's concerns were set aside on the basis that Bill had successfully moved from one organization to another previously and had always established himself with the people in quick order. Besides, it was argued, over time the culture would change to be more like the attributes that Bill brought with him, which was one of the objectives everyone had in mind for him.

As Bill later recounted, he should have listened to the psychologist, who at least had some idea of what he was getting himself into. Things started out poorly at Bill's first staff meeting and went downhill from there. The marketing "team" who seemed so interested in what Bill had to offer them when he met them before accepting the job clearly had no intention of changing their ways of operating. As Bill described it, "They functioned more like independent operators of booths at a county fair, doing what they wanted the way they wanted when they wanted." The only thing that seemed to unite them was their pleasant, passive-aggressive way of agreeing to everything and then going about doing things the way they always had. Bill's attempts to institute formal reporting and measurement systems were ignored, as were any of his initiatives to professionalize their relationships with customers and the back office support people. Not only were the touchstones of his previous job situations—professionalism, clear lines of responsibility, and a premium placed on communications, discipline and accountability—not present, within weeks it was evident to Bill

(continued)

that this group was not under any circumstances going to conform to his standards of management. His stomach churned at the thought of moving his family across the country for a situation that was, right from the start, so disheartening. While Bill would have fit nicely with the executives at the parent company's headquarters, his lack of fit with the subculture of the team he inherited was painfully real. Within a month he threw in the towel, which came as no surprise to his boss who, like everyone else, could see that the entire group would have to be fired before any one of them would accept Bill's leadership. Bill negotiated a small severance package and returned to the West Coast, bruised but wiser, to reinitiate his job search since the two other positions had been filled during his brief encounter with the power of an established and unified subculture.

Myth 6: When selecting new leaders, cultural considerations are not all that essential for success and need not be central to the process. The story of Bill is case in point of the importance of getting the fit between the individual—the entire person—aligned with the cultures at play in the situation. Bill was a great fit with the parent company's team's values and beliefs, but it was an impossible situation in which he found himself when his inherited marketing team marched, in unison, to a different drummer.

The Subtle Implications of Culture

Over the years of working in this field, we have come to regard cultures as if they were living, breathing organisms. And just like other organisms, they can, and will, reject anything that feels like a threat to their well-being. In this way they aren't much different than a human body that will reject a perfectly functioning transplanted organ if the chemical match is not just right. Bill's chemistry for this particular cultural organism was just "not right enough."

The premise of this book is that most leaders fail not because they cannot do the job, but because they do not fit well enough with one or more of the cultures at play in a new situation. In Chapter 5, "The Character Bucket," we pointed out that if the culture of the organization is one in transition; the values of the selected leader not only need to approximate those of today's organization, but just as importantly, those of the tomorrow's as well. So before selecting a leader it is critical to look not only at the values of the organization *now*, but at where the organization is headed. Today's values can be measured; tomorrow's may be reflected in the company's value statements or in its mission or vision codicils. If not, then higher management or the board must clarify them in conjunction with the company's strategic planning, preferably before initiating the search for the right leader. It is certain, however, that what exists today is the starting point for whatever may evolve tomorrow, and the organization cannot possibly select the right leader if it does not know where it is starting from, regardless of where it may be going. It cannot—and that is the point.

Moreover, if a company does not measure, define, and teach its leaders all about the culture and the impactful subcultures that they must lead and continue to mold, the odds are that these leaders will fail at the task. Without a clear understanding of the shape of the particular hole into which the peg is supposed to fit—as defined by the real needs of the organization and its culture and subcultures—selecting the properly shaped peg is a hit-or-miss proposition. Having had success at leading similar companies on similar journeys will not help the new leader. It may even be a disadvantage since it tends to breed reliance on assumptions as opposed to facts.

The Insider vs. the Outsider

At first blush the importance of understanding culture may lead to the erroneous conclusion that inside candidates are automatically better suited than those from outside the organization for any senior position because they obviously know the culture. Indeed, in a 2007 *Harvard Business Review* article, Joseph Bower reported that "company performance was significantly better when insiders succeeded to the job of CEO," and "other researchers, including Jim Collins in *Good to Great* have come to similar conclusions working from different sets of data."[34]

While I would not take issue with these conclusions in the broadest sense, I cannot agree that the difference is significant. Recent research conducted by Crenshaw Associates involving HR leaders, executive search professionals, senior-level executives, and entrepreneurs from a variety of industries strongly affirms that internal appointees only fare slightly better than outsiders when transitioning into top leadership positions. The three-year success rate of inside appointees was found to be approximately 60 to 64 percent, which is not overwhelmingly better than the likelihood of success of an outside appointee, which is in the 50-percent range.

Moreover, there is also research indicating that outsiders do better in certain situations and over certain time frames than insiders. In one study, for instance, Booz Allen Hamilton found that outsiders outperform insiders during the first five years; after that, insiders do better.[35]

So why is it that leaders who come from within a company and presumably already know the "cultural ropes" do not have appreciably higher success rates? There are several plausible reasons:

- Just because a leader comes from within the company does not mean his or her values automatically align fully with those of the larger organization, let alone those of the new subcultures they are joining.
- Nor does it mean that the particular cultural unit from which they came accurately reflects the overall culture or that of their new boss or their new team, leaving the new leader unaware of important differences and operating on invalid assumptions.
- As Marshall Goldsmith points out in his book, *What Got You Here Won't Get You There*, some people hold on to old behaviors that worked for them to *get* the job, mistakenly believing that they are the same behaviors that are expected of them *in* the new job. They rarely are.[36]
- Recognizing that culture tends to become diluted the farther from the center the cultural unit is located, a new leader being repatriated home or moved to an overseas headquarters for the first time may confuse implicit aspects of the new culture with those from his or her previous experience—elements that may not exist or worse, may not even be acceptable at the new site.

Among the reasons internal candidates do not fare much better than external candidates is that the means for improving the chance of success—measuring the culture and understanding the candidates' fit—are not used. Only by defining and measuring culture can hirers be sure they select someone who is not only best qualified and prepared to lead the changes that are truly needed (their match), but also best aligned with the powerful cultural elements at play (their fit) regardless of whether they are insiders or outsiders.

John Rogers, a member of the Goldman Sachs' fifteen-member Management Committee, described the importance of fit for all new executives when he said:

> *Our bankers travel on the same planes as our competitors. We stay in the same hotels. In a lot of cases, we have the same clients as our competition. So, when it comes down to it, it is a combination of execution and culture that makes the difference between us and other firms. . . . That's why our culture is necessary—it's the glue that binds us together. We hold onto the values, symbols, and rituals that have guided us for years, and anything new that we add to the culture always supports what already exists.[37]*

Our experience indicates that this enlightened perspective applies to all newly appointed leaders regardless of whether they happen to come from within the company or from outside.

It's All About Trust

As mentioned in Chapter 5, when talking about the importance of character to attaining proper fit, so it is with culture. The reason it is so very important to get the matter of fit correct when selecting a new leader is that without the close alignment of the leader's values with those of the culture, there cannot be trust, and without trust, there is no followership and, hence, no leadership. As Stephen M.R. Covey states in *The Speed of Trust*:

> *Simply put, trust means confidence. The opposite of trust—distrust—is suspicion. When you trust people, you have confidence in them—in their integrity and their abilities. When you distrust people, you are suspicious of them—of their integrity, their agenda, their capabilities, or their track record. It's that simple. We have all had experiences that validate the difference between relationships that are built on trust and those that are not. The experiences clearly tell us the difference is not small; it is dramatic.*[38]

Trust is at the center of every human relationship, and the relationship between an organization and its leader is no exception. Organizational trust is the essential element that makes a leader a leader and makes people willing to follow him or her. This trust is based on both the leader's competence (the proper match for the job requirements) and the leader's character (the proper fit with the company's culture). Both qualities must be evaluated against the needs and the cultures of the particular organization to be led. When there is misalignment, as Barrett aptly puts it, individual members of the company are placed in very difficult, very conflicted positions:

> *This mismatch of personal and corporate values is perhaps the most pervasive problem facing companies today. To be successful in organizations that focus on self-interest, you have to compromise your personal values, and you have to learn to live in a climate of fear. Because there is no trust, there is very little participation and empowerment. No one feels safe . . . we know that what is being said or done goes against our higher values, but we feel powerless to stop it. The choice is simple—speak up and risk losing your job or an important promotion, or suffer in silence.*[39]

When placed in such a position, a person may be powerless to do anything individually. However, the same is not true for groups, and that is how the culture derives its power. The resistive power of culture can be seen in Bill's experience with his marketing department. Informal communication networks express and expand the dissonance of a few to others. These others may not be directly involved in a particular situation, but because of their shared values with those who are, they become equally conflicted and upset. Very quickly initiatives are undermined, routines are abandoned, rumors abound, politics increase, morale is sapped, and a seemingly huge effort is needed to realize the simplest of changes. If prolonged, people soon start to leave the organization, and quality and efficiency begin to decline. The sense of belonging experienced by those in the network strengthens the power of culture that eventually undermines many leaders. Bill's lack of fit was his undoing. He never had a chance.

The greater the sense of belonging, the stronger the culture, and the greater the potential resistance the organization can produce. What's more, the most startling characteristic of such resistance is that very little of it occurs at an overt, cognitive level. Strong cultures do not plot or connive. They do not need to, since their shared beliefs have already been hardwired into every member. The automatic reaction to violated trust is resistance. In some cases it becomes revolt. In Bill's case the revolt was a passive-aggressive one—people pleasantly said one thing and then did another. The resistive power of culture is the counterweight that keeps the anticipated benefits of an action from ever occurring.

What's more, the lack of trust in a new leader who does not share the same values as those of the organization usually results from *how* the leader does things more than *what* the leader does. Most leaders are well versed in the development of strategy and processes and organizational structures. They can determine what the optimal direction is for the long-term good of the company and put together plans to achieve it. But lacking the appropriate knowledge of how to best leverage the specific cultural realities and overcome the resistive power of cultural inertia, their likelihood of success can be greatly impaired. Again, looking back on Bill's situation, he had changed companies before but had never encountered a culture like this one. He did not know how to deal with it.

Until businesses (and business schools as well) devote as much time and attention to building, leading, and sustaining strong organizational cultures as they already do to developing well-conceived business strategies, they will continue to assume the unnecessary and costly risks associated with leadership failure—the failure of selected leaders to deliver what is expected of them through the people they are supposed to lead. As Schein put it over twenty years ago:

> *The bottom line for leaders is that if they do not become conscious of the cultures in which they are embedded, those cultures will manage them. Cultural understanding is desirable for all of us, but it is essential to leaders if they are to lead.*[40]

Some Clues to Lack of Fit

When there is an inconsistency in values between a leader and the organization's culture, it gives rise to several conditions, which were described well by Eric Clemon and Jason Santamaria in a *Harvard Business Review* article on how modern military strategy applies in business.[41] These conditions are as follows:

- **Friction**, which makes the simple difficult and the difficult seemingly impossible
- **Uncertainty**, which will cloud decision-makers' judgment
- **Fluidity**, which merges events, permitting few breaks or opportunities for decisions to be made sequentially

In an environment where these conditions exist, a state of disorder will eventually occur. Just as when we are in poor health, a business that is suffering from the strains caused by differences between the values of the leader and those of the organization will present a number of symptoms, including:

Symptom 1: Forecasts and targets are missed—people are fearful of reporting emerging reality because they are not certain of the consequences (or certain that there will be repercussions if the news is not good).

Symptom 2: Milestones for key initiatives are not actioned on time, and delivery dates are rolled further and further into the future. Sometimes dates that were set were overly ambitious because the new leader imposed his or her will on the organization without realizing its true capability to execute. In other instances the organization collectively dragged its feet, since it was not certain whether the new leader's vision could be trusted to produce a better future or a sufficient likelihood of ever getting there.

Symptom 3: "Death by 1,000 memos." Lacking assurance that values are aligned, the organization becomes fearful of making decisions—even routine ones that have been accepted as a part of one's job for years. Everything then gets bumped up, and ultimately the new leader's desk becomes the place where all the bucks pile up and eventually stop. The leader is overwhelmed and, being new, either cannot figure out why all these decisions are ending up on his or her desk and/or what to do about them. Everything "bogs down" in the organization. Fears that the new leader intends to change the historical way of doing things becomes a self-fulfilling prophesy.

Symptom 4: Turnover of high-potential people and key contributors increases inexplicably. People who are needed "on the bus" are also the most mobile. If they do not trust the new leader's values, they are the ones most likely to move to a new place where their values align more comfortably—to join a former boss, a company where former colleagues have gone, or a competitor who is known to them.

It is these symptoms that are usually presented as reasons for the leader's failure and justification for his or her termination or resignation. But as you can see, these are just symptoms of a deeper, root-cause problem—the lack of proper fit between the personality (style), energy and character (values, beliefs, and philosophies) of the leader and the cultures and/or subcultures of the organization, and the teams through which the leader must deliver results.

Takeaways

This chapter is one of the most important in the book. Its intent is to change the perceptions of business leaders regarding what culture *is* and what culture *is not*. Until executives stop hiding behind the "soft stuff smoke screen" that has obscured the true nature of culture and start to deal with its importance on a more purposeful, planned, and measured basis, just as they do every other critical element of their profit equation, problems with fit will continue. In that regard, here are some of the key points addressed in this chapter:

- Culture can be taught to new entrants of an organization, but to do so, the teaching is best done by senior leaders who possess a factual description of their culture.
- A good, operative definition of culture is, "Historically created designs for living, explicit and implicit; rational; irrational, and non-rational that serve at any given time as the potential guides to the behaviors of its members."
- Cultures are neither "good" nor "bad"—they simply are. The strength of a culture is the degree to which there is alignment between the values of the organization and those of the individual members. The relative importance of those values to the members is *very* relevant when trying to understand the extent to which cultures will affect behavior.
- Cultures can be viewed as possessing three critical elements: the organization's artifacts, including its rites and rituals and other observable aspects; its values and beliefs (the level with the greatest impact on behavior); and the organization's assumptions (the hardest level to discern).
- Since the notion of culture came on the business scene twenty-five years ago, several myths about it have been perpetuated. These myths prevent business leaders from leveraging the full potential of their organizations. Six myths of culture are.

  Myth One—Culture is that "soft stuff"—it does not really directly affect business results or shareholder's return.

Myth Two—Corporate cultures are what they are and cannot be appreciably shaped or changed.

Myth Three—Cultural changes require a strong-willed leader who is willing to "shake things up."

Myth Four—Culture must be experienced to be understood—it cannot be easily described, measured, or taught.

Myth Five—Organizations only have one dominant culture—it is pretty much the same everywhere you go in the company.

Myth Six—When selecting a new leader, cultural considerations need not be central to the process and are not all that essential for success.

- The importance of selecting new leaders whose values approximate those of the cultures in which they are embedded is critical because it is the fastest, most assured way to create organizational trust in the leader. Leadership is all about trust. Without trust, leaders become irrelevant functionaries who will fail to accomplish what they have been hired to do—lead.

Part Two

Fixing a Flawed Selection Process

8

The New Hiring Process

"Hit my smoke"

Blade [Flight Leader], *watch it—I just found out the hard way there are two guns* [14.5 mm heavy machine guns] *down there. Hit my smoke!*
—Radio transmission from Forward Air Controller Dick "Dusty" Conyer (call sign, Herb 13) to the flight leader of four F-100 Super Sabres (call sign, Blade) over Hua Cu village, II Corps, South Vietnam, October 11, 1967.

H aving established the need and the underlying rationale for changing the way in which senior executives are selected in Part One, the purpose of Part Two is to describe what changes are necessary and how to implement those changes in order to improve the likelihood of selecting the right leader for any given situation. Chapter 8 is an all-important bridge between the more theoretical considerations of Part One and the tangible, "how to" elements of Part Two. While shorter than any of the other chapters in the book, it should not be glossed over because in it we:

- Create a metaphor that is critical to understanding the concepts and terminology employed throughout the remainder of the book
- Outline the content and flow of each of the remaining chapters as a guide to what lies ahead

A Useful Military Metaphor

As a former Air Force pilot during the late 1960s, I greatly admire all men and women who have served in the armed forces. I have an especially high regard for those pilots who flew as Forward Air Controllers (FACs, pronounced [faks]) during the Vietnam War. I was not one of them. The men who flew these missions were incredibly brave, unselfish, and as dedicated to their missions as any combat group I have ever known.[1]

The Forward Air Controllers who worked with the Army in Vietnam were all former fighter pilots experienced at delivering air-to-ground ordnance.[2] During the early years of the war they flew unarmed, single-engine light aircraft called the O-1 "Bird Dog" (a trail-dragger version of the popular Cessna 170 with a top speed of 130 MPH) right into the midst of very harrowing combat situations.[3] On average nearly 400 FAC sorties were flown daily, of which 75 percent were preplanned. The remainder were in support of immediate, "troops-in-contact" requests from ground commanders who were in need of close air support.

When troops on the ground needed quick support from the air, commanders at headquarters would dispatch fighter aircraft to the scene for an air strike. Before the fighters arrived, however, a FAC assigned to that area would fly in low over the battlefield and determine the exact location and nature of the enemy and precisely where the friendly forces were situated. The FAC would also identify the location of any anti-aircraft (Triple-A) guns or missiles that might represent a threat to the incoming fighters along with unique terrain features that would either aid or hinder their approach of the target. They would assess the situation with an understanding of the capabilities and limitations of the inbound fighters and, before marking the target with a white phosphorous ("Willie Pete") smoke rocket, would brief the pilots about the situation, wind direction, how to approach the target, and the best escape routes in the event they were hit by enemy fire. The FAC would then direct them to the target with the phrase, "Hit my smoke."

During the strike the FAC would stay in radio contact with both the commander on the ground and the fighters to determine if additional support would be necessary. After the strike the FAC would assess the success of the mission and report back to the fighters and to headquarters in a damage report indicating if their drops had been on target and what they had achieved. Most importantly, the FAC remained in contact with the troops on the ground to ensure that they were, indeed, safe.

The importance of the FAC's role in these kinds of close air support (CAS) missions cannot be underestimated. Without the aid of an on-site FAC, even the most highly trained and experienced fighter pilots would have found it very hard to find the proper site, assess the situation, and deliver their ordnance appropriately. At the speeds at which attack aircraft move, it is difficult to find the right target, let alone hit it with the precision required to keep from mistakenly hitting the friendly forces they were trying to protect.

It was the advance preparation the FACs provided—by identifying exactly what was needed to dramatically change the situation on the ground and to provide mission-critical information about the overall lay of the land—that allowed the fighters to accomplish their missions successfully. The quick assessment of the facts of the situation, the identification of which targets should be hit and in what sequence, made all the difference in the success of close air support missions in Southeast Asia. Without the courage, dedication, and heroism of the FACs, untold numbers of additional American soldiers would have perished on the ground, and even more pilots would have been lost.

Since leaving the service for a career in business many years ago, I have been intrigued about why, in analogous situations, businesses and other organizations fail to employ a comparable approach to making leadership changes. After all, the reason for almost every leadership change is that someone in a position of authority (like the ground commander) has decided that some kind of a significant change must occur to improve a company's performance, and often it must be done quickly. In the military analogy, headquarters (the board of directors or top management), wants to call in the fighters (a new leader) to make a quick and decisive strike (improve executional excellence, implement the right changes in direction, and the like) to improve the fate of the troops on the ground (the corporation and its various stakeholders) in an ongoing combat situation (be it a battle for market share, industry leadership, or even for the company's survival). Just like their military counterparts (the fighter pilots), business leaders are highly trained professionals who must meet rigorous requirements and have sufficient experience to carry out their assignments successfully.

Unfortunately, however, this is where the parallel ends. And it is also where the success rates for close air support missions and new leader performance statistics part as well. In Vietnam the U.S. military (Army, Air Force, Navy, and Marine) CAS missions had a combined on-target ordnance delivery rate of 97 percent. In business only 36 percent of newly appointed CEOs (the only segment of the leadership group for whom data is available) will hit their expected targets within the first four years and 40 percent of them will be replaced in eighteen months or less. Clearly the element that appears to be missing from the business scenario that was present in the combat setting is the involvement of a qualified Forward Air Controller—the FAC.

Instead, most businesses expect operationally or functionally skilled leaders to swoop in entirely on their own and immediately grasp everything they need to know about the very complex situation they have inherited, usually in a setting (culture) that is new to them (and not necessarily the friendliest, either). Under these conditions, from their position in "the cockpit," and at the speeds at which they are asked to move, it is understandable how they can mistakenly believe that what they are seeing below seems to resemble situations they have experienced previously. Rarely, however, is this the case.

Furthermore, these fast-moving, high-powered leaders are then expected to possess all the skills and knowledge necessary to detect all relevant subtleties in the lay of the land fully and accurately for themselves; to be able to intuitively identify the "friendlies"—in the business sense, those who are aligned with what needs to be done—as they sort out their new organization's structure and design; and to be able to avoid unforeseen political threats that may be in store for them that are every bit as dangerous as Triple-A and Surface-to-Air Missiles. As if this is not a big enough challenge, they are expected to do this at an extremely high speed while simultaneously keeping a multi-billion dollar and highly complex entity aloft and, oh yes, to successfully deliver the right changes in the right manner at the right time.

Unlike Vietnam-era fighter pilots, newly appointed business leaders selected under the Traditional Selection Process do not get a clear description of where the enemy is located and certainly no "smoke" to help locate the proper targets (changes) for them to go after. Rarely is factual, current targeting information provided by the headquarters because, frankly, they are not close enough to the battlefield to know the true lay of the land at that level of detail. Headquarters knows the enemy needs to be driven off, but they are rarely in a position to know exactly what that means in a fluid, ongoing, competitive situation. They certainly do not know it the way the troops in contact know it, yet nobody talks to the troops on the ground. Consequently while the statements of the desired outcomes that are given to a new leader during her or his initial briefings (the interview process) may be quite clear and very descriptive of what success will look like, the information about what needs to be done in actionable terms tends to be inaccurate and incomplete. Given the speed at which leaders must move, important nuances about the company cultures (the battlefield situation) tend to blur and, especially for the leaders coming from the outside, they are often misinterpreted. As those who have flown over a jungle canopy at high speed (or who have made a senior-level job change) know, "The next fifty miles of jungle looks just like the last fifty miles of jungle." Corporate cultures are rarely (if ever) the same, although they might look and feel that way to the newly appointed leader who finds him or herself in the midst of a "high-threat area" when expecting a safe haven.

Forced to operate without a FAC on-site to mark the targets, to locate the "friendlies," and to assess potential threats before the new leader arrives, it should come as no surprise that there is so much collateral damage and so many missed opportunities during the early days of a new leader's tenure. It is also why the success rate of business leaders is so abysmally low and why so many are "shot down" before they even know what hit them.

The Twin Benefits of Knowing the Lay of the Land

Over the course of my thirty-year business career I have held many different jobs, each with increased scale and scope of responsibility. Some were promotions from within the same company while, especially in my later years, many were moves into entirely different companies serving different market segments and different customer needs. I wish I could say that I made all these transitions successfully and that I always achieved all the objectives for which I was hired, but that was not the case. When I look back on each new situation I encountered, I can see how I could have done things better or faster. I could also have done them with less disruption or at a lower cost—if only I had received better factual information about the specific "combat situation" into which I was heading. In virtually every leadership position I held, I inevitably found myself flying by the seat of my pants. I often made snap, uninformed decisions about changes to be made (gathering my own "targeting information"), and I made quick judgments about people (Who is competent? Who can I use to fill gaps in the team? Who can I trust?). I consciously decided whether or not I should modify some aspect of my style and modus operandi to fit the culture as I perceived it (How do I quickly gain people's confidence? How do these people respond to directives versus a consensus approach? How do I get things done around here in ways that fit with people's expectations?).

From hundreds of conversations with other business leaders from companies of all sizes and industries, I now know that my experiences in these matters are widely shared. Most of us look back and can honestly say, "If only someone close to the situation had provided me with current, reliable facts—put 'smoke on the target' before I took the job and briefed me about the realities of the corporate lay of the land before I walked into my new office— think of how much more effective I could have been right from the start."

To be of the greatest value, gathering business data must be done by someone other than the new leader, and it must be done before the leader enters the "combat zone." In the business situation, the information that is gathered will actually have a twofold purpose: Not only will it be an invaluable aid to the Selection Team to help them select the right leader in the first place, the same information can be used by the new leader to hit the proper targets based on what really needs to be done. The nature of his or her transition plans and the decisions the new leader makes during the first hundred days, the first six months, and the first year are much more "on target."

Part Two of this book is all about how to gather the information necessary to address both objectives. It discusses how to define the true needs of the company in terms of what actions must be taken and how to analyze, measure, and define the organizational cultures the new leader must become a part of.

We have tested this methodology and found that by using current, fact-based data to "put smoke on" the needs and the key elements of the cultures in which the new leader will be embedded, the risks of leadership failure are greatly reduced. Besides increasing the speed at which the new leader can begin to make correct decisions on executional, directional, organizational, and personnel matters, the very process of gathering the information also helps prepare the organization to accept the new leader more easily and quickly. As has been proven time and again with virtually every other business process, the use of hard data always improves results otherwise based only on gut feel alone. A good feel for the situation when *combined with* hard facts can make an unbeatable combination for successful decision-making in any business situation. This is what we will help you to design for your own company in the following chapters.

What Lies Ahead

Before addressing elements that are currently missing from the selection process, Chapter 9 will focus on what can be done to improve the processes used by most companies in selecting leaders today. By applying the lessons learned in Part One about abilities, personality/energy and character, we will suggest places and conditions where various types of tests currently available to hirers might be incorporated. They can give hirers a better sense of candidates' talents, intelligence, strengths, energy levels, behavioral derailers, and, most importantly, insights into candidates' values and relevant business beliefs.

In Chapter 10 we then look at what needs to be *added* to the selection process to improve the odds of selecting the right leader and to equip that new leader with the necessary facts to know not only what needs to be done, but how to best go about it. It will help you select your own FACs (Forward Assessment Consultants) to put smoke on the targets, to brief your new CEO-fighter pilots and then help orient them to do things in ways that are acceptable and effective to everyone (both at headquarters and for the troops in contact on the ground). We will spell out what is involved in first gaining a sense for the business terrain through qualitative in-depth interviews with the new leader's direct reports and then, through quantitative inputs from the top senior managers to create Culturemaps by Mapping the Corporate Lay of the Land. As a result, you will be able to identify in a very granular way the executional and directional needs, cultures, and important subcultures. We will also describe ways to develop a team assessment (called Team Topography) and explain how to build a Field Guide of Vital Information to further acclimate the new leader to his or her new position.

The steps we recommend adding to the selection process will help guide the Selection Team in finding the right leader. In addition, this information will guide the new leader in determining *what* to do once in the job as well, and suggest *ways* to execute these changes compatible with the established cultural conventions and expectations. Based on current data instead of intuition and impressions, the new leader's decisions and actions can lead to improved execution and quicker results.

Chapter 11 uses real data from an actual Forward Assessment Consulting assignment to show how the information we gathered was used in selecting a new CEO for a medium-sized distribution company. It will give you a sense of how these techniques can lead to the design of a new process for selecting leaders. It also shows what Culturemaps look like and how they're used to develop the new leader's action plans.

Having identified the ways to improve the Traditional Selection Process in Chapter 9, the new elements to be added to it in Chapter 10, and how to use that information in Chapter 11, Chapter 12 pulls everything together. It introduces what we call the "Leader Selection Process."[4] We will show how the Accelerated Leader Selection Process can be implemented to achieve all of its intended benefits without adding any incremental time to the existing Traditional Selection Process. Each step in the process will be discussed in relation to the other elements on an optimal, time-phased basis. An Extended Leader Selection Process will be presented in Part Three (Chapter 13) for use in conjunction with CEO Succession Planning and other selection processes where longer lead times are available and time to complete the work is not so critical.

Both the Accelerated Leader Selection Process and the Extended Leader Selection Process are designed so the data gathered *before* the leader is selected can be used to select the right person and then to help the selected leader get started much more quickly. Their design also provides information that is much more timely and accurate for use in onboarding than anything gathered *after* the new leader has begun the job and the clock is running. The importance of having a "Forward Assessment Consulting Team" on-site before the new leader arrives is threefold:

1. To gather qualitative and quantitative data about the needs and cultures that can be used to select the right leader
2. To use the gathered data to ensure that all key stakeholders—the hirers, the new leader, the new leader's boss, and the new leader's organization— are all aligned and understand what actions and deliverables are expected of the new leader
3. To help the new leader to use the data gathered prior to his or her start date to formulate, track, and modify a fact-based transition plan covering the first hundred days, the second hundred days, and beyond

Besides introducing the Extended Leader Selection Process, Chapter 13 addresses one of the biggest issues facing boards today—the development of meaningful CEO Succession Plans in anticipation of planned and contingency changes in corporate leadership. This chapter discusses the relevance of the Match-Fit Model to the primary role of all boards—the selection, retention, compensation and, when necessary, the termination of the CEO. Given the extraordinarily negative impacts that a leadership change has on the company's P&L, its stock, and its organization—not to mention on the reputations of all those associated with it—the value of interpreting the principles presented in this book regarding the Leader Selection Process cannot be minimized. Specific suggestions for directors to consider concerning how to implement the principles during the search for a new CEO are also presented.

The final chapter, 14, answers several frequently asked questions about implementing the new Leader Selection Processes and then concludes with three points of particular significance.

Takeaways

Part One of this book focused on the reasons why the Traditional Selection Process needs to be changed to increase the likelihood of selecting the right leader. This chapter begins to focus on the design of a new Leader Selection

Process that will be detailed in the following chapters. Some of the key points covered here were:

- Unlike the U.S. military during the Vietnam War, companies have not adapted the use of a business counterpart to the Forward Air Controller (a Forward Assessment Consultant) to identify and verify the true executional and directional needs that must be addressed as well as the specific nature of the prevailing cultures that can be expected by the newly appointed candidate.
- By using a Forward Assessment Consultant to gather facts regarding the corporate lay of the land, hirers cannot only improve the likelihood of selecting the right candidate for any given leadership position, but they can also provide extremely valuable information to the new leader on which credible transition plans can be built and executed more quickly and purposefully.
- Chapters 9 through 14 will guide hirers through the steps they can take to refine and improve what they are currently doing as they interview candidates and then show them specifically what must be incorporated into their existing selection process to create a more effective Leadership Selection Process for the future.
- The missing information can be gathered in such a way as to not add additional time to the current hiring timetable for most senior leadership positions.
- By utilizing a FAC to "put smoke on their business issues targets," hirers can greatly reduce the risks and costs associated with leadership failures and address the root causes of the escalating turnover rates of senior business leaders today.

9

Changing the Way Candidates Are Vetted

It takes a higher order of thinking to fix a problem than that which created it.

—Albert Einstein

The Traditional Selection Process that has been in place in most U.S. companies for many decades does a very good job at what it focuses on. However, it clearly has not solved all the problems in the selection process.

As with so many facets of life, the greatest strength of the Traditional Selection Process is also its greatest deficiency—its in-depth focus on the abilities of candidates has now become so dominant as to overshadow other elements in the process. To a lesser extent the personality and energy of candidates for leadership positions are also factored into the traditional process. And a few companies use the interview process to evaluate character, but only a very few do so to the extent that is necessary.

This chapter will provide those with the responsibility for selecting senior executives with suggestions on ways to improve what they are already doing with their traditional screening of candidates. In the next chapter we will look at what needs to be added to these recommended improvements to create the new Leader Selection Process. Here we will look at the following:

- Three overall areas of process improvement
- Assessment tools for Personality and Energy
- Assessing Character and Values

Overall Process Improvements

Besides serving as an adviser to boards and senior-level executives for a number of years now, I have been in a position to work personally with many executives as they have transitioned between jobs, while my associates have assisted even more. This work has afforded us many insights into some sea-change shifts in the attitudes of senior executives who are representative of the kinds of candidates under consideration for top leadership positions in all functional areas and across all industry segments.

One indisputable change we have seen in job candidates is the willingness (or lack thereof) to relocate. Certainly the "temporary nature" of senior-level jobs is a factor driving this trend.[1] After all why should someone uproot his or her family if they'll just have to face another move in a few years? But there is more to this trend than that. As the war for talent has driven down the average age of candidates for senior-level positions in the United States, the less attractive moving has become, from both a lifestyle and a financial perspective. Younger leaders with school-age children and working spouses are more inclined to stay put or commute than relocate, a trend that demographics suggest will continue.

A second trend we have seen is the increasing willingness of even currently unemployed senior executives to turn down very attractive job offers simply because they do not think they are a "good fit" for the situation. Granted, at our firm we start talking to all of our clients about the importance of Match-Fit from the time they first walk in our door, so they may be more in tune with the importance of these realities than most, but eventually many job seekers will also become sensitive to it. As leaders become more aware of the importance of fit in their ability to succeed, they are more likely to step away from situations that are not right for them.

Both of these trends suggest that the ability of hirers to attract top people to participate in their selection process—regardless of whether the candidates are currently employed or already involved in making a transition—will only become increasingly difficult going forward. Improving the way hirers deal with people during the selection process can make a difference in their ability to get and keep top talent engaged until they have reached a final decision about who is right for the job. The trends we see strongly suggest that the way in which senior leadership candidates are treated— whether they are internal or external, employed or in transition, looking to make a change or happy where they are—will only become more important.

"Three to Get Ready . . . "

There are three general improvements that our firm has determined can increase the effectiveness of the selection process currently in use. These are in addition to the specific ones we will present later in this chapter.

In moving toward a new Leader Selection Process, we recommend changes in the following areas:

- Process management
- Participant training
- Relations with candidates

Let's examine these three areas in more detail before turning our attention to the specific recommendations concerning the three "buckets" that candidates bring to the interview table.

Overall Improvement Opportunity 1: Managing the Process. One of the biggest problems with senior executive searches is that the people who are involved in selecting executives hold senior positions themselves; these people are thus very busy and often difficult to manage. The consequence of all this bus-i-ness is a failure to take control of the process aggressively from start to finish.

At the outset of a selection process it is absolutely essential that *every* participant be informed of his or her role and in return, provides a commitment to perform that role as agreed to by everyone involved. The Six Sigma process to improve quality would never get off the ground if any single participant viewed it as optional. It is also imperative at the beginning of the process that one individual be officially designated as the Selection Team Leader and granted both the authority and responsibility to drive it on behalf of the organization. At the same time all other members of the Selection Team must be prepared to accept direction from the lead even if the Team Leader holds a more junior position in the organization. Rank has no privileges if you want to attract the best players. The process steps and the expected timetable of events need to be communicated to all those involved (*even* the founder/ chairman emeritus who may be retired in Bermuda if she/he is expected to play a role in selecting the right leader—to be effective roles must be scripted and rehearsed *before* the play begins). Obtain *everyone's* commitment to the process and document it. The application of good project management principles will help greatly.[2]

One of the biggest problems hirers have when selecting senior leaders is finding time on everyone's calendar to hold timely meetings with candidates. One way to deal with this reality is a best practice I learned from Robert Rigby-Hall, Senior Vice President of Lexis-Nexis. At the very start of the selection process, a timetable is laid out, and all those who will be involved in conducting interviews agree to set aside two back-to-back days six to eight weeks out. It is then up to the search firm or those screening internal candidates to fill those two days with candidates to be interviewed. Whatever time is still not scheduled two weeks prior to the interview dates that were put on hold are then released back to people's calendars for other purposes.

Regardless of the inherent difficulties in managing the availability of very senior executives involved in the interviewing process, the process must be structured and managed or else it will run amuck and end up being an unnecessarily drawn out series of disjointed meetings. The impression this leaves with top candidates is far from positive and will only make it more difficult to attract qualified candidates who fit your culture. I have seen it happen time and time again. As the old saying goes, Manage it or it will manage you. Just do it aggressively. Be respectful of everyone's time and manage your process professionally. Adhere to timetables, schedules, and agendas. Every candidate you come in contact with, either directly or through your executive recruiter, can potentially be your company's future CEO—so treat him or her that way from the first contact right through the end.

Overall Improvement Opportunity 2: Conduct Interview Training. During my years participating in the selection of key executives, I never felt that I was as good at the job of interviewing as was necessary; nor was my repertoire of interviewing techniques as broad as I would have liked. It was not until I became a principle in a firm that teaches clients how to be interviewed that I learned about different ways of interviewing. I now realize how, with a little bit of training, any business leader can become a better interviewer. In *Competence at Work*, Lyle and Signe Spencer focus on the Behavior Event Interview, an approach that is used within the HR departments of a number of companies and by many executive recruiter firms. Variations of the Behavioral Event Interview (BEI) are also known as Behavioral-Based Interviewing, competency interviewing, and competency-based behavioral interviewing. It is an extremely effective interviewing technique and is especially recommended for use in conjunction with a Character Interview, discussed later in this chapter. As described by Spencer and Spencer:

> *The objective of the BEI [Behavior-Event Interview] is to get very detailed behavioral descriptions of how a person goes about doing his or her work . . . to keep pushing for complete stories that describe the specific behaviors, thoughts, and actions the interviewee has shown in actual situations.*[3]

Learning to guide candidates through a behavioral-based interview like the BEI is not difficult, and the benefits are substantial. However, do not assume that everyone on the Selection Team is equally prepared to conduct effective interviews, especially at the senior levels. Even the most powerful corporate chieftains and highly experienced directors can benefit from refresher (or, possibly, initial) interview training to improve their interviewing skills. At the same time, mastering these skills does take a little discipline and practice. To be sure interviewers are proficient, we encourage everyone involved in the selection of key executives to allow themselves to become "trainable" and improve their competency in interviewing techniques. It is one thing for senior people to say they are committed to "attracting a top team" and "winning the war for talent," but being willing to take the time to improve their interviewing proficiency is an important step in walking that talk.

Overall Improvement Opportunity 3: Partner with Candidates. The shifting attitudes of candidates away from readily relocating and from accepting good job opportunities for which they feel they are a poor fit necessitate that hirers change their attitudes toward candidates. The most important key to senior executive success throughout the selection courtship lies in dealing with *all* candidates as partners: focus on mutual interests, describe the process to candidates, establish deliverables, share information freely and openly, and measure your performance by soliciting feedback from each one. In short, be transparent.

Ways to Achieve Overall Process Improvements

Here are a few suggestions of things you can do to achieve the three process improvements mentioned previously:

Focus On Mutual Interests. Obviously nobody wants to take a top-paying leadership job where the chances of being successful are low. As Jeffery Sonnenfeld, Chairman of the Yale School of Business, points out in *Firing Back*, only a few CEOs ever manage to recover from such a setback regardless of the reasons for their unplanned departure from the top job.[4] Consequently neither candidates nor hirers want to see the wrong leader selected.

If some candidates do not yet understand the importance of Match-Fit, then explain it to them and why it is just as important to them as it is to you to select the right candidate. Ask them how they see their fit with your organization's cultures and about the kind of situations where they have fit well before. Explain whatever concerns you may have about their candidacy and where you feel they may not be the "best shaped peg for this shaped hole." See how they respond. By focusing on the common ground between you, a more positive, open, and informative relationship will evolve—one that will serve you well when it comes time to tell all but one of the candidates (especially internal ones) that someone else has been selected because they fit better with the cultures in which they will need to work.

Describe the Process. The only oversight that will make your top candidates angrier than not returning their phone calls is not knowing where things stand and what the next steps are (even if those steps do not involve them!). Most candidates for senior leadership positions know what is going on behind the scenes at least in some general way—the selection process is not a secret. By *not* providing candidates (and your recruiters) with current, ongoing information, the selection process is hampered. Being a candidate for a top leadership job is, by its very nature, a harrowing experience for *all* candidates. The lack of concrete information (which often gets blamed on executive recruiters even though they are rarely at fault) is ultimately the responsibility of the company's hirers.[5]

Ensure that all candidates are briefed on the overall process design and timetables when they are first contacted. Provide them with updates about where the process stands and where they stand in it. Your feedback might go something like, "You are one of three candidates we intend to discuss with the Selection Committee next week. At that time we will eliminate one and set up meetings for the remaining two. We will let you know where you stand by next Friday. Does that work for you?" Proactively keep them abreast of changes in timetables (with a voice mail or e-mail message indicating, "The scheduled meeting of the Selection Committee was delayed by a week because two participants were stuck in an airport.") Be sure to put a reminder in your follow-up file to call back all candidates (or for your recruiter to do so) whenever you have given them an expected action date, even if the action did not occur. Do not leave them hanging.

The benefits to both the candidates and to you from this kind of treatment are many. Senior executives like having control or, more accurately, *do not* like feeling they do not have control. Furthermore not knowing what is going on and where they stand in the selection process is as big a source of stress and anxiety as can be found because it is so very personal. Keeping candidates abreast of the process and their status in it will not only help reduce their discomfort, but builds trust and goodwill.

The benefits to the company are the same only multiplied by the number of candidates in the queue at any given time. When dealing with internal candidates, the matter of building and maintaining trust is particularly important because they often feel forsaken by their own company when they are kept in the dark.

Establish Deliverables. Nobody likes surprises. As early in the process as possible, let every candidate know what they can expect from you *and* what you expect from them as well. Establish a two-way "social contract" right at the start. Find out if they can commit to the timetable you have in mind. Are they willing to participate in the assessment work you expect of all candidates? Are they under any noncompete commitments that could interfere with their candidacy? Are there any people on your interview team who, for competitive or other reasons, need to be handled in a sensitive manner to keep from compromising the candidate?

Make a commitment that your team, including your executive recruiter, will return all calls within twenty-four hours. In addition, you should give the candidate the phone number for the assistant to the leader of the Selection Team as the resource to contact for status information, to answer questions, and to let the company know if a communication breakdown has occurred. This will afford them some degree of control. Be sure to advise them that you would like their candid feedback at the end of the process regardless of its outcome.

Measure Your Performance. No business process should be exempt from ongoing, disciplined, and rigorous review for the purpose of continuous improvement. The Leader Selection Process is no exception. Nowhere does a Selection Team have a better opportunity to get relevant "customer" feedback about how well they performed or where improvements can be made than from candidates who have just gone through the selection process.

Once the right leader has been chosen, the head of the Selection Team should inform *all* candidates of the decision, thank them for their participation, and ask for their candid feedback. Recognizing that candidates rarely want to burn a bridge with another company or with a recruiter intentionally, the use of a third-party researcher to gather the results that are kept anonymous and confidential is advised. (In Chapter 10 we will introduce you to the logical person to do this for you, using a third-party interview.) Doing so will help generate better feedback from participants. A phone interview will suffice, but some may opt to use a short, structured survey questionnaire (paper or electronic) with ample space for open-ended comments for suggestions.

Getting the Most Out of the Assessment Tools

In addition to modifying your overall approach to selecting senior executives, there are a number of specific tools that can be used to maximize what you learn about the candidates. In the discussion of the Match-Fit Model in Part One, several chapters (3 through 5) focused on the "buckets" that contain the various qualities individuals bring to the workplace—their abilities, their personality and energy, and their character. While your company may be using some tools and techniques to assess those attributes, the following is a summary of ways hirers can further improve their understanding and appreciation of what each candidate potentially has to offer your company in terms of both his or her match and their fit. Three tools that may enhance the appreciation of a candidate's abilities have been discussed in Chapter 3: IQ tests, the Johnson O'Connor Aptitude Test, and the StrengthsFinder® Profile. The instruments presented below pertain to a candidate's personality and energy and their character.

If you are going to incorporate the use of one or more assessment tools into your new Leader Selection Process, as we strongly recommend, there are two very important points for you to keep in mind about their use:

1. Assessment tools are intended to help hirers make better decisions about the candidates they interview and with greater clarity. As stated by Dr. Gary Hayes, a Crenshaw expert and well-known clinically trained

psychologist focusing on leadership and organizational development, "In spite of what some people might want you to believe, assessment tools cannot provide black and white, 'absolute' answers about who to hire and who not to hire. They are not intended to be used in a binary fashion. Their value lies in adding efficiency and granularity to the selection process and giving interviews purposeful focus."[6]

2. There are a host of legal implications about when and how to properly use assessment tests of the types discussed below and those additional ones that appear in Appendix A of this book. Both federal and state statutes must be considered, especially when administering an assessment dealing with the abilities of candidates. The authors are neither qualified nor interested in providing you with legal advice, but we implore you to be sure that you understand the proper ways to incorporate any assessment tools into your selection of any candidates, be they internal or from the outside.

Moreover, it is vital to stay alert to how personality and energy align with needs. The focus of one assessment instrument can be quite different from that of another. The members of the Selection Team have to be sure they choose a tool that tests for the behaviors which are necessary for the new leader in order to accomplish their objectives. This may not be the tool the Selection Team members like best or with which they are most familiar.

In *Hiring Success*, the authors break down the steps in selecting and applying assessments as follows:

- Identify key performance requirements.
- Use job analysis to define and describe critical behaviors.
- Choose assessments that are valid for predicting critical behaviors.
- Collect and interpret data.[7]

Assessing Personality and Energy

Chapter 4 discussed the various aspects of a candidate's Personality and Energy Bucket and why these attributes affect both the match and the fit of the right candidate. Personality traits critical to success are particularly important, and there are quite a few of them to be considered for inclusion in the process of selecting senior executives.

In a field of study that, from an outsider's perspective, can be characterized as possessing numerous conflicting theories and strongly entrenched differing points of view, a fairly broad base of support has, nevertheless, evolved for the Big Five descriptive model of personality (also called the Five-Factor Model). It identifies the constituent traits of one's personality as:[8]

- **Openness**—appreciation for art, emotion, adventure, unusual ideas, imagination, curiosity, and variety of experience
- **Conscientiousness**—a tendency to show self-discipline, act dutifully, and aim for achievement; planned, rather than spontaneous behavior
- **Extraversion**—energy, positive emotions, urgency, and the tendency to seek stimulation and the company of others
- **Agreeableness**—a tendency to be compassionate and cooperative rather than suspicious and antagonistic toward others
- **Neuroticism**—a tendency to experience unpleasant emotions easily, such as anger, anxiety, depression, or vulnerability; sometimes called emotional instability

There are a number of personality tests hirers can use that are based on or related to the Big Five Factors. There are a host of others that, not surprisingly, are based on other factors.

Personality tests generally break down into two types that are easily distinguished from each other with respect to the presentation of the findings. The first type is called the "typological" test. It emphasizes discrete categories of personality types. The second type, the "dimensional type," reports the relative weighting of an individual's personality on a variety of fixed criteria. Researchers tend to favor the latter, while the former approach seems to be used in business settings more frequently.[9]

Personality Assessment Summaries

Depending upon the needs of the job, different aspects of candidates' personalities may need to be evaluated. Appendix A contains a list of thirty-four instruments frequently used in business, eighteen of which can shed light on a candidate's personality and/or energy. (Fifteen can be used to illuminate one's abilities, and ten can be used to better understand character as we have defined this term.) The following paragraphs summarize eight ways personality can be assessed that are currently popular among hirers. As a quick review of these various instruments and those listed in Appendix A hopefully makes clear, there are many ways that hirers can gain deeper and more meaningful insights into a candidate's behaviors, style, attitudes, motivators, and derailers than just through interviews.

Myers-Briggs Type Indicator®(MBTI®). The Myers-Briggs test is a sixteen-type indicator that was derived from Carl Jung's *Psychological Types* during World War II.[10] It is one of the most popular and frequently used tests in business. It categorizes respondents into one of sixteen personality types (typological results) and provides relative scoring on twenty subsets (called facets) of the four pairs of oppositional factors (dimensional results) for additional specificity. In companies where the Myers-Briggs Test is widely used, people generally know their four-letter personality type and will often use it as a kind of introductory shorthand when working with others from the same company for the first time ("Hi, my name is Nat; I'm an ENTJ," or something like that). Here are the eight factors:[11]

Extraversion (E)	as opposed to	Introversion (I)
Sensing (S)	as opposed to	Intuition (N)
Thinking (T)	as opposed to	Feeling (F)
Judging (J)	as opposed to	Perceiving (P)

The shorthand descriptors of the sixteen combinations that are derived from these eight factors are the following:

ESTJ	ESFJ	ENTJ	ENFJ	ISTJ	ISFJ	INTJ	INFJ
ESTP	ESFP	ENTP	ENFP	ISTP	ISFP	INTP	INFP

16-Personality Factors Test (16-PF). This is a multivariety derived dimensional test developed by Raymond Cattell in 1946 and one of the more popular of its type used in business. Respondents are asked to rate themselves on an array of descriptive terms, and the ratings are then plotted and reported in a number of ways by a trained psychologist or authorized consultant. The sixteen primary factors Cattell identified are, [12]

Warmth	Vigilance Abstractedness
Reasoning	Privateness
Emotional Stability	Apprehension
Dominance	Openness to Change
Liveliness	Self-Reliance
Rule-Consciousness	Perfectionism
Social Boldness	Tension
Sensitivity	

The Hogan Suite of Assessments. The four assessments in this suite include a variety of scales that create profiles to reveal a person's reasoning skills, competencies, values, and leadership characteristics. Data from the assessments produce easy-to-read reports that contain recommendations for hiring and development. The process is carried out with the help of the Hogan staff who serve as consultants, researchers, and advisers to every client. Of the four components, there are two that are particularly helpful in assessing the personality characteristics of candidates for senior leadership positions:[13]

1. *Hogan Personality Inventory (HPI)*. This was reportedly the first inventory of normal personality based on the Five-Factor Model developed specifically for the business community.
2. *Hogan Developmental Survey (HDS)*. Often used in conjunction with the HPI, this instrument assesses eleven behavioral tendencies, called derailers, which impede work relationships, hinder productivity, or limit overall career potential when the individual is under stress or is in a relaxed state and caught off guard.[14]

The Occupational Personality Questionnaire (OPQ32). This is a popular personality assessment tool encountered more frequently outside of the United States than within. It is available in more than thirty languages and has been administered over 3 million times since its inception in 1984. The OPQ32 targets the competencies required of managers, graduates, and experienced hirees. It provides information about an individual's preferred behavior on thirty-two personality characteristics. The OPQ32 dimensions are grouped into three areas: relationships with people, thinking styles, and feelings and emotions.[15]

Jackson Personality Research Form (PRF). Although not as widely used as perhaps some of the other tests, the Jackson Personality Research Form is one of the most frequently cited tests in the field of psychological testing. First introduced in 1967, the PRF has been used to study assertiveness training, consumer behavior, decision-making, emotional development, employee attitudes, job performance, leadership style, and risk-taking, to name a few. Besides providing an excellent template for understanding an individual's personality, it serves as a tool for gauging sources and drains on the candidate's energy.[16]

The Psycho-Behavioral Interview. In addition to using psychological and behavioral testing instruments like the ones described previously, another way that we have seen hirers effectively get a better sense of the abilities, personality, energy, and character of candidates is by using a qualified psychotherapist—either a psychiatrist or a clinical psychologist trained in the psychotherapeutic techniques. Dr. Kerry Sulkowicz, a Crenshaw expert who for many years has written regular columns for popular business publications, has demonstrated time and again how someone skilled in the psychotherapeutic technique can gain rich insights into the makeup of candidates in a period as short as just a two-hour interview.[17]

Energy Assessment Techniques

Beyond observing the displays of physical energy exhibited by candidates during the interview process, the formal assessment of an individual's energy is difficult to determine. One reason is that, as indicated in the discussion of energy in Chapter 4, energy is of a variety of types—physical, mental, emotional, and spiritual. In their book *The Power of Full Engagement: Managing Energy, Not Time, Is the Key to High Performance and Personal Renewal*, Jim Loehr and Tony Schwartz describe the importance of, and the steps involved in, managing energy to perform at peak levels.[18] Other insights into the interconnectivity of the various forms of energy essential for success for business leaders include Stephen Covey's *The 7 Habits of Highly Effective People*, Jack Groppel's *The Corporate Athlete*, and Jim Collins's *Good to Great*.[19]

Perhaps the most effective way to gain an appreciation of a candidate's approach to energy management is through the use of the behavioral-based interview technique, to inquire about the things that the candidate does to stay energized. The maintenance of energy takes discipline, practice, and consistency. By inquiring about his or her routines and regular health and fitness management practices, hirers can develop insights into the extent to which a candidate manages his or her energy resources on a purposeful, ongoing basis. Remember, however, that questioning someone about their personal life choices is off-limits, so keep the focus on the job requirements for energy and do not stray.

It should be noted that some of the personality assessments described previously in this section can also provide an indication of a candidate's energy levels and how he or she manages them, as can interviews conducted by trained psychologists and psychiatrists.

Assessing Character

For the reasons cited in the discussion of character in Chapter 5, there are not as many ways of assessing the nature of an individual's character as there are to determine personality. The tools that are available focus mainly on the candidate's values and not on the makeup of his or her entire character. Nevertheless, these values assessments can be very helpful, particularly if used in conjunction with the Character Interview, an important enhancement to the selection process of any company. A description of the Character Interview, followed by a brief summary of some ways that it can be used to gain insights into candidates' values, follows. A more complete list of ten assessment tools related to understanding character is contained in Appendix A.

Character Interview Tips

The experience I had in December 1988, talking with the CEO of Garden-Way in a coffee shop for four hours, although unplanned, is a good example of what I have come to call the "Character Interview" (see Chapter 5). Basically it is an open, two-way discussion of values and relevant business beliefs and philosophies that takes place between the final candidate(s) and the hiring executive to whom they will report and/or a trained psychologist or behavioral-based interviewer.

Conducting a Character Interview with the finalists for any senior leadership position is vital. The process builds a basis of trust, while the content helps each party explore their compatibility with the other and with the cultures through which the newly hired leader will have to accomplish certain actions. Information gathered from a variety of sources during the new Leader Selection Process can be drawn on as appropriate: individual and team assessments, research of the company's needs and cultures, and feedback from whatever psychologists or other outside consultants may have contributed.

Here are some important considerations to keep in mind when conducting a Character Interview:

- The Character Interview should be conducted by the person to whom the new hire will report—not exclusively by the Human Resources head (unless that is the person to whom the position reports), nor the executive recruiter, or even a psychologist or psychotherapist (although they may in some instances play a role). It is important that the hiring executive be fully engaged in this step because one of the by-products of a properly conducted Character Interview is the personal trust built between the participants. Building trust between the candidate and anyone other than that person's immediate superior is only of marginal worth, particularly if the company representative will disappear from the scene as soon as the selection is completed.
- The tone of the Character Interview should be open, conversational, and very collegial. The hiring executive should be prepared to share as much about his or her own values and beliefs as is expected from the candidate. Concerns about the candidate's fit are raised; questions about business philosophies, beliefs, and values are considered; and using behavior-based interview questioning, the candidate is asked for specific examples of how, where, and when that philosophy, belief, or value was put into practice or tested. Probe for specific situations—the problem, the action taken, and the result—but do it conversationally and empathetically. This is not an inquisition. There are no "right or wrong" answers, only clues. This is the best chance to really get to know

someone—someone you may end up working closely with for many years. So use it as your acid test to determine the extent to which he or she fits with your organization's cultures.

- When sharing your own beliefs and values with the candidate, it is preferable to do so *after* the candidate has expressed theirs on a particular subject whenever possible. Otherwise you run the risk of "leading the witness" and eliciting a response that may be more politically correct than a true reflection of their personal values and beliefs. This is why use of the behavior-based interview format becomes extremely important in determining whether their answers are truly aligned with what they have done. (If they are not, you have then obviously learned something very important about their character!)

- Take your time. A Character Interview is best conducted outside the office and over dinner when neither party has any pressing time constraint or hard deadline. If you do it at some other time of day be sure you have set aside enough time to let it unfold naturally and fully. A good Character Interview will invariably take longer than anticipated simply because of its nature.

- If the candidate has been asked to complete any assessment tools in conjunction with the selection process, review the findings beforehand and ask the candidate questions you may have about him or her as a result. Use the assessment materials as clues, not as concrete absolutes. Let the findings guide you to insights that will help you determine whether this candidate is the right leader or not. The Character Interview is a time of discovery.

- Before concluding the interview, share your impressions with the individual and ask for confirmation or push-back on the impression you have formed during the interview. Often you will gain as much insight and valuable information by "checking things out" in this manner as through any other means. People generally want to be understood and known for who they really are. If you ask them if you have missed the mark, they will usually tell you so.

Assessment Tools for Values

Values are a very large component of an individual's Character Bucket, and there are a few assessment tools available to hirers that shed light on these key traits. The Hogan Motives, Values Preferences Inventory is one of the best for this purpose, although many firms have had good experiences with the more general approach taken by Richard Barrett and Associates in this area. A brief description of each is following, along with an overview of the Crenshaw

Mapping the Corporate Lay of the Land Web-based assessment tool. Other resources are contained in Appendix A.

The Hogan Motives, Values, Preferences Inventory (MVPI). This is one of the four Hogan Assessment tools that constitute the Hogan Assessment Suite. This profile is a dimensional test that reveals a person's core values, goals, and interests—invaluable information for determining the kinds of environments in which the person will perform best and the kind of culture the person will create as a leader.[20]

The Richard Barrett Values Assessment Process. This tool is described in *Liberating the Corporate Soul: Building a Visionary Organization*, Richard Barrett's first book on the subject. In it he describes the process and underlying rationale used by his firm to assess the values of individuals and those of the cultures in which they are, or will be, involved. This process reveals the compatibility of the values of a new leader with those of the organization and where problem areas can be expected.[21]

Crenshaw's Mapping the Corporate Lay of the Land. In subsequent chapters, we will describe a process pioneered by Crenshaw Associates that can be administered either electronically to a large group of top executives or on paper to a smaller group of the new leader's direct reports. Either way, once maps of the corporate cultures have been produced, the final candidates are asked to complete the same questionnaire answering the questions in terms of the culture they are most accustomed to working in. Their predisposed expectations are then charted against the map of the cultures within the company to see where the candidate fits well and where her or his values may differ significantly from those of the organization. These Culturemaps then help the selected leader navigate the unique cultural elements with which they may not be familiar. Chapter 11 is devoted entirely to a very descriptive case study that shows how those tools are used in actual practice.

Takeaways

To sum up, the extent to which any of these assessment tools should be employed is best determined by the Selection Team in line with the needs of the job and all prevailing employment laws. Use them as the situation warrants. We encourage all hirers to adopt some form of assessment to gather additional insights and facts about candidates and explore these fully with finalists during a behavioral-based Character Interview as a way to help reduce very costly selection mistakes.

Some important points to bear in mind include:

- The Traditional Selection Process is good at what it is designed to do— determine if candidates possess the abilities that are necessary to address the company's perceived needs. For this reason the Traditional Selection Process will serve as the basis of the new Leader Selection Process into which we propose incorporating the missing pieces of principles of the Match-Fit Model.

- There are three general changes hirers can make to improve the effectiveness of whatever hiring process they utilize. They are,

    1. Aggressively manage the process.
    2. Conduct interview training of all participants.
    3. Partner with candidates.

- The value of these enhancements will increase in the war for talent[18] as demographics and lifestyle choices make top candidates less willing to relocate and as candidates become unwilling to accept positions where they do not consider themselves to be a good cultural fit.

- Partnering with candidates requires a significant change in both the attitudes and behaviors of some hirers. The key to success in this area is achieved by focusing on mutual interests, describing the process to hirees, by establishing deliverables, sharing information openly and freely, and by measuring performance through follow-up interviews from all candidates upon conclusion of the process.

- There are a variety of means by which hirers can augment the traditional interviewing process to gain a sharper perception of candidates' personalities and energy, either by using trained psychotherapists or verifiable testing instruments (many of which are based on the Big Five Factors).

- The most effective way of gaining insight into a candidate's character is through a technique referred to as the Character Interview which, to be effective, is best conducted by the hiring executive utilizing behavioral-based interview techniques. The incorporation of findings from administered values assessment tools can help sharpen the focus of the Character Interview.

10

The Missing Links to Selecting the Right Leader

This is a great process. . . . It is so much easier for me to be candid with you than with a new CEO. . . . I applaud the Board for putting us through this process.
         —Participant in a new Leader Selection Process

The previous chapter identified several ways to improve the Traditional Selection Process by implementing current practices differently. Now let's look at those elements that have been missing from the Traditional Selection Process altogether and that must be added to it to create a new Leader Selection Process.

The additional steps we will be adding all involve gathering data about the true needs of the organization and its cultures—information essential to selecting the right leader. They include:

- Selecting your FAC (Forward Assessment Consultants)
- Developing the Business Terrain Research
- Assessing Team Topography
- Mapping the Corporate Lay of the Land
- Creating the Field Guide of Vital Information

The information gathered as the result of implementing these steps can then also serve as the basis for the new leader's transition into the company.

Selecting Your FAC
(Forward Assessment Consultants)

Similar to the role played by the Air Force FACs (Forward Air Controllers), your own FACs—Forward Assessment Consultants—identify and "put smoke on" the priority needs as well as define the cultures before the new leader is selected.

As described in Chapter 8, the Forward Air Controllers in Southeast Asia were specially trained pilots who performed many different functions before the high-powered fighters arrived on the scene. They coordinated with the headquarters responsible for dispatching the fighters, and they were in direct contact with the troops on the ground. They were close to the situation and were able to pinpoint the exact location of the friendly forces, the enemy targets, and any possible threats to the incoming jets. They highlighted the targets the fighters should go after by firing a smoke rocket directly at them so when fighters arrived on the scene, they knew exactly where they were to go to make the biggest difference immediately. When the fighters arrived, the FACs briefed them about the exact nature of the situation, explained what to watch out for, and helped them plan their attack. After the initial engagement was over, the FACs remained in the area long enough to make sure they had been successful at what they had been brought in to do.

The Functions of the Forward Assessment Consulting Team

The assignment of a Forward Assessment Consultant is comparable to that of the Forward Air Controller. The business FAC is responsible for scouting and mapping the territory where the new leader will need to take action.

To gather the necessary information, analyze it, communicate it, and help translate it into a plan of action requires several different functions and skills. In fact, there are generally five separate participants required to gather and analyze the information that is needed to identify the right leader. At Crenshaw we have designed our FAC team to include the following members: Project Leader, Research Expert, Business Assessment Expert, Behavior Assessment Expert, and Confidential Administrative Support.

Project Leader

The Project Leader is a very senior executive with a broad base of business experience. He or she is often a retired CEO, former senior HR executive, or professional business consultant. It is extremely important that the Project Leader be able to assess information and interpret data, as well as provide feedback to board members on a peer basis. The experience of the Project Leader is extremely relevant because the work being done is not theoretical or conceptual—it is very pragmatic, purposeful, and related directly to the delivery of tangible business results. Depending on the specific assessment tools that are utilized to measure the needs and cultures of the organization, the Project Leader may need training in specialized software applications.

Research Expert

The Research Expert plays a critical role on the FAC team. Since this individual does the basic Business Terrain Research, he or she must interview everyone who will report directly to the new leader (the group we call the Executive Leadership Team or ELT).[1] The Research Expert should be experienced at working with very senior executives one-on-one. Often the questions used in the Business Terrain Research serve as triggers to conversations and sources of input that go well beyond traditional research, Q&A processes, and protocols. The Research Expert must be skilled at stimulating and hearing the very relevant and rich information that would not come out if strict adherence to a questionnaire were maintained. The

Research Expert needs the sensitivity and capability to follow themes and threads through the discussions with senior executives to gather relevant, sometimes unexpected, information. The Research Expert also needs to be able to help develop protocols, analyze data, and have a personal presence that sets interviewees at ease.

Business Assessment Expert

The data generated by the Research Expert often total over 300 pages of critical information. However, the information is not organized in any meaningful way. This is where the Business Assessment Expert comes in. The Business Assessment Expert works with the Research Expert and the Project Leader to cull the reports and organize findings into relevant, manageable elements for communication to the company's Selection Team. To ensure objectivity, this role is best played by someone who is *not* closely engaged in this particular situation—preconceived notions can be very dangerous.

Behavior Assessment Expert

The Team Topography Assessment Process is an integral part of the Leader Selection Process. It can be conducted by many trained industrial psychologists or psychiatrists, or it may be developed through the administration of the various testing tools described in chapters 3 and 9. Regardless of the specific techniques used, a highly trained professional is essential in this role. If your company already uses someone in this capacity whom the Executive Leadership Team trusts, then that person should be considered for the role of the Behavior Assessment Expert.

Confidential Administrative Support

It is important that the FAC provide Administrative Support capable of handling highly confidential research findings and reports for the various parties. Confidentiality is vital because the business data, as well as the team assessment information, can present significant legal issues if not handled properly. Furthermore, the support staff schedules appointments, serves as a "clearinghouse" for candidates' questions, and gathers feedback from participants, among other administrative tasks. When a CEO to whom the company's HR head will report is being selected, some additional tasks normally handled internally may need to be delegated to the Administrative Support element of the Forward Assessment Consultant to keep from compromising the HR head, the candidate, or the integrity of the process.

The Role of the Forward Assessment Consulting Team

Collectively the Forward Assessment Consultants work with the company's Selection Team to establish protocols for each element of the work and then use those protocols to develop the specific questionnaires and processes to be used. The FAC also helps to identify the company participants who will be involved in each phase of the work and helps to coordinate timetables with all the participants. Throughout the work the FAC must utilize the essential tools of project management while gathering, analyzing, interpreting, and reporting the data. The FAC is responsible for developing and communicating reports and for providing input to the chair of the Selection Committee and other directors as required. Liaising with the executive recruiter(s) involved in the process to keep them abreast of the information and its potential implications for the profile of the right candidate as it becomes available is also part of the Forward Assessment Consultant's role.

It is *highly* recommended that the FAC team be made up entirely of people who come from outside of the company. Rarely would all of the necessary skills required of a Forward Assessment Consultant be available in-house when necessary anyway, but even if they were, the matter of anonymity at the senior levels is extremely important in order to gather candid, relevant information. Only if people are confident that they can speak freely and without any threat of reprisals or "back-channel leaks" will they come forward with the information so essential to the success of the new Leader Selection Process. Furthermore, since the FAC's allegiance must be to the company's Selection Team and not to anyone else, the detached, objective perspective offered by outsiders is essential.

When a new CEO is being selected, the senior HR executive is a member of the team that needs to be assessed and must, therefore, be treated as a part of the ELT, not as someone exempt from it or with special insights or special access to the deliberations of the Selection Team. In these circumstances the FAC must pick up some of the responsibilities usually performed by the HR head.

The four reasons that outside consultants are best used for this purpose are,

1. An independent Forward Assessment Consultant can offer the insiders involved in the data-gathering processes the anonymity necessary to ensure that accurate information is obtained about the organization's true needs and cultural elements.
2. Hirers already have full-time responsibilities and, without the aid of the FAC, the necessary research will inevitably come at the expense of

something else—either the selection process itself or some other important part of their responsibilities.

3. Not unlike their military namesakes, effective business FACs require a particular set of skills, experiences, knowledge, and some unique training, most of which cannot be found in people within the majority of companies.

4. With the possible exception of the largest of companies, the development and maintenance of this type of internal capability is not cost-justifiable.

Determining the Business Terrain

Of the four elements to be added in creating the Leader Selection Process, the Business Terrain Research is possibly the most important. It is an in-depth, two-hour interview of each member of the Executive Leadership Team. The Business Terrain Research is conducted by the Research Expert who is highly experienced at conducting personal interviews with senior executives.

The reason that this research is so important is that the Executive Leadership Team that will report to the new leader is made up of the people with the clearest view of the organization's strategic intent (its directional needs) *and* its operating realities (its executional needs). The group comprised of these executives also constitutes one of the three subcultures that will potentially make or break the new leader. Knowledge of its inner workings is valuable information. Further, the individuals who make up this team have seen the outgoing leader perform, and each from their particular vantage knows what has been going on, as well as where the cover-ups have been buried. They are the architects and champions of key initiatives, and they know the people who are critical to the success of the company. Most importantly, the Executive Leadership Team members have the greatest personal stake (their jobs, their legacy, and their professional reputations) in the success of the new leader, making them highly motivated to provide input and guidance if asked in a way that will not come back to haunt them if what they have to say is politically unpopular. To claim they yearn to have a say in the new leader's plans and success is an understatement. As one senior individual said when speaking about the Business Terrain Research conducted in conjunction with a CEO search:

> *This is a great process. I don't know how many companies are going through this, but looking at this from the CEO's perspective, it is great to get this information from the team and not to have to spend weeks doing it. From my perspective, it is much easier for me to be candid with you than with the new CEO. I wouldn't want to wax on*

about some of this stuff because the new CEO might find it infuriat-
ing or whatever. So this is a great process. I applaud the board for
putting it in place.

Developing the Business Terrain Research

The protocol established for the Business Terrain Research defines the parameters and the purpose of the work and the basic ground rules regarding the use of respondents' comments. After explaining the reasons that the individual's input is so valuable, the normal protocol is for the interviewer to ask respondents to put themselves in the shoes of the new CEO for the duration of the interview. The following points are then stressed:

- The remarks that they make will all be held in confidence; no comment will be made to anyone within the company with their names attached to it as the source. To underscore the anonymity of the work, not even any outside FAC team member will be provided the names of the respondents attached to any remark.
- The research will be used to help the Selection Team select the right leader and to aid that leader to focus on the proper priorities.
- The Research Expert conducting the interviews has signed non-disclosure and confidentiality agreements with the company so the respondents are free to discuss *anything* that is pertinent.
- Whenever possible, the interviews will be tape-recorded so the interviewer can concentrate on what is being said instead of on taking notes. After the session the tapes will be transcribed and destroyed by the transcription service.
- The final report will be provided to the new leader as well as to the head of the Selection Team and other directors or members of the Selection Team that the chair feels have a need to know.
- The interviews are only a part of what will make up the final report.
- Everything will be covered in two hours.
- No cell phones or BlackBerries during the course of the interview, please.

Once the purpose and intentions for the interview have been established, the interviewer outlines six areas (described following) to be examined in the course of the Business Terrain Research. The line of questioning covers both business issues and aspects of organizational culture. The interviewees are encouraged to talk about, and embellish on, other concerns as they see fit in order to help the new leader focus on the important aspects of his or her job right from the start.

Vision and Mission. This section of the Business Terrain Research focuses on the degree to which the Executive Team shares a common understanding of the corporate vision and mission. It also explores the extent to which each member believes that his or her team understands their roles and whether or not they have the resources to accomplish them. Some of the key concerns that are addressed are,

- Is there is a commonly held vision or mission statement for the company? What is it?
- If unaware of one, what do you feel it is or should be?
- Is the mission of the company meaningful and realistic?
- Do you agree or disagree with it? How would you change it?
- How far down in the organization does the understanding of the mission go?
- Do people really believe in it?
- What role does your department play in making the vision a reality?
- Does the culture help or hinder the attainment of the mission? How?
- Do you have the needed resources to accomplish it?
- What are the top two issues regarding the vision and mission that the new CEO should be aware of?
- Will you and your team be adequately recognized and rewarded for achieving your portion of it?

Strategy. This area focuses on the commitment to, and concerns about, the existing strategic direction of the company. Some of the key questions include:

- Is the strategic direction of the company clear to you?
- What is your understanding of the strategy?
- Are you committed to it? Why or why not?
- Do you have concerns about the strategic direction that the company is taking?
- What is the biggest threat to the company from outside? From within?
- What is the likelihood of these events occurring?
- Do you see any solutions to these concerns?
- Do significant opportunities exist that are being overlooked?
- Do you know the quarterly and annual objectives for your part of the company and for the company overall?

- Are the financial objectives realistic for the current year and the next one?
- Does culture play a facilitating or distracting role in the company's strategic direction? How?
- What are the top two issues regarding strategy?
- Do you have adequate resources to achieve the portion of the strategic plan for which you have responsibility? If not, what is missing?
- If you achieve your portion of the strategic plan, will you and your team be adequately recognized and rewarded?

Critical Success Factors. The purpose of this section is to identify those factors that the Executive Leadership Team member believes *must occur* (or perhaps *must be avoided*) in order to achieve certain make-or-break milestones of key initiatives needed to produce expected results. Critical path roadblocks that must be eliminated of a functional or corporate nature are also identified. Questions here include items such as the following:

- If you were the new leader, what would you be most concerned about in the areas of people, organization, strategy, competition, and the like?
- What do you believe must change in the company? (Name three things.)
- What things should *not* be changed? (Name three things.)
- What are the critical milestones coming up that must happen without fail to achieve your functional objectives? (To achieve the corporate objectives?)
- Are there any unresolved issues within your functional area or elsewhere that require decisions by higher-ups so things can move ahead?
- What are the top three critical success factors for the new leader?

Early Wins. The questions regarding early wins serve to identify places where action can be taken by the new leader that will start to build momentum while establishing his or her credibility without the risk of derailing major initiatives. Often these involve reinstituting abandoned programs or processes, while others require the adoption of new policies and practices that had been promised but never delivered:

- Can you identify any place where a quick victory could be achieved without derailing major initiatives? Are these tangible or intangible activities?
- What can the new leader do to build followership and win peoples' hearts and minds?

- What new programs, processes, or attitudes will send the right messages to the organization?
- What are your two best ideas for potential early wins?
- Where will the new leader find the greatest resistance to implement changes?
- What would be the first thing you would do if you were in the new leader's shoes?

Culture. The Executive Leadership Team member is asked questions about the culture of the company and about that of the new leader's team itself. The term "culture" is defined simply as "the way things are done here—the personality of the company." Answers to questions about the company-wide culture are often used as a basis for exploring and contrasting aspects of the Executive Leadership Team subculture:

- How would you describe the cultures here (the company's and the leadership team's of which you are a part)? What are the basic values and beliefs held in common here?
- What are the strengths and weaknesses that these cultures provide the business?
- Would you like to see the cultures remain the same, or do you feel they need to change in some fashion? If so, how?
- What leadership style do you feel the new leader should possess to have the most positive effect in dealing with his or her direct reports?
- What type of leadership style do you feel would be most effective in the eyes of the overall organization? Is this a change from the previous CEO's style?
- Of everything we have discussed, what are the top three strengths of the organizational and team cultures? The three most significant drawbacks of each?
- How can the new leader gain the support of the organization at the "gut level" over time?

Human Capital and Bench Strength. The purpose of this section of the interview is to identify areas of the business that are weaker than others; to identify "rising stars," "key contributors," and "high pots" (high potential people); and to assess the extent to which "silos" (rigidly bureaucratic, vertical chains of communication and control) exist in various functions and between functions. Since these are very sensitive areas and of a highly subjective nature, the Research Expert will usually conduct this portion of the interview at the end of the process when rapport has been established. Reminding the respondent of the confidential and anonymous nature of this work is essential here. It is helpful to have an organization chart available as a reference tool so the Research Expert can understand specifically what areas are being discussed.

Some of the questions here involve:

- Are there areas in the company that you feel make major, exceptional contributions?
- Are there areas or functions that do not quite measure up?
- Are there areas in the company that need new blood or revitalization?
- Looking at all the functional areas in the organization and at the strength of the people in them, which ones do you feel are meeting, exceeding, or falling short of expectations and can significantly help or hinder the company moving forward?
- Who are the "rising stars" who possess strong leadership qualities within your organization and elsewhere in the company?
- What is it about these individuals that makes you feel they are highly capable?
- Are any of these people ready to be utilized in a different or bigger role elsewhere in the company?
- Who are the "key contributors" whose departures, if unexpected, might hinder the organization going forward? How?
- Describe the kind of people who are best suited for success in your organization's culture. What are the characteristics of those who have a hard time "fitting in" here? Can you cite any examples of people who "don't fit"?
- What is the top issue regarding people and human capital here?
- Who would you be concerned might leave during this transition time? Why?
- If you were the new leader, what people and organizational changes would you make? Why?

At the end of the Business Terrain Interview, the Research Expert will often ask some general questions to ascertain if there are any other "burning issues" that have not been addressed:

- If you had a magic wand and could change any three things about the company overall, what would they be?
- Is there anything else you can think of that would be helpful to the new leader?
- If one of the internal candidates does not get the appointment, what do you think his or her reaction will be? How will that affect the

organization? What can the new leader (or his or her boss) do to mitigate the problem?

- How do you feel about this process? Is there anything we can do to help make you and the new leader successful?
- If I have any follow-on questions or have the need to clarify anything you have said here, may I call you?

Processing and Use of the Business Terrain Data

All of the material that is collected in the Business Terrain Research is qualitative in nature. As indicated at the outset of the interviews with the Executive Leadership Team members, tapes are usually made of each of the meetings, transcribed, and then destroyed. The transcriptions are sent to the Research Expert, the Business Assessment Expert, and the Project Leader of the Forward Assessment Consulting Team. After having reviewed them, the three get together to organize, cull, discuss, and interpret the input by looking for areas of agreement or disagreement, common themes, the subleties of things *not* discussed by different team members, and, of course, the literal importance of specific points. Depending upon the number of interviews conducted, several hundred pages of transcription are produced, and the analysis can take over a week. The information derived from the Business Terrain Research is used for several key purposes:

Report of Preliminary Findings. The Business Terrain Research is first used to develop an initial snapshot of the business and the implications that these findings have on the profile of the leader who would be best suited to address them in this culture. The report of preliminary findings focuses primarily on the nature of the specific challenges that the new leader will face and the kinds of actions that will be required to be successful. Aspects of style, energy, and character that will be most effective in this situation are also identified. The FAC Project Leader will relay this information to the head of the Selection Team and usually, at the chairperson's request, to other members of the Selection Team, key directors (during a CEO search), and the executive recruiter involved in the process. The information gathered in the Business Terrain Research interview is *extremely* helpful in fine-tuning everyone's focus of the final candidate's desired traits, capabilities, and character. Without question, this is one of the most valuable pieces of information in the new Leader Selection Process, and its timeliness is usually quite critical.

Ghosts in the Office. Frequently one of the ways people learn what it is they want is by first discovering what they *don't* want. Quite often during the course of interviewing the new leader's direct reports, the interviewer gathers great insights into the problems created by the style, demeanor, or other behaviors of the leader being replaced. The frequency that these "ghosts" are mentioned (or the intensity with which they are brought up) can often provide insight into the kinds of characteristics that should be avoided in the new leader. The kinds of ghosts in the office that can be heard rattling around during the Business Terrain interviews are contained in remarks like:

- "He frequently reversed his decisions and changed his mind all the time; he had a priority du jour."
- "She yelled at people for bringing bad news—this was particularly embarrassing in public."
- "He was more worried about having a strategy to show the world than a strategy that could be delivered."
- "He intimidated people in front of their subordinates and peers."
- "He used things people said to him to pit people against each other."
- "She undermined the authority of senior managers by going to lower-level employees to 'get the scoop' and then confronted the senior manager with what she had learned."
- "He is constantly micro-managing the entire leadership team and their people."
- "She was not a good judge of executive talent and filled three key positions with 'fast-talkers.'"

Input to Team Topography. The comments made during the Business Terrain Research frequently provide direct insight into the overall Team Topography (to be discussed later) and are often directly incorporated into that work. Such comments can also serve as an initial thread of questioning to be subsequently unraveled during the course of the Team Topography Assessment.

Input to Mapping the Corporate Lay of the Land. The Business Terrain Research interviews provide great insight into what should be examined in greater detail in the quantitative research conducted with a broader base of individuals. This quantitative research, which we call "Mapping the Corporate Lay of the Land" or "Mapping" for short, is discussed in depth later in this chapter. However, it is worth noting here how important it is that various processes, programs, and initiatives as seen by the new leader's direct reports be examined more closely through the eyes of a broader population during the Mapping phase. Knowing what specific questions to ask in the Mapping phase often comes directly from the Business Terrain Research. Also, the "insider vocabulary" of the company (its jargon, acronyms, and buzz words) picked up in the Business Terrain Research are incorporated into the Mapping questions to make them more specific, relevant, and "user friendly" to the respondents.

Leader's Team Subculture. Comments made by the executives interviewed during the Business Terrain Research regarding the culture of the organization and that of the of the leader's team are invaluable. They provide information about the dynamics of the overall culture and the key success traits (values) that the right leader needs to possess. They also provide insight into the two most important subcultures in which the new leader will be enmeshed—that of the team the new leader will lead and that of the team on which the new leader will be a member. Understanding how decisions have been made and the expectations of the people who make up the different subcultures can greatly facilitate the new leader's introduction to these groups.

Assessing the Team Topography

This second element of the Forward Assessment Consulting work creates a behavioral snapshot of the Executive Leadership Team—the term used for the direct reports of the new leader. The Team Topography documents the dynamics of the group, as well as the characteristics and perceived competencies of each individual. It is prepared by the FAC Project Leader in conjunction with the psychologist or psychiatrist who is the Behavior Assessment Expert on the Forward Assessment Consulting Team. Sometimes all or portions of the report are provided verbally rather than in writing due to their confidential nature.

The Individual Assessments

Part of the Team Topography Assessment consists of a compilation of data from company files pertaining to each member of the Executive Leadership Team. Information regarding hire dates, job history, a current bio, compensation history, performance reviews, and current year objectives are usually included. A written summary of findings from the various testing instruments administered and interpreted by the Behavior Assessment Expert for assessment purposes may also be included.

The Behavior Assessment Expert usually reviews all of the information about each team member with them before sharing it with anyone on the Selection Team or with the new leader. Providing feedback to the individuals affords them information for development purposes as well as insight into what is being said about them to the new leader. It fosters trust.

Information from the Behavior Assessment Expert is combined with input from the Business Terrain Research interviews to prepare brief summaries of issues, concerns, and sensitivities relating to each team member (not the things they said, but the things said about them—the psychologist's "take" on them, and the like). These are sometimes presented as color-coded flags—red, yellow, or green—to indicate the degree to which concerns may exist regarding the match and fit of each member. The following are examples of the kind of descriptions that are provided in this section of the Team Topography Assessment:

Joan Doe, V.P. Sales. (Red Flag). A strong past contributor and leader with recent serious health problems. Does not see herself as long-term player with the company. Needs to retire with honor. Has lost credibility with other team members but is still well liked.

Clark Rogers, CIO. (Yellow Flag). There are conflicting views regarding Clark. Concerns about business judgment and the fact that he is not seen as having been successful in his role. On one hand it is possible he was asked to do things that weren't humanly possible. On the other hand there's a question as to whether he has his organization on track to fix what needs to be fixed. Has made questionable acquisitions of resources but is also seen as having a brilliant mind and future potential if properly applied and developed.

Lisa Smith, V.P. Development. (Green Flag). Highly effective. Pragmatic, drives for results, looks for trends, and is willing to listen to new points of view. Proactive. Mature leadership style. Could be a flight risk if she does not feel she's a valued member of the new leader's "inside group."

The Team Assessment

Based on the inputs provided to the psychologist or psychiatrist serving as the FAC Behavior Assessment Expert, combined with the insights uncovered while developing the Business Terrain, a narrative description of the team is prepared. The purpose of this narrative is to provide a picture of how well the team has coalesced and how the various members cooperate with one other. It provides insights into the new leader's team's subculture, the nature of communications among peers, and the strength of social ties and connections among the individuals. In some instances a sociogram will be created describing the dynamics and relationships among the team members.

Uses of the Team Topography Assessment

The Team Topography Assessment, then, is made up of two pieces: a summary of each team member as an individual (the Individual Assessments) and a look at the team as a whole (the Team Assessment Report). It can be a key tool in selecting the right leader for a particular situation, especially when trying to decide between two closely qualified candidates. The Team

Topography Assessment can be used to compare and contrast the degree to which the finalists will fit with the expectations, behaviors, and processes of the management team they inherit. The insight the Behavior Assessment Expert obtained from having interviewed and done an assessment of each member of the new leader's team can clarify how one candidate would relate to the group as compared to another. Given the depth of knowledge that the Behavior Assessment Expert has of the group dynamics from having conducted the Team Topography, a very accurate sense of the relative fit of the final candidates can usually be provided—a very helpful piece of information in the Leader Selection Process.

The Team Topography Assessment work also serves an extremely important element in the new leader's onboarding plan. It provides clues as to how to manage early interactions with each individual team member and can be especially helpful in forging early alliances. In particular it can be useful as a guide for the new leader in dealing with internal candidates who did not get the position. It also provides the new leader with a framework to facilitate quick organizational design decisions if necessary. Quicker people and organization decisions can be made with this enlightened perspective.

The Team Topography Assessment is not, in itself, a *plan* of action for the new leader, but it is the best source of relevant data for new leaders to use in building their own plans once they have had a chance to observe their situation for themselves. Possessing an objective assessment like this regarding each individual and the team dynamics upon arrival is not only extremely helpful, but will greatly reduce the amount of time required to reach critical people decisions quickly and accurately.

The two keys to making the Team Topography Assessment most effective are,

1. When possible, utilize the same instruments for the overall Team Topography Assessment as are used in assessing the internal and outside candidates. Not only does this provide comparable data, but the experience the selected leader has with these instruments will enable him or her to know how to best use the information gathered to evaluate others.

2. Ensure that the Team Topography is completed *before* the final candidates are interviewed. The Team Topography Assessment Report can provide extremely helpful clues to be closely explored during the final interviews before selecting the right leader.

Because of the *highly* confidential nature of this Team Topography, only one copy of it is prepared by the FAC for review with the Selection Team leader and with the new leader once selected. Quite often no written copies are prepared at all simply to avoid the potential accidental mishandling of such sensitive data. This material is reviewed with the new leader as a part of the new leader briefing (described in Chapter 12).

Mapping the Corporate Lay of the Land

Concurrent with the development of the Team Topography, the FAC Project Leader works closely with the HR head and the Selection Team leader to Map the Corporate Lay of the Land. This process provides a more granular picture of the Business Terrain—one that can be examined from a number of different perspectives on a wide array of needs-related and cultural factors. Quite often it is based on information gathered in the Business Terrain Research, which provides the qualitative information to determine what needs to be more closely targeted in this phase of research.

The purpose of the Mapping process is to identify *exactly* where the "targets" (the actionable needs of the organization) are that the incoming leader must focus on. The process of Mapping the Corporate Lay of the Land identifies the true needs of the organization—both executional and directional—as well as the extent to which each functional and geographic operating unit is prepared to execute them. Of even greater importance to the success of the new leader, Mapping also defines the key elements of the cultures through which the needed changes must be achieved. This information is equally valuable to the Selection Team in deciding which candidate possesses the best combination of Match-Fit characteristics for a particular situation.

Historical Roots of Mapping

When we first began Mapping the Corporate Lay of the Land, it was primarily a culture-assessment tool that looked at eight basic factors. The members of the Executive Leadership Team were asked to indicate on a scale of 0 to 10 where they felt their company's culture existed for each of the items. We also asked them to describe the subculture of their peer team in a similar fashion. The eight aspects we looked at are shown in Table 10.1.

Final candidate(s) were also asked to complete the same questionnaire relative to the culture in which he or she was most accustomed to working. We called the results their "predisposed" cultural expectation. The candidate's predisposed cultural expectations are an indication of what they are most accustomed to experiencing and what they will be most inclined to interpret those "explicit and implicit, rational, irrational, and nonrational" behavioral guides as meaning.

The combined responses of the Executive Leadership Team members were then plotted on a spider graph (sometimes referred to as a "radar diagram") which we have come to call "Culturemaps." The "predisposed

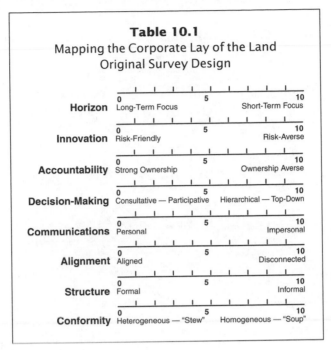

Table 10.1

Mapping the Corporate Lay of the Land
Original Survey Design

	0	5	10
Horizon	Long-Term Focus		Short-Term Focus
Innovation	Risk-Friendly		Risk-Averse
Accountability	Strong Ownership		Ownership Averse
Decision-Making	Consultative — Participative		Hierarchical — Top-Down
Communications	Personal		Impersonal
Alignment	Aligned		Disconnected
Structure	Formal		Informal
Conformity	Heterogeneous — "Stew"		Homogeneous — "Soup"

expectations" of the new leader candidate are then plotted on the Culture-maps for purposes of comparison. The greater the distance between any two points on a given axis, the greater the potential for a misunderstanding or disconnect to occur. The greater the distance between the expectations of the new leader and the reality of his or her direct reports, the greater the potential for the new leader to misread the situation or to behave in ways that will not be understood or accepted by the organization. Such a comparison, taken from an early Crenshaw Mapping study, appears as Figure 10.1.

Figure 10.1 shows an actual comparison between an incoming CEO candidate and the organization into which she will soon be enmeshed. Eliza comes from a large corporation where, for instance, alignment (see "alignment" axis in Figure 10.1) on corporate mission, vision, strategies, and annual goals was always very clear. The company into which Eliza would now move is much smaller and has gone through a lot of significant changes. As you can see, the organization is *not* well aligned on those key factors, and the gap between the reality that exists in this company and what Eliza will naturally expect to exist is considerable. If Eliza assumes that everyone understands and buys into the marching orders for the current year as she is accustomed, she will be making a *very* big mistake. Achieving alignment can take time, and clearly, one of Eliza's initial tasks is to understand exactly where alignment exists and where it does not so that she can build the necessary shared

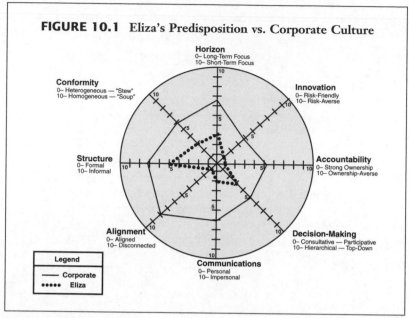

FIGURE 10.1 Eliza's Predisposition vs. Corporate Culture

foundation, without which whatever new initiatives she might seek to implement will fail. By using this information as a map Eliza can navigate the cultures of the organization to avoid problems and pitfalls.

The value of these analyses of corporate culture were immediately evident and provided the opportunity to look at the Executive Leadership Team's team subculture. Taking the work further, we now have an expanded Mapping Process that examines both needs *and* cultures as seen through the eyes of the top several hundred executives, as well as the top Executive Team. It pinpoints exactly where, continuing with Eliza's alignment conflict, alignment does and does not exist on a number of key, success-related executional and directional needs or initiatives.

The New Mapping Research

The practice of using research techniques to measure the true needs of an organization is not new. Work in this area has been done in a variety of forms with different methodologies for many years, particularly in research settings. In a business setting, however, the notion of measuring aspects of culture is still in its infancy, and there are not many ways to be found that are specifically designed to assess the fit of candidates for senior leadership roles. We anticipate and hope that this will change as the importance of this kind of work is accepted and expands.

The Crenshaw Mapping process is intended for use with a company's top 100 to 200 senior executives. Our partner in the development of the software and methodology used for this tool was Genesys Solutions, LLC. Their work in identifying the readiness of large organizations to execute their strategies and other initiatives is well known and highly regarded. By adapting the Genesys software we have created an online survey totaling 154 questions (instead of the eight original ones shown in Table 10.1), of which 54 pertain to the needs of the organization (26 related to executional needs and 28, to directional needs), while the remaining 100 questions focus on culture. More information on this survey can be found at *therightleader.com*.

Our survey asks respondents to rank statements according to how accurately they reflect the respondents' perceptions of their company (or business unit) on a seven-point scale. Some questions are used more than once in the assessment of the data. For instance the statement, "Within my company (or functional area), people frequently and freely talk with others from different levels and areas of responsibility," is used as an element in assessing not only the structural rigidity of the corporate and functional cultures, but also the extent to which the cultures are "open" ones. The scoring of this statement is also used to shed light on the nature of "internal communications" within the company, yielding three different uses for this single question.

Table 10.2 shows the different areas that constitute the design of the online survey used in Mapping the Corporate Lay of the Land today.

Table 10.2
Mapping the Corporate Lay of the Land Current Survey Design

Executional Needs (26 Questions)

- Key Issues
- People
- Resources
- Communications — External

Directional Needs (28 Questions)

- Vision
- Strategic Plan
- Operating/Annual Plan
- Readiness to Execute

Culture (100 Questions)

- Alignment
- Climate
- Communications — Internal
- Decision-Making
- Empowerment — Accountability
- Momentum

- Nature of Work
- Processes — Formal
- Processes — Informal
- Rewards & Recognition
- Structural Rigidity
- Values

Working with the Forward Assessment Consulting Team, the company's Selection Team identifies the specific individuals who will participate in the Mapping research and prepares a spreadsheet containing basic demographic data that is attached to their records, so that when they sign onto the survey Web site, their answers can be categorized anonymously for the purpose of analyzing the data. The following demographics are generally used to analyze and present the data:

- Functional Area
- Supervisory Level
- Gender
- Hire Date
- Geographic Location

To further ensure the anonymity of respondents, all of the data are processed by a third-party provider, and nothing is reported back to the Forward Assessment Consultants or to the company in aggregated groups of less than three people, nor are there any verbatims containing names or departmental affiliations that could reveal individual identities.

Verbatims are often very helpful in crystallizing a nugget of insight and in bringing the data to life in a colorful and memorable way. Opportunities for respondents to provide their comments, thoughts, and open-ended inputs to the topics at hand are included at several junctures in the survey. Together, the data and the verbatims furnish the insights into the true needs and cultures of the organization that are essential to help select the right leader and to aid that selected leader to successfully transition into his or her new role more effectively and quickly.

The current survey design (Table 10.2) focuses on those categories of executional and directional needs as shown. Needs are described in terms of the *actions* that must be taken to achieve the *results* that are desired from making the leadership change. By learning what specific actions are required, the company's Selection Team can focus its behavioral-based interviewing more closely on the kinds of experience the new leader will need to have had to address the challenges facing the organization. This information can be of particular value to the executive recruiter who is charged with responsibility for identifying qualified candidates for the position, as well as to those who are screening the slate of candidates. It is also why use of behavior-based interviewing is so highly recommended. It is through the use of this technique that interviewers gain the clearest understanding of *exactly* what each candidate has done and the true extent of his or her involvement in the kinds of things they will face if selected. It is the best means available to determine exactly *how* the candidate's experiences may or may not relate to the actions expected of them if chosen.

Table 10.2 also lists the areas that are examined when looking at the cultures of the organization. Based on input from the Business Terrain Research, the statements used in the Web-based Mapping survey are modified and tailored to incorporate the company's terminology, as well as to dive more deeply into areas where there are indications that chronic problems may exist.

Because cultures change slowly, the Mapping data pertaining to cultures do not become obsolete quickly and can be therefore used in different selection processes at different levels for up to twelve months with a fair degree of confidence. Given the fact that 25 percent of the Executive Team will, on average, become "forced resignations" following the appointment of a new CEO, having this data already available when their replacements are being selected is of great value.[2] For senior management these data can also provide an excellent basis for identifying where aspects of the overall culture or of a particular functional or geographic subculture need to be changed. These cultural data can also provide a baseline to track longitudinal studies of improvements or changes to the culture over time—a practice that is highly recommended in order to provide the tools necessary to manage the process of culture creation to gain competitive advantage.

One of the greatest values of the Mapping data lies in the creation of the Culturemaps for the selected new leader. As you will see in the case study that appears in Chapter 11, the cultural predispositions of the new leader are plotted onto the Culturemaps of the organization at large as well as those of the leader's team (comprised of the ELT) and the boss's team of which the new leader will be a member. During the initial briefing presented by the FAC Project Team Leader, a specific set of potential cultural pitfalls are identified and discussed—places where the new leader will find him- or herself at odds with the values and expectations of one or more of the organization's cultures. We refer to this list of potential pitfalls as the leader's "cultural compass" because it serves as a tool to help the new leader navigate through or around obstacles that would not otherwise be seen as a source of contention. Charting one's course with the use of a compass and maps truly helps a new leader from getting lost.

Chapter 11 provides a case study of Specialty Distributors, Inc. that shows how, by Mapping the Corporate Lay of the Land, the process of selecting the right leader is greatly enhanced. Beyond selecting the right leader, however, Mapping the Corporate Lay of the Land also provides invaluable data for onboarding the new executive. The research provides very clear snapshots of the varying degrees to which functional areas or geographic regions are prepared to achieve their objectives and what is needed to improve their readiness to execute. This use of the data is far too extensive to include in Chapter 11, but we have included some examples of these important uses of Mapping on a Web site created especially for the purpose of providing further insights into topics raised in this book. Again we refer you to *therightleader.com*.

The Malleability of "Pegs"

This brings us to an important point regarding the fit of pegs into the corporate holes, the true shape of which the FAC work now permits us to see. Unlike wooden pegs, human "pegs" can be quite malleable if they choose to be. Their ability to be shaped is in stark contrast to organizations whose holes are shaped by their needs and cultures, neither of which are very easily changed. An individual can adapt quite quickly to the normative behavior of the organization, but it takes much longer for an organization to embrace the new behaviors of an individual (even those of a powerful leader).

Consequently, if a newly appointed leader is *aware* that differences exist between his or her expectations and predispositions about a new environment and what actually exists, they can, and will, usually make significant changes and adjustments to fit their style and approach into that of the culture. Human "pegs" can modify their shape to better fit into certain holes in regard to their personalities (style), and they can even reallocate their energy levels to some degree.

The one place where significant changes cannot be made is in the area of character. Like the cultures of organizations, the characters of individuals change slowly over time. Since values make up a large component of both character *and* culture, the initial alignment of values between the individual and those of the culture is extremely important. If close alignment of values does not exist coming into the job, trust will not occur, and ultimately success, will not ensue. When it comes to values, leaders do not have the option of adjusting themselves to fit the situation better.

Our experience shows that what causes many senior leaders to fail is that they simply do not have the knowledge of what they should change to fit the cultures at play better, in what direction, and how much. They don't have an accurate compass and set of maps for the particular terrain. By the time they figure out that what worked for them elsewhere is not working well here, it is too late. Many *think* they "get it" when, in fact, they do not; what they see is *not* what exists. Others are convinced that the "my way or the highway" approach is the rule of the road and are not *willing* to consider making any changes. Our experience, however, has been that when given a choice between modifying their behaviors to be successful or not, most senior leaders will opt for success.

This is an important factor to keep in mind when using the Mapping tools to select the right leader. For any given situation there is no *one* right leader, and there is certainly no such thing as the "perfect" leader. However, given clear, factual information and the chance to learn where the potential gaps and problem areas regarding fit exist, most candidates will come to the right decision along with the Selection Team that is hiring them. Clearly this is one of the benefits of Mapping the Corporate Lay of the Land—it gives the selected individual the information necessary to improve his or her fit and, with it, the likelihood of his or her success.

The Field Guide
of Vital Information

The Field Guide of Vital Information is a very simple yet *extremely* beneficial step in the Leader Selection Process. It is included in the Leader Selection Process even though it plays little or no *direct* role in the actual selection of the leader. It does, however, play a meaningful role in the swift and successful onboarding of the new leader, and it is included in the Leader Selection Process because it must be initiated sufficiently in advance of the new leader's arrival to be of optimal value.

The Field Guide of Vital Information is a purposeful collection, review, and organization of relevant management and planning documents. It is material that the new leader needs to either be familiar with or at the least aware of. The contents of the Field Guide of Vital Information often become the new leader's "motel-room reading"—documents and reports that the individual takes home after a day of work to review before going to bed. The contents of the Field Guide of Vital Information serve to establish a solid foundation of knowledge on a number of important topics.

Creating the Guide

The creation of a Field Guide of Vital Information begins with the Forward Assessment Consulting Team's Project Leader preparing a message for the head of the Selection Team to forward to the Executive Leadership Team members and to selected peers of the new leader, requesting them to submit copies of *all* relevant documents, reports, policies, and the like, that are deemed important for the new leader to read and to know about. A due date is established in the message. Specific examples of what should (and what should *not*) be provided are included in this "call for input." A list of the kinds of material that is requested appears in Appendix C. The FAC Project Manager then reviews everything that is submitted, culling out unnecessary items and returning them to the senders. Everything that is kept is reviewed and organized—a process that can take several weeks to complete.

The FAC organizes the materials into several tabbed binders (usually between four and seven 3-inch binders) and/or electronic files and develops an overall annotated table of contents, as well as specific tables of contents for each binder. The annotated table of contents includes:

- A description of each document
- The name of the person and department who has responsibility for it
- The distribution list of those who receive copies
- The frequency and date of publication of the document
- The degree of confidentiality of the document

Once created, efforts should be maintained to keep the Field Guide of Vital Information current. The Field Guide of Vital Information can then serve as an orientation tool for other newly hired senior executives and outside directors.

By creating the Field Guide of Vital Information, the Forward Assessment Consultant will eliminate the need for the new leader to have to scour the organization looking for those key policies, procedures, plans, and programs that are at the core of the "way we do things here"—the organization's cultural artifacts. They will be available to him or her *before* the time comes when their need is recognized.

The Contents of the Field Guide of Vital Information

The contents of this Field Guide will vary from situation to situation because it is truly a function of both what is available and the position being filled. The specific information needed by a functional head, a country leader, a division president, a CEO, or a chairman will all be different. Generally, however, the following nine sections will serve as an outline when starting to assemble a Field Guide of Vital Information.

1. Board and Shareholder Information
2. Enterprise-Wide Information
3. Human Resources Information
4. Financial Information
5. Operations Information
6. Marketing and Sales Information
7. Product Information
8. Manufacturing and Sourcing Information
9. Legal Risk/IT Information

Appendix C contains a compilation of the contents from several field guides of vital information from different leader selection processes. It is provided as a checklist for hirers looking to create a Field Guide of Vital Information for individuals being selected for a new position.

Create It Now, Not Later. There are many reasons that it is essential that the Field Guide of Vital Information be created by the FAC before the new leader is in place besides the obvious one—so he or she can have it available as soon as they need it, even before day one. If possible, he or she should have access from the day they are hired, so that they can review it before they start.

Better Information Is Gathered. When the head of HR—or the director leading the Selection Team in the case of a new CEO search—puts out a call for contents, the likelihood of full cooperation is quite high. Surprisingly the response to the same kind of request is *not* always as enthusiastically supported when made by the new leader. This is possibly because "information is power," and until trust is built, some team members may withhold key pieces of information for use at a time that might be more advantageous to them. With no one other than the new CEO to "police" the request, it is easier for something to "drop through the cracks" than when the process is being managed by the FAC's Project Leader.

Follow-Up Is Key. The Forward Assessment Consultant is in a position to follow up on the call for information to ensure things have not been withheld, forgotten, or overlooked. Having seen a number of these, the FAC Project Leader is also in the position to have a good idea as to what should be forthcoming. Sometimes the requests for Field Guide materials simply get lost in the course of normal business. Nevertheless the FAC Project Leader must stay on top of the information that is coming in and know what to look for. Gathering the right information takes time and is rarely a particularly straightforward procedure.

Cull Out the Excess. Often the call for contents will generate an overwhelming load of material. Some participants may see this as a chance to acquaint their future new boss with their view of the world, including documentation of old political battles won or lost, examples of recent affronts to their "good judgment," samples of the outstanding work done by them and their people on pet projects, and so forth. In the end, keeping the focus on what is essential to the new leader and not what may be of greatest importance to each and every one of the leader's direct reports is what matters most.

Create Key Documents That Do Not Exist. Sometimes things that will be needed by the new leader simply do not exist at the company and must be created, which is something that the FAC Project Leader is in a position to do. Generally, the two most helpful items that companies do not always have readily available are the Corporate Calendar and a Business Process Summary or Checklist.

- **Corporate Calendar.** The Corporate Calendar is a cross-functional, integrated date book of events all brought into one place where the upcoming "givens" that drive the business are clearly identified. These "givens" include such things as monthly and quarterly financial closings, industry events and trade shows, sales meetings, board meetings, recognition and retirement events, analyst meetings, secular and corporate holidays (regional and global), planning conferences (such as strategic planning, operational planning, succession planning reviews, and due dates), staff meetings, and even the scheduled vacations of the new leader's direct reports. Without this information, the coordination of even the simplest of meetings that the new leader may want to hold can become an endeavor of galactic proportions—one that is time-consuming and could inadvertently cast the new leader in a very bad light with various constituencies without even knowing it (by, for example, scheduling an off-site meeting in Toronto on the second Monday in October, which is when Canadians celebrate Thanksgiving).
- **Business Process Summary (or Business Process Checklist).** Another extremely helpful tool, especially for leaders who come from outside of the organization, is a descriptive summary of the key business processes that are in place at the company. Having pulled together the Field Guide of Vital Information and having reviewed all of the Business Terrain and Mapping data, the FAC Project Leader is in a good position to create such a summary. The summary should indicate the name of the process, its "owner," how long it has been in place, when (how frequently) it is employed, produced, or updated, the degree of rigor surrounding it, and the like. Crenshaw expert Bob Aquilina, who developed this idea, recommends that the checklist include processes such as capital planning, budgeting, strategic planning, business reviews, operating dashboards, sales inventory-production planning, merit reviews, and succession planning.

Takeaways

Chapter 10 has been focused on the four key elements that have been missing from the Traditional Selection Process for years. When added to the Traditional Selection Process along with the enhancements to it that were discussed in Chapter 9, the end result is a new Leader Selection Process. The following is a summary of the new research elements and how they can be gathered by a Forward Assessment Consulting Team:

- Use of an outside Forward Assessment Consultant (FAC) to perform a variety of functions in the new Leader Selection Process is recommended. The involvement of outside professionals to perform the necessary research helps to assure the company's participants that their anonymity will be maintained. Without that assurance, the desired information (which the participants dearly wish to convey provided they can do so safely) will not be forthcoming.

- The Forward Assessment Consultant is not a single individual but a number of specialists whose involvement is coordinated by an outside Project Leader. The Project Leader should be a former senior executive (CEO, Operating Head, or HR Chief), or a very senior professional business consultant. Other experts making up the FAC Team include a Research Expert, Business Assessment Expert, Behavior Assessment Expert (psychologist or psychiatrist), and various administrative support specialists.

- In addition to other changes and modifications, there are four key elements to be added to the Traditional Selection Process in order to create a new Leader Selection Process. They are the Business Terrain Assessment, the Team Topography Assessment, Mapping the Corporate Lay of the Land, and the Field Guide of Vital Information.

- Researching and understanding the Business Terrain is a crucial first step. It is developed from in-depth interviews with each Executive Leadership Team member that are conducted anonymously by the FAC's Research Expert.

- The Business Terrain Research interviews focus on the company's mission and vision, strategies, current success factors, early wins, culture, and human capital.

- The Business Terrain Research has many uses. Its input is used as a basis for fine-tuning the selection parameters and also as input to the Team Topography Assessment. The data is also used to tailor many of the normative statements used in Mapping the Corporate Lay of the Land. The Business Terrain Research is particularly helpful in understanding the subculture and inner dynamics of the new leader's team of inherited direct reports.

- The Team Topography Assessment looks at the individual members of the Executive Leadership Team and at the team dynamics as a whole. Human capital and bench strength issues that were touched upon in the Business Terrain Research are explored in greater detail through the use of selected interview techniques and assessment instruments employed by the FAC's Behavior Expert.

- Mapping the Corporate Lay of the Land ("Mapping") is a deeper dive into the true needs and cultures of the organization. It identifies the readiness of the organization to execute its strategic and operating plans and initiatives on a regional, functional, departmental, and overall basis. It identifies the prevailing values of the organization's culture and of key subcultures that will determine, in large part, the ultimate fit of the leader.

- Mapping usually breaks down the major elements of culture into tangible, manageable, and quantifiable pieces that can be examined on the basis of supervisory level, geographic location, gender, years of service, and functional area. (This will be seen clearly in the next chapter.)

- Mapping takes "culture" out of the "soft stuff" category and gives it a hard, descriptive shape to be used and molded by the right leader.

- Although the Field Guide of Vital Information plays only a small direct role in selecting the right leader, its value to the new leader is great. It reduces the time it takes the new leader to learn about the various policies, programs, and processes that serve as anchors for the organization. It furthers understanding of where the company has been, where it currently is, and where it is headed.

- If properly maintained, the Field Guide of Vital Information can benefit future new hires, as well as assist new directors seeking to do due diligence or learn more about the inner workings of the company.

- Upon occasion pieces of critical information of great value to the new leader simply do not exist, and the FAC Project Leader may need to create them for the incoming leader. The Corporate Calendar and a Checklist of Business Policies are two such helpful items that can greatly facilitate a new leader's transition.

11

The FAC Process at Work

The case of SDI, Inc.

The real voyage of discovery consists not in seeking new landscapes but in having new eyes.

—Marcel Proust

T he following case study incorporates actual data from a Crenshaw Mapping the Corporate Lay of the Land process. The data shown for the corporation and for the individual are real. Everything else, however, has been changed to ensure the confidentiality of the participants.

We have broken this example of the process into three parts:

- The situation we found when we began to evaluate the selection process ongoing at the client
- What Mapping told us
- What we recommended to the client in terms of making the selection

This case study provides an excellent view of how the injection of this kind of research into the needs and cultures of an organization can give the Selection Team "new eyes" capable of seeing not only their own corporate landscape more clearly, but also the extent to which a new potential leader will fit into it.

The Situation

Specialty Distributors, Inc. (SDI) is a company that has been in existence for twenty-five years. It is headquartered in the Midwest and has annual sales of $350 million. Specialty Distributors, Inc. is publicly traded on NASDAQ and has enjoyed above-average industry growth in sales and earnings for the past several years. Their success has come as the result of a growing customer base in the markets they serve and through aggressively managing the mix of the products they offer. Their customer service is viewed to be better than any of their competitors'.

Their current chairman and CEO, Fred B., has informed the board of his intention to retire at the end of the year. When he retires it has been agreed that he will stay on as chairman for one year and then leave the board altogether, at which time a nonexecutive chairman, probably the current lead director, will be appointed.

Fred started with SDI right after graduate school and became CEO ten years ago following the company's initial public offering (IPO). Two years ago he became chairman as well. Over the years Fred has done an excellent job communicating the long- and short-term goals of the business to employees. He allows his direct reports to "do their thing." His bimonthly staff meetings serve as a clearinghouse for issues, updates, and cross-functional communications. In addition Fred holds a staff meeting after every board meeting to provide feedback that quickly disseminates throughout the organization. While he acknowledges that there are opportunities for process and people upgrades, his conservative, low-risk approach to making changes has worked well, and at this point in his career he is not interested in "fixing something that isn't broken." He agrees with several of the directors that potential opportunities exist for SDI by expanding their geographic base of business and has even looked at the acquisition of other specialty distributors in adjacent regions. At this juncture, though, all agree that the orchestration of such a growth strategy is best left in the hands of Fred's successor.

A High-Altitude Snapshot of SDI

Imagine yourself flying over SDI's main location, well above 10,000 feet and taking a picture of the company with a special camera that allows you to see, on an overall basis, how the top 100 leaders and managers feel about their company—how they perceive the future direction (directional needs); how they view the current outlook (executional needs); and how they relate overall to the ways things get done there (its culture). Figure 11.1 shows just such a

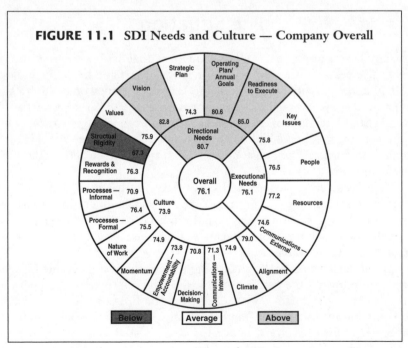

FIGURE 11.1 SDI Needs and Culture — Company Overall

high-altitude picture of SDI taken with the Mapping tool described in the previous chapter.

If you glance back at Table 10.2 in Chapter 10 and compare it to Figure 11.1, you will notice that the categories are the same. The numbers in each category in Figure 11.1 are the average ratings of the respondents on the seven-point scale converted to a percentage, so the higher the number, the more positive the attitude of the respondents. This conversion makes comparisons and contrasts between the areas a bit easier.

Overall, SDI is a solid company and does indeed possess a clear understanding of where it is going. However, it is not as clear about how it intends to get there. This discrepancy is indicated by the relatively lower rating for "Strategic Plan" and for all of the "Executional Needs." The SDI culture is, with the exception of "Structural Rigidity" (a symptom of entrenched "silos") indicative of a solid "B team" company—one that is not outstanding at anything, but where nothing is terribly wrong either. Most importantly people feel quite connected to the future of the company.

Other, more detailed maps make it clear that people are comfortable here. Things work predictably. Nobody rocks the boat—people do their jobs, feel pretty good about themselves and their team members, are adequately paid, and feel challenged but not pushed or driven. The parking lot does not empty out at 5:05, but it is not still full at 6:30 either. People express a great deal of pride in their company and trust Fred and his team. As one verbatim states, "SDI is a good place to work, although that may not always be a good thing. It may be more of an easy place to work than just a good one."

The CEO Search

In anticipation of Fred's upcoming retirement, the board has initiated a search for his replacement under the direction of the lead director. A special committee made up of independent directors has been created for this purpose. The internal candidate who was being groomed to succeed Fred was hired away by a bigger, national competitor a few months ago, just before Fred announced his intention to retire. No other internal candidates are ready to assume the position, although one has expressed her interest in the position.

Working with the head of HR, the chair of the Special Selection Committee has engaged a well-known, reputable search firm and, after developing a comprehensive job description, they have initiated a search for someone "with ten years of industry experience who has successfully led a distribution operation of scale." Among other attributes, the ideal candidate would "possess an MBA and be able to work well in a strong team environment."

The Final Candidate

After two rounds of meetings with very attractive candidates, the consensus view of all those involved in the search, including Fred B., is that James R. is the preferred candidate. James is a very personable, poised executive, age 45. His undergraduate degree is from an Ivy League school, and his MBA is also from a very competitive Eastern university where he finished near the top of his class. James has been a fast-track performer for his entire career and has worked for two Fortune 500 companies for most of it.

Currently James is employed by a very large, well-known consumer durables company noted for its focus on new products and its speed to market. Its growth rate had slowed in recent years, and a new CEO was recently appointed from within the company. James has been with this employer for six years, having started there as the SVP of Global Supply Chain operations. Four years ago he was promoted to president of the Distribution Services Division which, although not in the exact same industry as SDI, nevertheless possesses many similar characteristics and faces many of the same issues, challenges, and pressures.

James has received rave comments from references almost across the board and has, himself, expressed keen interest in the prospects of becoming the CEO of a public company and "taking SDI to the next level." Initially there were some concerns that James might be too aggressive and goal-oriented for the more staid SDI environment, but as people spent more time with him in the second round of interviews, he seemed to lose some of his edge and came off as a regular guy—"very likable and easy to talk to." The consensus was that James was a high-energy "people person whose abilities and background make him exactly what we need" in the eyes of everyone who had spent any time with him at all.

The Findings

In the following paragraphs are six Mapping figures that shed considerable light on James' candidacy and his potential fit with SDI's cultures. Three of them (11.2 through 11.4) compare the overall cultural traits of SDI with James's predispositions and cultural expectations, and the other three (11.5 through 11.7) compare James's cultural predispositions with those of the subculture of the Executive Leadership Team. In each of these figures the darker line connecting squares represent the expectations, attitudes, and perceptions that James would bring to SDI, while the lighter, triangular points are those of the organization's culture, climate, and values.

James's predispositions—which are the product of his past cultural experiences—will shape the way he will interpret his new experiences and how he will form impressions of SDI if he gets the job. As you look at these maps and formulate what you would do as the head of the Special Committee, keep the following in mind:

- Leaders fail more because they do not fit the cultures they must lead and through which they must bring about change than because they cannot do what is necessary.
- If the values of the leaders do not approximate those of the culture, people will not trust the leader, and without trust there is no followership.
- There is never a perfect candidate for a situation. All candidates will have pluses and minuses, making trade-offs and judgment calls a necessary part of the selection process. Ultimately, the selection of the right leader comes down to making the best judgment based upon the best information that can be obtained.

James and the SDI Culture

James's Fit with the Company Overall Culture (Figure 11.2). James's predispositions are by and large a function of the cultures of which he has been a part. When compared to the culture of SDI, James is most closely aligned

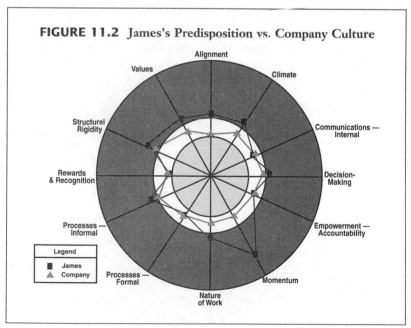

FIGURE 11.2 James's Predisposition vs. Company Culture

with the manner in which internal communications occur, the types of rewards and recognition processes that exist, and their linkage to performance, as well as with the more formal processes used to operate the business. In addition, the extent to which people are empowered and their sense of accountability at SDI are not too dissimilar from James's past experiences and expectations, which is another favorable finding.

But there are some differences too. The most apparent difference is the speed with which the two companies operate. James comes from an organization where changes occur rapidly and without end. At the same time, a lot of "wheel spinning" goes on there so that, in spite of their corporate slogan that the company is "driven for speed," it does not have much forward traction. The people at James's current company are bombarded with new initiatives and rush programs but do not have much in the way of results to show for it. Its structural rigidity ("silos") is in contrast to the more open climate that exists at SDI.

Since the SDI culture is generally more positive than the one to which James is accustomed, these differences should not pose as great a challenge for him as if the conditions were reversed. The SDI culture may, in fact, represent a refreshing change for him, provided he is willing to adjust to it right from the start and work *with* it instead of trying to change it too drastically too quickly.

James's Fit with the Company Climate Detail (Figure 11.3). In spite of its public persona, James's current company is one where people resist the

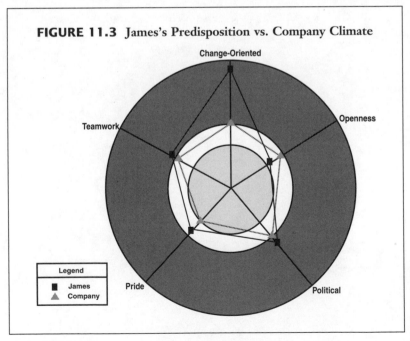

FIGURE 11.3 James's Predisposition vs. Company Climate

Legend
■ James
▲ Company

internal changes with which they are regularly hit and which they are expected to implement quickly. Being a product of that culture, James is predisposed to expect resistance to whatever initiatives he decides to take. Given this predisposition, the manner in which James plans to lead changes at SDI should be an excellent topic for the final round of interviews. It will be especially relevant in the Character Interview to be conducted by the chairman and, in this case, the lead director who is heading the Special Committee. How James plans to go about initiating changes at SDI will make a big difference in how his new organization accepts both James and his initiatives. Using the behavioral-based interviewing techniques, the interviewers should not ask, How would you go about leading a change initiative here? but rather, Describe how you have led change initiatives previously. Please take us through the details of one of them and tell us why you did it the way you did.

Then, after handing him the map shown in Figure 11.3 and explaining it to him, they should ask, In light of this picture of you and SDI, how might you go about leading a change initiative here? Have you ever had to change your style to lead a more effective initiative before in your career? Where? When? How did it go?

James' Fit with the Company Values Detail (Figure 11.4). Relative to SDI, the culture in which James is accustomed to operating is less trusting, more disrespectful, and more tolerant of individuals with lower integrity than

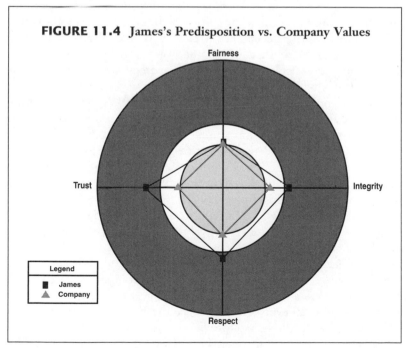

FIGURE 11.4 James's Predisposition vs. Company Values

Fairness

Trust

Integrity

Legend

■ James

▲ Company

Respect

SDI's more principled culture. Only in the area of fairness (primarily inclusiveness and diversity according to the even more detailed maps not shown here) does James's background provide him a similar predisposition to that which he will find at SDI. The fact that James comes from an organization that is low on trust, respect, and integrity does *not* mean that James, himself, is low on these important character traits, but it *is* critical that these topics be explored and understood before a decision about James can be made. The Character Interview discussed in Chapter 9 is the best method to do this. In dealing with other people James must understand that his background will tend to make him more suspicious, distrusting, and more inclined to tolerate people who are disrespectful toward others than what people will expect to see from him. In his old culture it was "okay" to promise to do one thing and then not live up to your word 100 percent of the time. But that is not the case at SDI. If James becomes the new CEO, he cannot behave that way or bring in others who behave that way if he hopes to become the company's leader in any way other than name.

James and the Executive Leadership Team Subculture

As stressed in Chapter 7, a leader must contend with more than one culture when stepping into a new role. The culture of the country (or region) can have a big impact on his or her acceptance, as can that of the overall organization, as we have just examined. In addition there are two other very important subcultures to be considered—that of the team the selected leader must lead and that of the "boss's team" on which the new leader is a member.

In our Mapping process, the SDI board (the boss's team) was not, for a number of reasons, included in the research, but the team made up of James's direct reports was. Comparisons similar to those made previously, but this time comparing James and the Executive Leadership Team, are shown in Figures 11.5 through 11.7. As you are about to see, it appears that James's predispositions are going to make it more difficult for him to work within the subculture of the ELT (his direct reports) than with the company overall.

James's Fit with the ELT Subculture (Figure 11.5). James will have a difficult time relating to, and effectively dealing with, the SDI Executive Leadership Team if he projects his cultural predispositions onto them instead of seeing and accepting them the way they are. On every single key element of culture, James is accustomed to working in an environment different from his team's except for the matter of internal communications. In that one category they see eye to eye. In every other instance the Executive Leadership Team holds closely aligned views of a more positive nature than James (or SDI as a whole, as per Figures 11.2 through 11.4). Consequently James will have to

FIGURE 11.5 James's Predisposition vs. Senior Management Subculture

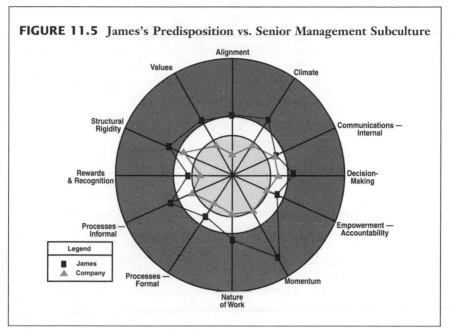

bridge a greater gap in properly "reading," understanding, and relating to the team he inherits than to the overall organization. He will also have a more difficult time being accepted as the leader of his management team than he will by the SDI organization as a whole.

James' Fit with the ELT Subculture Climate Detail (Figure 11.6). The differences between James and his future direct reports are significant in terms of the kind of climate in which he is accustomed to operating. In the area of teamwork James's background will be a disadvantage for him in dealing with the SDI Leadership Team. They will expect him to trust them to work things out among themselves as they are accustomed to doing, while he will tend to approach things with them individually and feel he must interject himself in areas to resolve differences. The bigger gap in their attitudes toward change can potentially exacerbate the tension between James and his direct reports as well. Fortunately the fact that James and the ELT share similar views toward openness may enable them to discuss their different expectations on this score and help everyone get through it. The more closely aligned elements in the "political" area will be helpful to James in this instance since he will not be naïvely expecting them to be less political than what he is accustomed to. Overall, however, he may have difficulty trusting his new team to the extent they expect to be trusted, which could become a critical problem area for James if appointed CEO.

James's Fit with the ELT Subculture Values Detail (Figure 11.7). Because the differences between the values of the culture to which James is

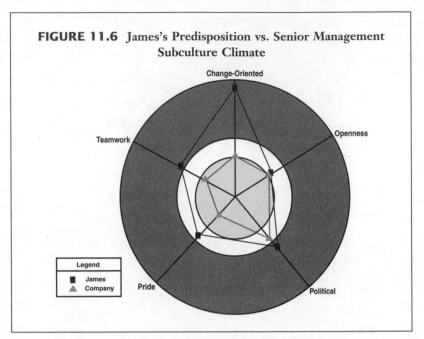

FIGURE 11.6 James's Predisposition vs. Senior Management Subculture Climate

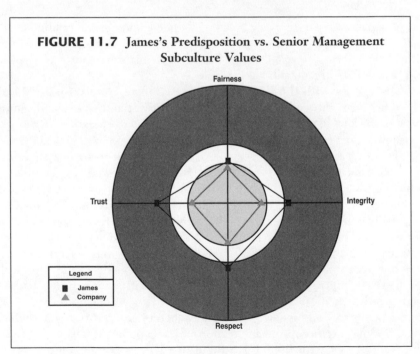

FIGURE 11.7 James's Predisposition vs. Senior Management Subculture Values

accustomed and those of the SDI leaders is large, they are potential sources of conflict and disruption. If the Character Interview determines that James's personal values are similar to those he depicts for his current organization, then his divergence from the values of the SDI culture could be a significant problem area affecting his candidacy. If they are, then his lack of trust, respect, and integrity will alienate his new management team. They, in turn, will lose trust and respect for him, eventually pushing him out of the company. Remember, though: How James depicts the values of the culture he comes from does not mean that they are necessarily the same values he personally embraces. The fact he has been there for six years and has been successful, provides good reason to delve into this area in the Character Interview and understand whether a future problem will arise if James gets the job.

What to Do About James?

So, as the lead director and head of the board's Special Selection Committee, what would you do about James? Would you make him an offer, or would you relaunch the search and look for someone else in light of this information? Would you see if the abilities, personality, energy, and character of the internal candidate align with the needs and fit better and ask Fred to stay for another year until that candidate could possibly be ready?

While there are no right or wrong answers, the recommendation of this Forward Assessment Consultant is that the head of the Special Committee do an in-depth Character Interview with James (either together with the chairman or one separate from him, depending upon the extent to which Fred B. has taken the fundamental principles of the Leader Selection Process to heart). In this case it might be worthwhile to also include the Forward Assessment Consultant's Project Leader or the Behavior Assessment Expert in this interview in order to get as many relevant points of view as possible about James's values and his willingness to mold his personality to better fit the SDI cultures. The focus of this special Character Interview should be to explore James's values and beliefs regarding trust, integrity, and respect.

If it turns out that James's personal values are closely aligned with those of the environments from which he has come, then there is probably another candidate better suited for this slot. Many individuals, however, hold values different from their organizations at large, and it may be that one of James's reasons for wanting to leave the organization is to find a place where the cultural values are more aligned with those of his true self. If that appears to be the case, the head of the Special Committee may wish to share these Culturemaps with James in order to engage him in a conversation about their potential implications and the nature of his source of concern. This conversation would represent an opportunity to begin to establish some key behavioral parameters for James's transition. It may help ensure that James is focused on building followership with his executive team in areas where he might otherwise have a difficult time—the kind of difficult time that so often leads to the turnover rates seen at the CEO level today.

If the decision is made to make James an offer and he decides to accept it, he can use the Culturemaps shown in Figures 11.2 through 11.7 while he is transitioning into SDI. The places where his predispositions and expectations differ from those of the overall culture and those of the key subcultures with which he must contend are specifically identified. Knowing where these potential traps or pitfalls exist will provide James with the greatest chance of navigating around them by initiating changes in ways the organizations expect of, and accept from, their leaders.

Regardless of the decision taken by the head of the Special Committee, the value of Mapping the Corporate Lay of the Land is undeniable. The use of the Mapping information allows hirers to make better decisions in selecting the right leader for a particular situation because it pinpoints where potential problems will arise. It puts "smoke" on the specific "targets" that would otherwise go undetected only to ultimately impede the successful transition of the new leader.

Readers interested in finding out what came out of the Character Interview go to *therightleader.com*, then cast your vote whether James should receive an offer from SDI or not. The consensus opinion of others who also voted will be shared with you there.

Takeaways

The case of SDI demonstrates several key points about the importance of Mapping the Corporate Lay of the Land in order to understand and measure corporate cultures as an essential part of the Leader Selection Process:

- By Mapping the Corporate Lay of the Land before final interviews occur, the Forward Assessment Consultant Team can determine with relative ease when a candidate whose credentials match the needs of the company very closely may still have problems due to a poor fit with one or more of the prevailing cultures with which he or she will have to contend.
- In those circumstances additional interviews that are focused on the specific concern will shed light on how to interpret the data.
- The Culturemaps developed in Mapping the Corporate Lay of the Land are only a starting point; they serve as an important addition to the Leader Selection Process. Mapping is complementary to, not a replacement for, the ultimate decision for which the Selection Team is responsible. Nevertheless, the information it provides is invaluable in shedding light on the area that causes more newly appointed leaders to fail—their lack of cultural fit.

12

Putting It All Together

A recipe for success

You don't run twenty-six miles at five minutes a mile on good looks and a secret recipe.

—Frank Shorter, 1972 U.S.
Olympic Marathon Gold Medalist

n Chapter 1, Figure 1.2 depicted a Gantt Chart of the Traditional Selection Process used by most companies today. The current chapter will show how to apply the modifications and enhancements discussed in the intervening pages to the basic framework of that chart. The resulting process is referred to as the new Leader Selection Process and is comprised of two major portions which we will discuss in this chapter:

- The Preselection Actions (Steps 1–23)
- Postselection Actions (Steps 24–26)

The new Leader Selection Process improves the chances of selecting senior executives for top leadership positions who are, indeed, the *right* leaders. By "right" we mean people who not only possess abilities that match up well against real needs, but whose characters and personalities fit the cultures of the companies they will lead. This new Leader Selection Process will help companies reduce the risks and costs of leadership failures so common today.

Creating Your Leader Selection Process

In preparing to implement the Leader Selection Process, hirers need to be mindful of the following variables.

Best Practices to Choose From

The Leader Selection Process has been used successfully in two different forms: the accelerated version and the extended version. The steps involved in each of the two are the same, but the sequence in which the steps are performed is different.

The Accelerated Leader Selection Process. Of the two choices, the Accelerated Process is used more frequently. It is the process that will probably be implemented when a leader has resigned or been terminated without the benefit of executing some of the longer lead-time elements of the Succession Plan or where no such plan exists. The beauty of the Accelerated Leader Selection Process is that the research is all conducted concurrent with other elements of the process so *no incremental time is added* to the time it would have taken to fill the vacancy without the extra research.

Because the traditional process generally produces short-list candidates who have appropriate abilities, personality, and energy there is not much risk allowing that aspect of the work to occur simultaneously with the gathering of data by the Forward Assessment Consulting Team. When undertaken in parallel like this (as in the Accelerated Leader Selection Process), it is important that the FAC deliver preliminary Business Terrain findings in time to more sharply focus the short list. The balance, however, should be completed before final interviews are conducted. Thus, without adding time to the process or compromising the integrity of the work, the Accelerated Leader Selection Process gives hirers the information they have been lacking to make good, timely decisions about the right candidate fit.

The Extended Leader Selection Process. The extended version is recommended for situations where lead times are longer, and the time from start to finish is not a critical issue. In the Extended Leader Selection Process, all of the research is completed *before* any search activities are initiated. This process will be discussed in detail in Chapter 13 in conjunction with issues dealing with Succession Planning. The current chapter will focus exclusively on the Accelerated Leader Selection Process.

The Meaning of Time

Figure 12.1 depicts the Accelerated Leader Selection Process. While lapsed time from the start of the process to the new leader's start date is the same in the Accelerated Leader Selection Process as in the Traditional Selection Process (sixteen weeks), this time frame is only a *representation* of the time required to select a new leader. There are no hard and fast rules, although the higher in the organization the position to be filled, the longer it takes to complete *any* selection process satisfactorily.

Consider the Variables. The time required to fill senior positions can actually vary greatly in the real world. You will recall the story from Chapter 1 about a "match made (quickly) in heaven" where the entire time from "first sighting" to acceptance was sixteen days as opposed to the eight to nine weeks reflected in the Accelerated Leader Selection Process. What was not mentioned before is that that selection process had already taken over six months of executive search and interview time. When the search-related activities are outside, they can move more quickly or slowly than than ten-weeks represented in Figure 12.1.

The times shown for completing the Forward Assessment Consulting research are fairly typical of what can be expected, although even here some positive variance can be achieved when everything falls into place. In one instance, Crenshaw Associates completed all the Business Terrain Research and the Team Topography in four weeks instead of the nine weeks depicted. Keep in mind also that the scale changes from *weeks* for the steps leading up to the new leader's start date to *months* for those that occur after it.

FIGURE 12.1 Accelerated Leader Selection Process

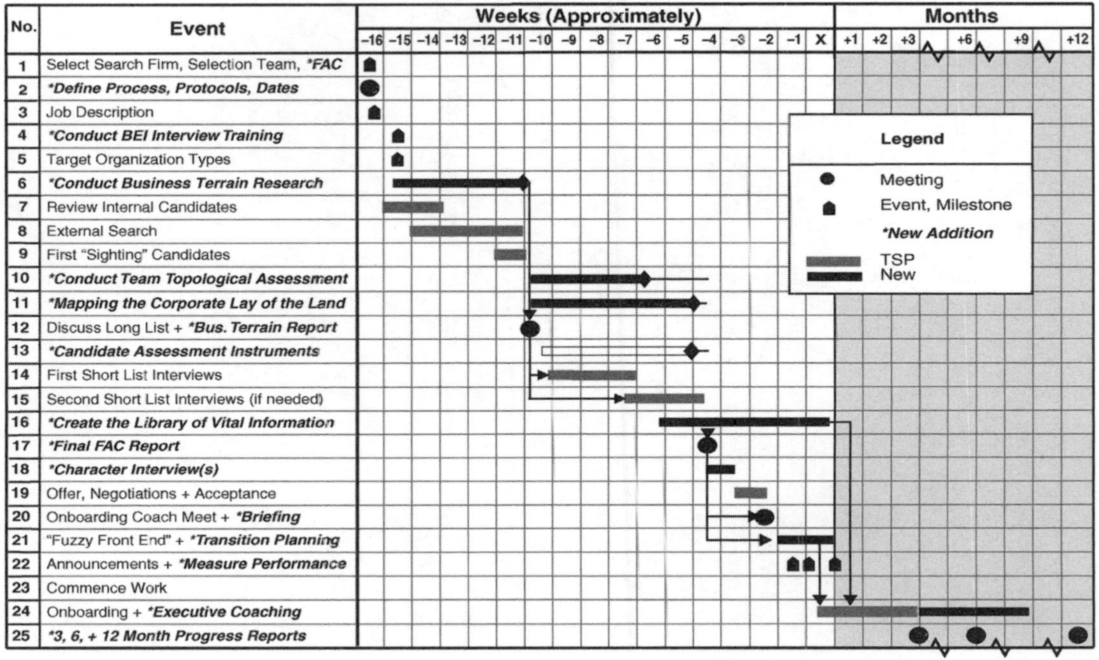
No.
Event
Weeks (Approximately)
Months
–16 –15 –14 –13 –12 –11 –10 –9 –8 –7 –6 –5 –4 –3 –2 –1 X
+1 +2 +3 +6 +9 +12
1 Select Search Firm, Selection Team, *FAC
2 *Define Process, Protocols, Dates
3 Job Description
4 *Conduct BEI Interview Training
5 Target Organization Types
6 *Conduct Business Terrain Research
7 Review Internal Candidates
8 External Search
9 First "Sighting" Candidates
10 *Conduct Team Topological Assessment
11 *Mapping the Corporate Lay of the Land
12 Discuss Long List + *Bus. Terrain Report
13 *Candidate Assessment Instruments
14 First Short List Interviews
15 Second Short List Interviews (if needed)
16 *Create the Library of Vital Information
17 *Final FAC Report
18 *Character Interview(s)
19 Offer, Negotiations + Acceptance
20 Onboarding Coach Meet + *Briefing
21 "Fuzzy Front End" + *Transition Planning
22 Announcements + *Measure Performance
23 Commence Work
24 Onboarding + *Executive Coaching
25 *3, 6, + 12 Month Progress Reports
Legend
Meeting
Event, Milestone
*New Addition
TSP
New

Consider the Costs. Rarely have we seen a job search where time was not of the essence for many good reasons. In fact the higher in the organization the position, the greater pressure to fill it rapidly because the selection receives more attention from insiders and outsiders alike. Resist the pressure. Those applying it may never have run a business. Only where a well-conceived Succession Plan exists and a fully capable candidate just happens to be ready at the right moment can the process time be optimized.

Speed for the sake of speed can be a deadly trap. While each day that passes may cost the company momentum and inertia, the costs of selecting the wrong leader as previously described are many times greater. If the situation the company is in was created by the failure of an executive to meet the expectations set for him or her, *the* most important issue facing the hirers is to make sure that does not happen again. Do not succumb to the pressure of filling the job quickly if doing so comes at the expense of doing the job right. The stakes are simply too high. Remember: no one will remember if you filled the job in twenty-two weeks or twenty-six weeks. They will remember if you fail to fill it well forever.

The Preselection Actions: Steps 1–23

The following paragraphs provide brief descriptions of the specific steps that comprise the Leader Selection Process. They are also listed in Figure 12.1, where additions to the steps are shown in bold italics to draw attention to them. (For detailed descriptions of these new elements turn to Chapters 9 and 10, or, for the exact page references, refer to the index at the back of this book.)

Step 1: Choose Search Firm, Selection Team, and FAC

Rudiments of this step have been an implicit part of virtually every senior executive selection process for decades. It is needed whether the candidate is an internal one or will come from the outside. While the selection of the search firm has always been a formal step because contracts are required, the formation of the Selection Team is not always as purposefully done. It needs to be, however. The team needs a charter and a leader who has authority along with the responsibility. Team members must be committed to live up to standards they all agree to uphold.

Adding the Forward Assessment Consultant to undertake the necessary research and analysis that has heretofore been missing in the selection process is also a formal step. Everyone who will be involved in the Selection Team (those who will do interviews, assessments, and administrative work) must make themselves available and commit to the process at the outset to ensure continuity and maximum effectiveness.

Step 2: Define Process, Protocols, Dates

This part of the process should happen at a meeting organized by the FAC and the internal head of the Selection Team. It marks the beginning of the process and sets the tone to aggressively manage it. The purpose of this meeting is to bring all those involved in the selection process together and to review and agree upon the process that will be followed, the roles and responsibilities of all participants, to block dates for interviews—short-list, final, and Character Interviews—and to book dates to discuss the long list and to review the Business Terrain Research Report. The date for the final Forward Assessment Consultant's report should also be set. In addition, protocols pertaining to the three pieces of research to be undertaken need to be discussed and reviewed for appropriate tonality and communications materials, then prepared accordingly. A script should be developed for the executive search professional to use with candidates to describe the company's process, and it should include a company (or FAC) administrative contact numbers. A roster of Selection Team members with office, home, cell phone contact numbers, faxes, and e-mail addresses, as well as the location to which packages should be sent for overnight delivery, needs to be prepared for use by the team. The commitment to follow up and measure their performance with all of the candidates should also be discussed and agreed upon at this meeting. This kickoff meeting is one of the most critical steps in the entire process since it empowers the various members (the head of HR, the executive search professional, and the Forward Assessment Consultant) while also committing the entire team to certain performance standards.

Step 3: Create a Job Description

The job description developed at this point should be labeled "preliminary" to make sure that everyone knows that it cannot be finalized until the specific actions required of the right leader have been defined by the research that will be completed over the coming weeks. At this stage only perceived issues and expectations can be identified, all of which will need to be verified or modified as the result of the Business Terrain Research undertaken with the Executive Leadership Team. When developing the preliminary job description, it is important to avoid boilerplate and meaningless, "nice to have," and politically correct imperatives. Like a good advertisement or résumé, keep the position specs pertinent and relevant.

Step 4: Conduct Behavioral Event Interview Training

An interview is *not* a conversation. It is not the place for "what if" speculations or invitations for candidates to ramble on in response to traditional "tell me about yourself" questions. The interviews conducted by all participants need to focus on behavioral events—what, specifically, has each of the candidates done and what were the results? As the old saying goes, "everyone is the parent of success," and it is important, therefore, for interviewers to ascertain exactly what role candidates played in the work for which they were responsible and how active that role was in its success.

Interviewing improves with practice, and most senior executives stand to benefit from a refresher course from time to time. Most seem to know how to avoid legal issues, but not many know how to go after the nuggets of information that will help tip the selection scales one way or the other.

Step 5: Target Organization Types

Identifying the types of organizations from which potential outside candidates might come is a good place to start. However, when Mapping the Corporate Lay of the Land is complete, this step can be revised or replaced so that the search will focus on the type of *culture* the ideal candidate will come from rather than the industry segment or the size of company they worked for. Remember: A square peg that fits well in a square hole does not mean that the same square peg will fit well into the triangular-shaped hole that you are trying to fill.

Step 6: Conduct Business Terrain Research

As described in Chapter 10, this is a key step in the Leader Selection Process. The output from the in-depth interviews with the direct reports of the new leader is used as a basis for refining the search parameters (Step 2) and for defining areas in need of deeper exploration in both the Team Topography Assessment (Step 10) and in Mapping the Corporate Lay of the Land (Step 11). Ultimately the Business Terrain Research also serves as the basis for defining what the "fit" parameters for success look like in regards to the subculture of the team the new leader will have to lead directly.

Step 7: Review Internal Candidates

In addition to being interviewed by the Selection Team members, internal candidates should take the same assessment tests required of outside candidates. To keep the playing field level, it is also important that insiders receive the same information about the process, their status, timetables, and the like, as outside candidates do. Often, internal candidates are overlooked and not given equal consideration and opportunity to understand the process and how and where they fit into it. It is important to pay particularly close attention to the communications with these key executives. If an outsider becomes distracted by the excitement that your position holds and then does not get it, you lose nothing. If, however, an internal candidate becomes distracted by the process of being considered for a big promotion, you could lose considerable momentum, inertia, or the ability to deliver results regardless of whether he or she gets the job. In the event the internal candidate does not get the job, then an entirely separate set of issues must be dealt with delicately.

Step 8: Conducting the External Search

This step is strictly the domain of the executive search professional. It is what recruiters do and, by and large, do extremely well. Regular reports and phone contact with the head of the Selection Team during this period are very helpful to both the recruiter and the company to ensure everyone stays on track and within the agreed-upon parameters. Keep the recruiter in the loop! They cannot do their job as well as they would like (and as well you need them to) if you do not keep them abreast of changes to the process timetable, internal happenings, research findings from the FAC, and all other aspects of the process.

Step 9: First "Sighting" Candidates

Initial interviews with prospective candidates are conducted by search professionals, leading to a detailed write-up of each one relative to the parameters established in Steps 2 and 3.

Step 10: Complete Team Topography

This step is initiated immediately upon completion of the Business Terrain Research and incorporates various aspects of these findings into it. Each of the Executive Leadership Team (ELT) members are spoken to and/or communicated with in advance to solicit their support and understanding of the purpose of this step. Assessment tools may be administered to them as described in Chapter 10. It is unlikely that the team members will take *all* the same tests as the internal and external candidates, but whatever ones *are* administered to them should be the same as those given to the candidates for ease in making comparisons and getting the most out of them later on.

Step 11: Mapping the Corporate Lay of the Land

This step undertakes quantifiable research of the executional and directional needs of the organization, along with all in-depth exploration of the cultures involved, including climate, values, artifacts, processes, and communications. The top 100 to 200 managers throughout the company are asked questions that provide great insight into what is really going on inside the company.

Given the scope of this work, it is advisable to use a digital tool to gather and analyze the data.[1]

Step 12: Revise Job Specs Based on Review of Long List and Business Terrain Report

This step involves the marriage of two very key documents that are prepared and reviewed with the head of the Selection Team and, at his or her discretion, with other members of the Selection Team and Board of Directors. The long list of candidates is developed by the executive recruiter based upon their first sighting. The Business Terrain Report is prepared by the Forward Assessment Consulting Team based on interviews with the Executive Leadership Team members. Generally it takes a half day to go over the two reports in sufficient detail to understand and appreciate their interconnectedness and relevance.

Based on what the Business Terrain Research has revealed about the actions that must occur to deliver the expected results in both the short-term and long-term, the job description can now be revised. This work must be done quickly so that the first round of interviews can focus on selecting final candidates who have the experience in doing the work that will be required of them. Insights into the organization's culture, as well as that of the Executive Leadership Team's subculture (and often that of the boss's team) can also be factored into the upcoming interviews.

Step 13: Complete Candidate Assessment Instruments

The FAC's Behavioral Assessment Expert, a psychologist, or a psychiatrist administers tests (if any are used) and provides feedback from them while interviewing each individual candidate. The information and insights gathered through these steps are provided, selectively, to the head of the Selection Team at the end of each round of interviews. The data will augment the decisions made about each candidate's true "fit" with the cultures of the organization, which is being identified in parallel with the testing. Candidates must complete the assessments before being interviewed by Selection Team members.

Step 14: Conduct First Short-List Interviews

Candidates are seen for the first time by the company Selection Team members using behavioral-based interviewing techniques to explore their specific background experiences as they relate to the executional and directional needs of the company. The interview should also provide greater insight into factors identified in the assessment work completed in the previous step.

Step 15: Conduct Second Short-List Interviews (If Needed)

A second round of interviews with the same or new candidates may be necessary depending on the results of the first round. As with the previous candidates who were seen, the administration of assessment materials and their feedback should be completed *before* candidates are scheduled to meet with any of the company Selection Team members.

Step 16: Create the Field Guide of Vital Information

An e-mail or memo is sent to each Executive Leadership Team member and others in possession of necessary information explaining the purpose of the Field Guide of Vital Information and soliciting material for its contents. This information is sent to the Forward Assessment Consultant's Project Leader to be reviewed, culled, and then incorporated into binders and/or electronic folders for the new leader as described in Chapter 10. Refer to Appendix C for a list of some of the specific items that have been included in the field guides prepared for various companies.

Step 17: Final FAC Report

The quantifiable data obtained from Mapping the Corporate Lay of the Land are of particular help to the Selection Team in making the ultimate determination as to who is the right leader for a particular position. The final ranking of candidates is based upon the detailed findings of the Forward Assessment Consultant's report and includes the behavioral assessments and the Culture maps comparing the final candidates' predispositions against the cultures of the organization and the subcultures of both the boss's team and the Executive Leadership Team. Some of these maps were shown in the case of SDI in Chapter 11. The final FAC report is also of great value to the new leader once the individual has been selected because, along with the Business Terrain Research, it provides the hard data on which a fact-based transition plan can be built. However, the findings regarding cultures and needs are usually incorporated into the final round of Character Interviews.

Step 18: Conduct Character Interview(s)

In this step the final candidate(s) are interviewed one final time by the person to whom they are going to report. Upon occasion the Character Interview is conducted as a final part of the first round of interviews. Behavioral-based interviewing techniques focus on the individual's values and how they align with those of the cultures in which they will be enmeshed. The Maps comparing the individual's predispositions to the culture of the overall organization and to the subcultures of the boss's team and that of the direct reports often serve as a basis for these in-depth discussions. In some instances the Forward Assessment Consultant Project Leader or the Behavior Assessment Expert may be invited to join in this final round of meetings.

Step 19: Extend Offer, Negotiate, and Receive Acceptance

The term sheet, a letter of understanding, or contract is prepared, and negotiations are concluded. Depending upon the role and the position of the individual, an immediate public announcement may be required upon acceptance in principle.

Step 20: Conduct Onboarding Coach Meeting and Briefing

Having overseen the development of the Business Terrain Research, the Team Topography, Mapping of the Corporate Lay of the Land, and the creation of the Field Guide of Vital Information, as well as having participated in the development of the process protocols and the various updates and decisions to date, the value of using the FAC Project Leader as the onboarding coach is undeniable. If someone else is used in this capacity, they must first become thoroughly familiar with the contents of these undertakings.

In some instances, the briefing of the selected leader may actually occur prior to his or her acceptance (in conjunction with the Character Interviews in Step 18). The briefing will generally take four to six hours in order to cover the information and its implications. This is a great deal of information for the new leader to absorb, and for this reason, a follow-up session and second briefing are usually scheduled as a first step in the "fuzzy front end" that ensues.

It is during this initial briefing when the new leader's plan is created using the data that came from the Mapping process. The plan provides a concise description of how to read and heed those "explicit and implicit, rational, irrational, and non-rational guides to behavior" that make navigating a new culture so difficult to the uninitiated, as well as specific behavioral guidance to the new leader about what to do, what not to do, and how/how not to do it in specific situations based upon knowledge of the organization's culture and key subcultures.

Step 21: Complete Fuzzy Front End and Transition Planning

The term "fuzzy front end" was first used in this vein by Dan Ciampa and Michael Watkins in *Right from the Start*. Originally they defined it as "the period from the initial recruiting contacts to the first day on the job."[2] Through general usage, however, it has come to refer to the period between the time that the offer is accepted and the incumbent's first day on the job.

Originally, the importance of the fuzzy front end was that, during this period, the individual has "precious, uninterrupted time to assess the organization" and "to formulate hypotheses about what needs to be done."[3]

Today, with the use of the new Mapping tools presented here, the right leader can use that same precious time to begin to build concrete action plans based on *facts* rather than on hypotheses and theoretical possibilities. Clearly this is the second great benefit that will contribute to the success of the right leader from the new Leader Selection Process—the same data that were used to help select the right leader can help him or her in making crucial decisions regarding quick wins, organization changes, people, priorities, direction, communications and more. Additionally, the *manner* in which the individual can best approach these actions to ensure that they fit the expectations of the cultures at play can be factored in with a great degree of confidence, too.

Step 22: Make Announcements and Measure Performance

In some instances the announcement of a newly selected leader must be made at the time of acceptance. Regardless of whether it is made then or in conjunction with the individual's departure from his or her previous employer or when they start the new job, a detailed communications plan covering all the appropriate internal and external bases will be necessary. At this point the Forward Assessment Consultant initiates the steps to close off the search with candidates on behalf of the company and to obtain information from all who have been involved in the process regarding opportunities for continuous improvement of the company's Leader Selection Process.

Step 23: Commence Work

As a result of the new steps that make up the Leader Selection Process, the new leader can start to implement a fact-based transition plan beginning on day one rather than have to start the planning work on their first day in the new job. Knowing what is in store for them—knowing the company lingo, how the culture works, what the priorities are, which people they can count on, which things to change and which ones to leave alone, and where the pitfalls may occur in the lay of the land—is of incredible value to the new leader. Being very clear about where the targets are (since the FAC has already highlighted them with "smoke" as a result of the research) and in what sequence they should be pursued is of particular benefit. Most importantly, knowing *how* to go about making the necessary changes to be successful in this culture is key to getting off on the right foot.

Post-Selection Actions: Steps 24–26

Having now selected the right leader, the real work can begin—getting the right leader off on the right foot in the right direction doing the right things right. It is time to put all the research and knowledge accumulated during the Preselection Phase to its second use and to help the new leader transition successfully into his or her new role.

We have pointed out previously that "leadership is a performing art."[4] All eyes are on the new leader, particularly during their first year, and they are always on stage. Unfortunately, under the Traditional Selection Process, these new star performers are usually sent out on stage with no costumes, no rehearsals, no props, and no script. They are asked to perform in a flawless manner before an audience whose attitudes may range from indifferent to highly skeptical and to perform to the satisfaction of some of the most difficult and outspoken critics.

The steps added to the Preselection Phase of the Leader Selection Process will help the new leader's performance greatly, but they need ongoing support after the house lights dim. This support comes in the form of onboarding advice, executive coaching (Step 24), and a series of periodic reviews at the end of three, six, and twelve months (Step 25). This support will help ensure that continued alignment of expectations is maintained with all key stakeholders and that progress is being made toward them.

Step 24: Provide Onboarding and Executive Coaching

Over the past several years, much has been written about the value of onboarding and the kinds of techniques and tools that onboarding advisers use to help newly appointed leaders transition into their new roles effectively. Having served as an onboarding coach in numerous situations, there is little to add to onboarding *methodologies*—they are all fairly straightforward. However, I do have three perspectives to offer about the *importance* of onboarding assistance for leaders selected under the Leader Selection Process (either the accelerated format described here or the extended version discussed in the next chapter) as opposed to those selected through the Traditional Selection Process.

The first 100 days are 100 days too late. As depicted in Step 21 of the Accelerated Leadership Selection Process, the best time for transition planning work to be completed and tested with key stakeholders is during the fuzzy front end period. Because the research has already been completed by the FAC Team at that point, leaders selected under the Leadership Selection

Process can spend their earliest days focused on execution rather than on planning. Their onboarding resources can be applied to fine-tuning plans and helping leaders do things in ways that will build trust within the specific cultures rather than in trying to figure out what needs to be done.

Avoid the "Blind Leading the Blind" syndrome. Under the old Traditional Selection Process newly appointed leaders, particularly those brought in from the outside, who work with onboarding coaches (also hired from the outside) are at a great disadvantage. Not only does the new leader lack the necessary facts, hard data, and professional insights to the critical issues, people, structures, and cultures at hand, but so do their advisers. Two outsiders trying to build plans and sort out facts from a dead start have very little to go on and few resources. Because the gathering of needed planning data and facts does not even begin until *after* the leader has been selected under the Traditional Selection Process, usually two things occur: The new leader and the onboarding adviser spend much of their initial hundred days gathering the needed data, ferreting out facts, and waiting for needed research to be conducted; or the leader hastily builds plans with the onboarding adviser that are based upon the best assumptions, collective wisdom, and their own perspectives which, as we have already seen in regards to culture, may simply not be all that accurate. As a result the effectiveness of the new leader during the critical first hundred days may be significantly less than what it needs to be, or worse, the leader's initial reactions may be well off the mark. Without hard facts and data provided in the new Leadership Selection Process, even the best onboarding adviser's contributions are far from maximized.

Use data to avoid confrontations and expedite buy-in. Problems often arise during the onboarding period when the time comes for the new leader to present to the Executive Leadership Team (and ultimately to the board and the balance of the organization) his or her case for change. Having had a Forward Assessment Consultant conduct in-depth interviews with each member of the new leader's team, as well as having access to a complete Team Assessment and detailed Maps of the Corporate Lay of the Land, the new leader is able to create a powerfully persuasive platform that factually details the need to make certain changes. Much of the input actually came from the insights, comments, and views offered by the executives themselves. When serving as an onboarding adviser, the approach that we recommend for new leaders is to share as much of the Business Terrain and Mapping reports with as many of their direct reports as possible in the following context:

> *Here is the picture of our company that the people who were hired before I was selected have painted for me based upon your comments to them. What do you think of their report? Did they get it right? What's missing? This being the case, what do you think we should now do about it?*

This approach not only demystifies the new leader's perceived agenda, but it does so in a nonconfrontational and highly consultative manner. If any direct report wants to argue with the FAC's findings, they can voice their concerns without having to challenge their new boss directly. It is the FAC's report that is in dispute, not the boss's opinion. Leaders who are appointed through the Traditional Selection Process, however, have a much different and more difficult dynamic to deal with. Because they lack few if any third-party reports, the new leader is inevitably forced to say something like: "Here's what I think needs to be changed around here—what do you think about my ideas?"

Clearly the Executive Leadership Team member faced with answering this question is in a difficult spot, particularly if they happen to disagree with the new boss's views. Rather than take issue with their new boss's assumptions or conclusions and risk a range of unknown reactions, many executives might avoid raising their concerns or simply go along with the new leader to be supportive.

Executive coaching is not an extension of onboarding. Once the onboarding period is over, we feel strongly that new leaders need the benefit of an executive coach for a period of six to nine months. As a matter of opinion, executive coaching should be a *requirement* for every new leader to help with the strategic, operational, personal, and political issues that occur on an ongoing basis, as well as to continually update information, plans, programs, and action steps needed to achieve effective results. As in the case of onboarding much has been written on the subject of coaching in general and executive coaching in particular. Again we will refrain from a lengthy discussion of the merits, styles, techniques, and benefits of executive coaches except in regard to the following points that are highly germane to the new Leader Selection Process.

There are very big differences between executive coaching and onboarding. Onboarding is highly transactional. It has a beginning and an end, and it contains certain deliverables that are expected from it. Executive coaching is transformational, and often specific outcomes cannot be established until after the coach and the client have been working together for a while.

Those who have been both an onboarding adviser and an executive coach can attest that the difference between the two is huge. Being an onboarding coach is like being Steve Williams, Tiger Woods's caddy since 1999. Williams helps Woods to improve his game on a hole-by-hole basis by reading greens, knowing distances, and understanding Tiger's capabilities with each club. Being an executive coach is more like being Butch Harmon or Hank Haney. They have worked with Tiger on the practice tee for many long hours before he ever gets on the course. Their role is to help Tiger to continually improve and refine the capabilities of admittedly, the best golfer to have ever played the game. Just as Tiger Woods benefits from having a caddy *and* a coach, a newly selected leader—no matter how good his or her game may be—will benefit greatly from having both an onboarding adviser during the initial part of the transition and an executive coach during the latter stages.

Executive coaching is very different from "coaching." In the book *Taking Advice,* Dan Ciampa identified four types of advice needed by leaders: strategic, operational, personal, and political.[5] The areas of strategic and operational advice are the domain of consultants who come in a wide variety of types and forms. Personal advice is the area where coaches do their work. Most coaches (though not all) come from a psychological orientation, and their focus is usually on helping a leader to effect a needed change in his or her behavior. The work of a coach will often touch upon political matters, but primarily from the perspective of how the individual's behaviors are experienced by others. For advice on political matters, most leaders will turn to their various networks of trusted associates and friends (such as a former boss, an old college roommate, golf buddy, or their spouse). As shown in Figure 12.2, an executive coach (sometimes also referred to as an "adviser" or "mentor") is, in my estimation, someone uniquely qualified to provide some degree of advice in all four of these key areas—an experienced sounding board whose sole purpose is to help the new leader anticipate and think through issues, opportunities, and unseen problems regardless of whether they are of a strategic, operational, personal, or political nature.

A Forward Assessment Consultant's Project Team Leader who has been a CEO, a senior executive, or a professional consultant is often uniquely qualified to serve the newly selected leader in this capacity during the six to nine months after the onboarding period and sometimes beyond. In this

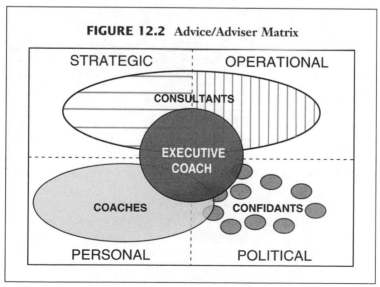

FIGURE 12.2 Advice/Adviser Matrix

STRATEGIC   OPERATIONAL

CONSULTANTS

EXECUTIVE COACH

COACHES   CONFIDANTS

PERSONAL   POLITICAL

instance the combination of having been in, or closely associated with, a similar role previously (experience) combined with the in-depth understanding of this particular situation (knowledge) makes this person a powerful resource for the new leader if the rapport and respect between the two (chemistry) is right. Chemistry is not as important when assigning or selecting an onboarding adviser due to the work's transactional nature, but it is *extremely* important in selecting the right executive coach for the leader due to the close nature of the relationship.

Executive coaching is necessary, not just "nice." When I started my career, the standard practice for hiring rookie salespeople was allegedly to "give 'em a catalog, a set of car keys, a few old leads, and turn 'em loose to see what they can do." While this is a bit far-fetched, the description was not all *that* far from reality for many companies back in those days.

Contrast that old approach to the elaborate and extensive training programs run by companies around the world today to ensure that their rookie salespeople understand the policies, programs, pricing, products, and the key selling features and benefits of every product before they are turned loose to "see what they can do."

But what about the "rookie" leader who is in a new role in a new situation, often with only limited direct experience with many of the issues they will have to face? For an individual cast into one of the most important jobs in the company where they can have a major effect on the strategic direction, operational effectiveness, and financial results of the firm, there is still little more training and support given to them to help them get up to speed in the most complex of situations than that given to the rookie salesperson of old. The value of having someone who has faced similar challenges and experienced the realities of making senior-level transitions in the course of their own life—someone who knows the ropes—is the least expensive senior level on-the-job training that can be found. Often, having someone to talk to who actually understands what you are talking about and who has felt the "loneliness at the top" that the rookie leader may first be experiencing can be invaluable.

Catch-22.1 of Executive Coaching. Although the composition of boards is changing, and there are fewer sitting or former CEOs and more directors selected for the particular abilities, experiences, and insights that they bring to the position, many CEOs still serve on boards. When the current generation of CEO-Directors was coming up through the ranks, "coaches" were not seen in the same light as they are today. Historically, having a coach meant something was wrong that needed fixing or else the individual was not going to be around for long. Consequently, few of today's directors ever had a coach, and many still hold a jaundiced view of the role that an executive coach can play in helping an executive's development. Consequently the head of the Selection Team may encounter resistance to offering a new leader the use of an executive coach. Continuing the analogy of a business leader to a fighter pilot, it is important for hirers to appreciate that there is a lot more going on in the cockpit of a high-speed business today than at any time in business history. New pilots (leaders) have their hands full and can benefit greatly from having an experienced senior pilot in the backseat giving them help with priorities, pointers, timely reminders, and calling out things for them to keep their eye on.

Catch-22.2 of Executive Coaching. There is a second Catch 22 to look out for when engaging an executive coach for a newly appointed senior leader, especially when that leader is the CEO. If choosing whether to have an executive coach is left up to the individual, there is a good chance that the offer will be declined, even if the leader might see the benefit of having one on an intellectual level. The reason, pure and simple, is a matter of pride. Having just been selected to lead a very complex organization to new heights, some find the notion of now asking for help as a signal of weakness or a lack of confidence that might cast them into a bad light. When I became the CEO of World Kitchen, I had a well-known executive coaching firm available to me to use if I felt they would be helpful. I decided to decline their assistance for the exact reason just stated—I thought that the Board had hired me to do the things that needed to be done and might think they had been shortchanged if it looked like I needed help. As things turned out, I *did* end up hiring an executive coach who helped me in a variety of ways with aspects of the job (most of which were political) that I had never encountered before. The point is this: Accepting the help of an experienced executive coach may be a difficult decision for some new leaders to make, even though it makes good intellectual sense to them. My recommendation is that hirers make it an expected part of the transition plan included in the terms of the new leader's package. The use of an executive coach is an important part of ensuring the right leader's full success and should not be an elective left up to the leader alone.

Step 25: Provide Three-, Six-, and Twelve-Month Progress Reports

Implicit in every change of leadership are the promises of better things to come: more growth, faster progress, greater stability, improved returns, and the like. Whether they are explicitly articulated in the internal announcements and outside press releases made at the time of the new leader's appointment or not, *all* stakeholders hold expectations and hopes for things to come. The hopes of some stakeholders are inevitably at odds with those of others, so not all stakeholders are going to be pleased with the new leader's performance as it unfolds. The communication gap is widened because few stakeholders are privy to the new leader's plans and timetables for execution.

This causes some to feel that not enough is being accomplished as quickly as it should be and certainly not as quickly as they would like.

Keeping key stakeholders—especially the new leader's boss and the board of directors—aware of the inevitable changes to plans, objectives, priorities, and timetables is especially critical during the leader's first year in the job. During the first year, three formal reviews are recommended that will contribute greatly to the ultimate success of the new leader: one at the end of the onboarding period (ninety to one hundred days), one after the first six months (which is of a slightly different nature from the others), and one at the end of the first year in anticipation of the questions that will, at that point in time, be on many stakeholders' minds.

Three specific progress reviews held with the new leader, the onboarding adviser or executive coach, and the leader's boss to go over accomplishments, new or revised priorities, surprises, problems encountered, changes to upcoming plans, and action steps, are highly recommended. Their purpose is to ensure that alignment of expectations is maintained for all key stakeholders.

Three-Month Update. By the end of the first ninety to one hundred days of transition, the new leader is almost fully enmeshed in the new work situation. Hopefully, as a result of the Forward Assessment work and the ensuing onboarding support, the new leader has also become enmeshed in the new cultures at this point. It is at this juncture that I usually inform transition clients, "Congratulations, you are now officially a part of the problem—so watch out." During this time frame, the new leader has been on a growth curve with a near-vertical trajectory. Before more time passes, it is a good idea for the leader to sit down with his or her boss and the onboarding adviser to recap the journey-to-date and to identify accomplishments, adjustments that have occurred to the original transition plan, timetable changes, and differences in expectations (both positive and negative). The goal of this review is to confirm for the hirers that the new leader is still on track and to make adjustments where necessary. Sometimes changes in the environment will require unforeseen changes to the plans or priorities under which the new leader is operating. Sometimes the expectations of the boss must be adjusted to a more realistic level. Regardless of where the "give and take" must occur, it is essential that alignment between the leader and the boss be reaffirmed before any more time passes. The onboarding adviser can play a very important role facilitating this process.

Six-Month Progress Report. Using very basic 360-degree interviewing questions, it is highly recommended that either the Research Specialist who originally conducted the in-depth Business Terrain interviews with the new leader's Executive Leadership Team or the Behavioral Assessment expert who did the Team Topography be called back in to do a follow-up survey to see how the new leader is perceived as progressing. The leader's executive coach or the Forward Assessment Consultant's Project Head can conduct these interviews as well. The basic questions to be asked are,

- What is the new leader doing that he or she should keep doing?
- What is the new leader doing that he or she should stop doing?
- What is the new leader not doing that he or she should be doing?
- Are the right issues being addressed?
- Are they being addressed in the right ways?
- What would you do differently if you were in the new leader's shoes? Why?

It is recommended that this information first be shared with the new leader and the executive coach if conducted by someone other than the executive coach. The new leader's boss should be presented with the findings as well. The purpose is to identify places for ongoing improvement in the culturalization of the new leader (fit), as well as to affirm that the proper organization needs (match) are being addressed. This is particularly important at this juncture because most of the changes to the new leader's team will usually have been made, and it is valuable to solicit the views and input of the new members, as well as those who have been there throughout the transition.

Twelve-Month Progress Report. In preparing for the first annual review, it is essential to measure performance against the agreed-upon objectives that were set down at the time of selection as modified (if modified) at the three- and six-month points. However, it is also important to go back to the start and review *all* of the internal announcements and external press releases, newspaper articles, and even board minutes to ensure that the company and/or the new leader is prepared to address the expectations of *all* parties at the one-year point. Analysts, shareholders, and the media will not have forgotten the glowing statements of optimism that were made at the time the new senior leader was appointed. Neither will employees or directors. One year later they and other stakeholders will want to know where things stand. Consider the announcement of Donna that read in part as follows:

> *Donna is a great addition to our team. She joins us from XYZ Corporation where she developed a well-deserved reputation for championing new products that led to above-industry growth rates on a global basis. She will take over the helm of our Core ABC Division . . . she will provide new energy to the organization and closer ties with our traditional dealer base.*

Based upon the Forward Assessment Consulting work that led to Donna's hiring, her first targets were to revamp and streamline the internal product development process at ABC, which had become slow and highly bureaucratic as a result of its success for many years. Donna's approach required her to terminate several pet programs and initiatives, to reallocate new product investment priorities, and to undertake a fairly broad-based housecleaning of both the marketing and engineering departments. With all the restructuring behind her, the new product pipeline was in the process of being refilled, although fewer actual new products were launched for market at the end of her first year than in any of the previous five. Even though the corporate CEO and Board of Directors supported Donna's strategy and timetable thoroughly at her twelve-month review, the company, and Donna in particular, came under considerable fire at the company's annual general meeting that occurred at about the same time as her first year anniversary in the job. Some of the questions and challenges that she faced were as follows:

> **Analysts and shareholders.** These concerned parties wanted to know where the new products were that had been foretold in the announcements. Why did new product launches for ABC Division drop off from their historical rate rather than increase? Where was the more aggressive organic growth they were expecting?
>
> **Dealers.** This group wanted to know how global product requirements were going to be integrated into new products for the domestic market. Would all dimensions and hardware now be in metric terms instead of U.S. standards? How was this going to affect the company's policy for replacement parts and service items?
>
> **Retirees.** These individuals wanted to know what kind of special incentives had been given to the marketing and engineering people who were offered "early retirement" that maybe had not been offered to them during an earlier reduction in force.
>
> **Local newspapers.** These media outlets wanted to know if more layoffs were coming and if the "gutting of long-term employees" at ABC's main headquarters was really a harbinger of things to come and possibly even foretold of a move to China, as Donna's former employer, XYZ, had done soon after she left.
>
> **A national business magazine.** This publication wanted to know if Donna's failure to deliver the kind of growth she had consistently produced at XYZ was because of provincial attitudes at ABC toward women or outsiders or both.

The point is that, before the end of the new leader's first year, not only must actual performance be reconciled with the agreed-upon expectations of those who selected the leader, but questions, concerns, and the self-serving interests of every other constituency should be anticipated and appropriate responses prepared. A proactive approach instead of a reactive one will usually produce more positive results. Full disclosure and transparency is, whenever possible, the best policy. Hoping to avoid a ticklish situation by "letting a sleeping dog lie" usually means the leader ends up being chased by a more rested dog and is eventually "chased up a tree" on a point of interest to one stakeholder faction or another. Understanding and anticipating the perceived promises and hopes generated at the time of the leader's appointment is an important element of the new leader's twelve-month review.

Takeaways

This chapter pulled together the various modifications and enhancements discussed in the preceding chapters and applied them to the basic framework of the Traditional Selection Process to create a new selection process for senior leaders, described here as the Accelerated Leader Selection Process:

- The Leader Selection Process is designed to help companies reduce the risks and costs of leadership failures plaguing companies today by ensuring that the leader who is selected for a top position has the abilities, personality, and energy to match up well with the real executional and directional needs of the organization, *and* whose character and style fit well with the cultures of the company.
- The Accelerated Leader Selection Process discussed in this chapter (Figure 12.1) is a real world, pragmatic approach that does not add any incremental time to the selection of a new leader than would be required under the old Traditional Selection Process.
- A second selection process called the Extended Leader Selection Process will be presented in the next chapter. It is particularly applicable to Succession Planning, where longer lead times are generally available for Forward Assessment Consulting work to be initiated sufficiently in advance so that it can be completed in full before the earliest steps in screening candidates are begun.
- The actual time required to complete an Accelerated Leader Selection Process will vary as the result of many factors just as in today's Traditional Selection Process. In the accelerated format, all of the Forward Assessment Consulting work is accomplished in parallel with other elements of the process to deliver their benefits on a timely basis to greatly enhance the final decision.
- The Accelerated Leader Selection Process contains twenty-five steps, of which thirteen are from the original Traditional Selection Process

currently in use. Six of these original steps have been modified or enhanced in some fashion to bring them up to a new level of effectiveness.

- Just as important as the steps leading up to the selection of the right leader are the steps that occur in the post-selection period. These steps include: onboarding; executive coaching; and periodic progress reports at the three-month, six-month, and twelve-month anniversary dates. Without support during the entire transition process, even the right leader can stumble and fall.

Part Three

Conclusion

13

Why Boards Should Care

Process to Give Prince Top Citi Job Was Flawed, Says Predecessor

"Weil Unhappy Over Plan of Succession"

Financial Times, p. 1, May 24, 2008

The purpose of this book is to fix the flaws in the process for selecting top executives, thereby reducing expensive mistakes and excessive turnover. In earlier chapters the steps in a new Leader Selection Process were detailed. Here we will focus on how they can be used for CEO Succession Planning.

The costs of leadership failures are huge. In aggregate, today's levels of turnover rob the U.S. economy of approximately $14 billion in unnecessary expense, inefficiency, and opportunities foregone. As described in Chapter 1, the impacts of a failed CEO transition are felt in the value and stability of the company stock as well as in its P&L. The greatest toll, however, is felt within by the organization where uncertainties, doubts, and fears bring out the worst of times throughout the company.

Probably every director has seen, if not experienced firsthand, the pain caused by a leadership failure at one time or another during his or her career. So this is not news. What *is* news is that the chances of its occurring can be reduced through better Succession Planning and better implementation of that plan.

An outspoken advocate for improved Succession Planning, Dr. Ram Charan has ranked Succession Planning as the number one area where boards should place their emphasis ahead of (in his order) strategy, compensation, monitoring risk, and board composition.[1] In order to better understand its importance and the solutions we propose, this chapter will look at:

- Some of the changes that have occurred in the nature and scope of the CEO's job during the past ten years
- The state of CEO Succession Planning today
- Reasons that many boards have not yet initiated CEO Succession Planning
- Why the new Leader Selection Process can make the difference
- A number of new best practices for directors to incorporate into their CEO Succession Planning process

Putting the Problem in Perspective

Ten years ago, the average tenure for a CEO was nearly ten years; many remained in office much longer. Today, according to James Melican, chairman of the shareholder advisory firm Proxy Governance, Inc., the average time for a CEO to hold that job is less than five years.[2] Sixty-four percent of CEOs

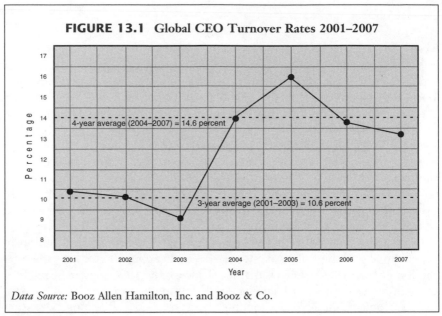

FIGURE 13.1 Global CEO Turnover Rates 2001–2007

Data Source: Booz Allen Hamilton, Inc. and Booz & Co.

appointed four years ago will be gone by the end of this year, and 40 percent of them were out the door just eighteen months after their name went on it.[3]

The global turnover rate of CEOs is very reflective of the U.S. experience. As shown in Figure 13.1, the global CEO turnover rate averaged 10.6 percent during the early part of this decade (2001 to 2003).[4] The rate during the next four years (2004 to 2007) was roughly 40 percent higher at 14.6 percent. As more and more CEOs have been replaced on a quicker basis, the pressure has increased for all CEOs to deliver results *or else*. Yet while the time frames in which CEOs are expected to produce tangible results have shrunk, the time frames required to execute the changes that will produce those results have not. If anything, it can be argued that in our increasingly complex world they very well may have increased.

Ten years ago, it was much less frequent for the CEO of a Fortune 500 corporation to be forced from office for *any* reason, let alone for failing to achieve expected performance standards. The three most notable exceptions that occurred during the entire final decade of the twentieth century were GM, IBM, and American Express.[5] Today the forced turnover of corporate CEOs is much more prevalent. Between 1995 and 2006, the performance-related turnover of CEOs increased 318 percent.[1] In 2006 more than one in three left office involuntarily, and, interestingly, another one in ten left due to power struggles on the board (11 percent in 2006 versus only 2 percent in 1995).[6] Through the first seven-and-a-half years of the twenty-first century, Disney, Merck, Pfizer,

Bristol-Meyers Squibb, Boeing, Hewlett-Packard, Fannie Mae, Citigroup, Merrill Lynch, UBS, Motorola, HBO, Ford, Sara Lee, 3M, Chrysler, Alcoa, Home Depot, Toys R Us, Starbucks, Bear Stearns, and Sallie Mae (SLM Corp)[7] led the list of major corporations where CEOs have been ushered out under pressure from the board.[8] And they are only a few among many.

Ten years ago, being a CEO meant holding a very prominent, powerful, and prestigious position with a degree of stability that offered a chance to develop and refine strategies, shape corporate culture, and execute plans in response to changing market conditions. It was a job to be cherished. Today, "the CEO position is a temporary job (with) less job security than most (employees) have," at least according to Leslie Gaines-Ross, Chief Reputation Strategist at Weber Shandwick.[9] Not only has the time frame in which CEOs are expected to deliver results shrunk significantly, but so has much of the positive aura that used to come from simply being the "top dog."

Ten years ago, there were no long shadows across American boardrooms caused by the scandalous and illegal behavior of a handful of executives—the most frequently cited being those at Enron, Global Crossing, Tyco, AOL, Time-Warner, Adelphi Communications, and WorldCom.[10] The wrongdoing of a handful of executives who represented less than one-tenth of 1 percent of the market capitalization of all public companies has had an astonishing effect on the image of the other 99.9 percent of corporations, resulting in a new level of vigilance expected of boards today.

Ten years ago, there was not the same degree of aggressive state attorneys general looking to gain political mileage for themselves by pursuing corporations, executives, and directors for actual or alleged wrongdoings that were costly to defend. And there were nowhere near as many SEC, NYSE, or Financial Industry Regulatory Authority (FINRA) regulations and regulators with broad, sweeping powers to charge, adjudicate, and punish corporations. As a result, being the CEO of a public corporation today comes with a higher degree of risk of being investigated for possible violations of a host of regulations, both civil and criminal. Moreover a sea-change in public opinion toward business and business leaders has further affected the nature of being a CEO in U.S. society today.

Ten years ago, when most of today's directors first became board members, the allocation of power in the governance triangle resided primarily with the CEO, most of whom wielded it wisely. With Sarbanes-Oxley and other governance reforms, some of the power shifted away from the CEO and was divided between the board and shareholders. Today only independent directors can sit on the audit, nominating, and compensation committees, and directors must attest to the financial statements reported by the company. These moves have been purposely designed to distance the board from management and thereby prevent conflicts of interest.[11] The CEOs have lost some of their ability to personally appoint a board comprised of friendly cohorts, and they are losing the power to select their own successors.[12]

State of the Planning Art

While all these factors—trends, pressures, and shifts in power—have come onto the scene, one thing that has *not* changed over the course of the past ten years is the fundamental responsibility of boards of directors—to monitor performance, counsel management, and most importantly, select, compensate, and, if need be, replace the CEO.[13] Looking at their two most important functions—the hiring and firing of the CEO—it appears that boards are doing a much better job dealing with the second half of the equation. The statistics we have cited previously are evidence that boards have become much more aggressive about firing CEOs whose performance does not measure up. In fact they are grappling with underperformance of CEOs by terminating them more quickly than at any time in the history of the free enterprise system!

Although such action generally wins kudos for the board in the business press and with certain groups of shareholders, their seemingly courageous action warrants applause only if we overlook the fact that *they*—the board members— are the ones who put the CEOs in the jobs in the first place. In this light, firing the CEO may be as much an indictment of how *poor* a job the board did in performing its hiring duties as it is worthy of praise for taking action to rectify it. Would you cheer a fireman who rushed into a burning building to save the lives of its inhabitants if you knew that the fireman had set the fire originally?

Dr. Charan puts it this way: "The problem isn't that more CEOs are being replaced. The problem is that, in many cases, CEOs are being replaced *badly*."[14] When a CEO fails, the board owns a piece of the failure, and by no means is this some sort of passive "failure by association." Since the board and the CEO share responsibility for corporate performance, then the boards, too, have failed if the CEO they selected fails.[15] In short a CEO's failure is also the board's failure to properly fulfill their most important responsibility—selecting the right CEO to begin with.

Unfortunately another element that has remained relatively unchanged in ten years is the status of Succession Planning. In 2004 research sponsored by the National Association of Corporate Directors (NACD) found that only half of the 579 companies surveyed had current Succession Plans in place for the CEO. More significantly the research also showed an apparently low level of confidence in those plans, since 68 percent of the respondents indicated that they did not have a successor identified by name.[16] Additional research conducted at about the same time by ARA International on behalf of the Directorship Search Group (now RHR Partners), revealed that among companies that had CEO Succession Plans in place, over one-third of them (39 percent) still expected the transition to be difficult.[17] Boring down deeper, the Corporate Leadership Counsel (CLC), a human resource research organization, found in the same year that only 20 percent of responding HR executives were satisfied with their top management

Succession Plans.[18] So not only was the percentage of companies with CEO Succession Plans surprisingly low, but the confidence placed in those plans to work when needed was also quite low. Data indicates that the picture has not improved significantly over the past few years.

In the 2004 NACD research cited previously, two-thirds of the companies who did *not* have formal Succession Plans stated that they anticipated having one soon, as they were either "working on one" (29 percent) or "would have one in the very near future" (39 percent). If completed, these planned additions would have raised the overall percentage of corporations with CEO Succession Plans to 83 percent.[19] In November 2007, however, Joseph Bower reported in the *Harvard Business Review* that he was "appalled to learn recently that 60 percent of the respondents to a poll of HR directors of large U.S. companies said their firms have no CEO Succession Plan in place."[20] If Bower's data is comparable to the earlier NACD sample, that would represent *a decline* of ten percentage points for companies with active CEO Succession Planning processes versus 2004 and less than half of the number that were anticipated to be in place by that point in time. Even more recently, research conducted by Epsen Fuller/IMD in March 2008 revealed that, on a global basis, only 27 percent of companies surveyed had identified a successor for their CEO.[21] Describing their conclusions from their tenth annual survey of CEO turnover, researchers at Booz Allen Hamilton put it this way in a 2008 report:

> *Moreover, we have found many North American companies continue to pursue CEO succession practices that seem questionable. In short, our research suggests that there is substantial scope for improvement in the way companies oversee chief executives, plan for successions and develop pools of top leadership talent.*[22]

Clearly, large strides must be made to get effective Succession Planning up to where it needs to be.

Why It Is Taking So Long

Why is it that only 40 to 50 percent of public companies have Succession Plans—and of those, only a small number are seen as being of a satisfactory nature? The lack of meaningful succession plans is particularly difficult to understand when you consider the amount of pressure being placed on boards from a variety of regulatory agencies and investor groups to develop those plans as a best practice in fulfillment of the board's most important fiduciary responsibility—selecting the CEO.

The reasons for the current situation are many and varied. What's more, none of the research done to date explains exactly which of these reasons contribute most to the lack of progress.

The following are some of the reasons that more boards have failed to put adequate Succession Plans in place:

No Regulations. It is not a statutory or regulatory requirement for boards to develop CEO Succession Plans. The NYSE rules do state that "Succession Planning should include policies and principles for CEO selection and performance review as well as policies regarding succession in the event of an emergency or the retirement of the CEO," but they do not specifically require a company to adopt a Succession Plan.[23] Moreover, companies are not required to state whether or not they have developed a Succession Plan in any of their corporate filings, which have tended to keep this particular governance practice beneath the radar of investors, shareholders, and regulators much of the time.

Insufficient Time. There is no question that being a board member today takes more time in preparing for, and attending, board and committee meetings than just a few years ago. Board and committee meetings are often so crammed full of topics that it is difficult to get through everything on the agenda let alone to add something new—even something as important as Succession Planning. Since the passage of the Sarbanes-Oxley Act, the additional time required to address required items for compliance purposes has further reduced available meeting time for things like Succession Planning.

A Potential Source of Unpleasant Confrontation. If the sitting CEO happens to be an individual who holds strong opinions and feels uniquely qualified to have the final say in who his or her successor should be, there is a good chance the topic of a board-driven succession process is *not* going to be warmly received. In an NACD study released in 2006, 26 percent of the companies surveyed reported that the responsibility for leading Succession Planning rested with their CEOs, even though 94 percent of the same respondents indicated that they do not endorse such an active role for the CEO in Succession Planning.[24] Clearly a struggle over control of the process exists in many boardrooms. Rather than create an immediate confrontation over responsibility for Succession Planning, many directors simply choose to go along with the CEOs course and avoid the issue for as long as possible. I know of some instances where the futility of trying to put a meaningful Succession Plan in place as long as the current CEO was still in control was so great that the board, in executive session, simply agreed they would rely on doing an outside search at the time that events triggered the need to make a change. Sometimes it is not worth the disruption and distraction it can create, especially in the highly charged political atmosphere of some boardrooms.

Sending Smoke Signals. If a CEO is performing well, raising the topic of Succession Planning may generate unnecessary concerns on his or her part that the board may harbor hidden concerns—that his or her time is possibly running out. Such questions can cause a schism between management and directors at a time when it is completely unnecessary. Raising the topic of

Succession Planning can be even more difficult when the CEO is struggling, because then it inevitably sends a signal (whether intended or not) that the board may be preparing to replace him or her.

Rather than risk unintended signals, many boards take the course of least resistance and avoid introducing Succession Planning today in favor of dealing with it under better circumstances tomorrow. This problem can be avoided by making Succession Planning a routine part of the ongoing board work. Doing so will separate its strategic intent from short-term circumstances and keep principles ahead of short-term issues.

No Individual Accountability. Some critics argue that more boards would have Succession Plans in place if directors had more individual accountability. Since Succession Planning is not a required element of board behavior, no single committee or chairperson has specific accountability for it. Succession Planning can fall within the purviews of the compensation committee or the nominating committee, or a special committee made up of independent directors. Without specific ownership stipulated in the by-laws or by board resolution, there is no one specific committee to be looked to for accountability.

Little Perceived "Real" Value. Many directors are, or have been, CEOs at other companies. Like anyone, their thinking is largely a product of their experience, and most of them have experienced making it to the top-floor, corner office by having been "plucked" from a previous position somewhere along the line by an executive recruiter who offered them a career opportunity "too good to refuse." According to recent research, 37 percent of the CEOs of Fortune 1000 companies were hired from the outside.[26] On a global basis, 30 percent of CEOs were brought in from the outside.[27] If a director has not been "plucked" specifically for the top job, the chances are he or she has been actively recruited for one, or has made an earlier career change as the result of the executive search process. Consequently it is quite understandable for many to feel that since that approach has worked for them in the past, as it obviously has for many other CEOs, it can certainly work again if and when something comes up. In some instances, this line of thinking *may* actually be exactly correct—an outside candidate who fits the company culture may be just what is needed to address the directional or executional needs at hand. While the strategy works in some instances, data indicates however, that the strategy of "plucking" someone from somewhere else just *does not* work very well at the CEO level. Research shows that there is no correlation between having been a success previously as a CEO and doing so again in a new company:[28]

- CEOs who had successfully served as the CEO of a publicly traded company previously and were subsequently recruited to a new public company actually "delivered slightly worse returns to investors in eight of the nine years studied" (1997 to 2006) than those who came from within their company, according to recent research.[29]

- The extent to which an outside CEO can be viewed as being successful is often a function of time. The same study also showed that, although outside CEOs do excel in the short term, insiders perform better over the long term.[30]

- Finally, earlier research conducted in 2003 (the last year for which these data are currently available), showed that, of the CEOs who had been brought in from the outside who lost their jobs that year, 55 percent of them were forced out of office; whereas only 34 percent of CEOs who came from within their own company were dismissed.[31] This suggests that insiders either did a better job of delivering expected results or possibly built stronger relations with their boards than those from the outside.

Lack of Experience. As Charan points out, "Another problem is that the vast majority of search committee members have had no experience working together on a CEO succession. As a result they seldom coalesce into deep-delving bodies that can get to the pith of their company's fundamental needs."[32] Some boards may therefore avoid engaging in Succession Planning because it is uncharted territory and so more than a bit daunting.

The Pressure Is On

Invariably, the best that can ever be said about almost every change in leadership once it is over is that "its impact wasn't as bad as it could have been." There simply is not an easy way to mitigate the difficulties, financial implications, and organizational disruption that accompany the replacement of a CEO. It is no wonder that so many advocates for improved corporate governance view the development of meaningful Succession Plans as being so important. Moreover, as the significance of other governance issues ebb as changes already initiated in these areas begin to produce their intended improvements (such as better controls, fewer restatements of earnings, executive compensation), the focus on CEO succession will naturally increase.

Besides the fact that Succession Planning is an idea whose time has come, additional factors are encouraging its adoption. Pressure from shareholder interests and activists will continue to mount as new fulcrums for the shifting balance of power in the governance arena continue. Changing business conditions (economic, market, and/or political) may trigger more CEO fallout as will the natural demographic impact caused by the trend toward earlier retirements and the glut of baby boomers who are approaching the end of their careers.

Under these circumstances, perhaps the greatest source of pressure to be exerted on boards to create meaningful Succession Plans will come from the directors themselves: Succession Planning makes sense and is the right thing to do.

How the New Leader Selection Process Can Help

Even though Succession Planning is already, or soon will be, a top priority for many boards, there is still a lot of work to be done. In our experience, adapting the new Leader Selection Process to CEO Succession Planning can significantly improve results. Here's why:

Good Planning Equals Good Results. Research indicates that among HR leaders whose companies have already developed a Succession Plan, 80 percent report that they are not satisfied with it. Clearly this is a danger signal for directors to examine. Something must be greatly wrong with the current planning process if so few HR professionals are satisfied with the end result.[33]

The World Has Changed But the Selection Process Has Not. What is missing from the Traditional Selection Process used by most companies for decades as the mainstay of their approach to Succession Planning are steps to gather and analyze substantive, empirical data about the true needs of the company and about the various cultures in which the future CEO will be enmeshed. It is the lack of relevant data to drive the individual development plans of internal candidates and to establish the selection criteria of outside ones that, in our estimation, leads to such a level of dissatisfaction with their company Succession Plans and with the increase in CEO failures.

As in any other planning processes—be it strategic planning, operational planning, or acquisition planning—Succession Planning can only be as good as the accuracy of the facts and assumptions upon which it is built. Max Landsburg, leadership consultant for global search firm Heidrick and Struggles, describes the lack of hard data in Succession Planning this way:

> Yet this "bet the company" decision (to change its CEO), is still often tackled too late, with no recourse to a contingency plan, and without the benefit of enough data—as a recent client commented, "There was less data in the process than in a footnote of a monthly board pack."[34]

Addressing the chronic lack of hard data in selecting senior executives is one of the central themes of this book. It is what the Leader Selection Process is all about. The keys to selecting the right CEO are no different from those used to select any other senior executive, although the stakes are higher and risks are greater. The first requirement for success is in factually knowing what the individual must be required to do, expressed not in terms of results, which is so often the case, but in terms of future actions.

Secondly, success lies in factually describing the specific nature of the cultures into which the newly selected CEO must fit. Like brands and personal character, cultures change slowly, so knowing definitively what the culture is today will go a long way in understanding that of the future. Regardless of the

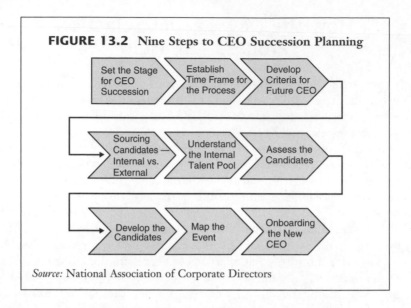

FIGURE 13.2 Nine Steps to CEO Succession Planning

Set the Stage for CEO Succession → Establish Time Frame for the Process → Develop Criteria for Future CEO

Sourcing Candidates — Internal vs. External → Understand the Internal Talent Pool → Assess the Candidates

Develop the Candidates → Map the Event → Onboarding the New CEO

Source: National Association of Corporate Directors

reasons driving the implementation of a CEO Succession Plan, it is time for all boards to address this matter rigorously and with updated tools and techniques to get the job done properly and fully.

In 2006 the National Association of Corporate Directors (NACD), in collaboration with Mercer Delta Consulting, published a Best Practices Study detailing the role of the board in Succession Planning.[28] In that report they identified nine broad steps to CEO Succession Planning that are shown in Figure 13.2.

While the NACD's nine steps provide a general sense of direction, they are hardly specific enough to be of much help in implementing a rigorous Succession Planning process. For that reason we have developed an extended version of the Leader Selection Process. This version incorporates the same critical, up-front, fact-finding steps (see Chapter 12) that have been missing in the flawed Traditional Selection Process on which so many Succession Plans have been built. However, the sequencing of these steps is changed to take advantage of the longer lead times afforded by the proactive nature of the work.

All the principles and practices advocated as a part of the Accelerated Leader Selection Process introduced in the previous chapter are completely applicable to the CEO Succession Planning Process. Only the timing of when various elements are conducted may vary depending upon whether the CEO is being replaced on a planned or reactive basis.

The Extended Leader Selection Process appears as Figure 13.3. Please note that the scale in Figure 13.3 is in *weeks* leading up to the CEO's start date and in *months* for the important post-selection dates. All the times are

FIGURE 13.3 Extended Leader Selection Process

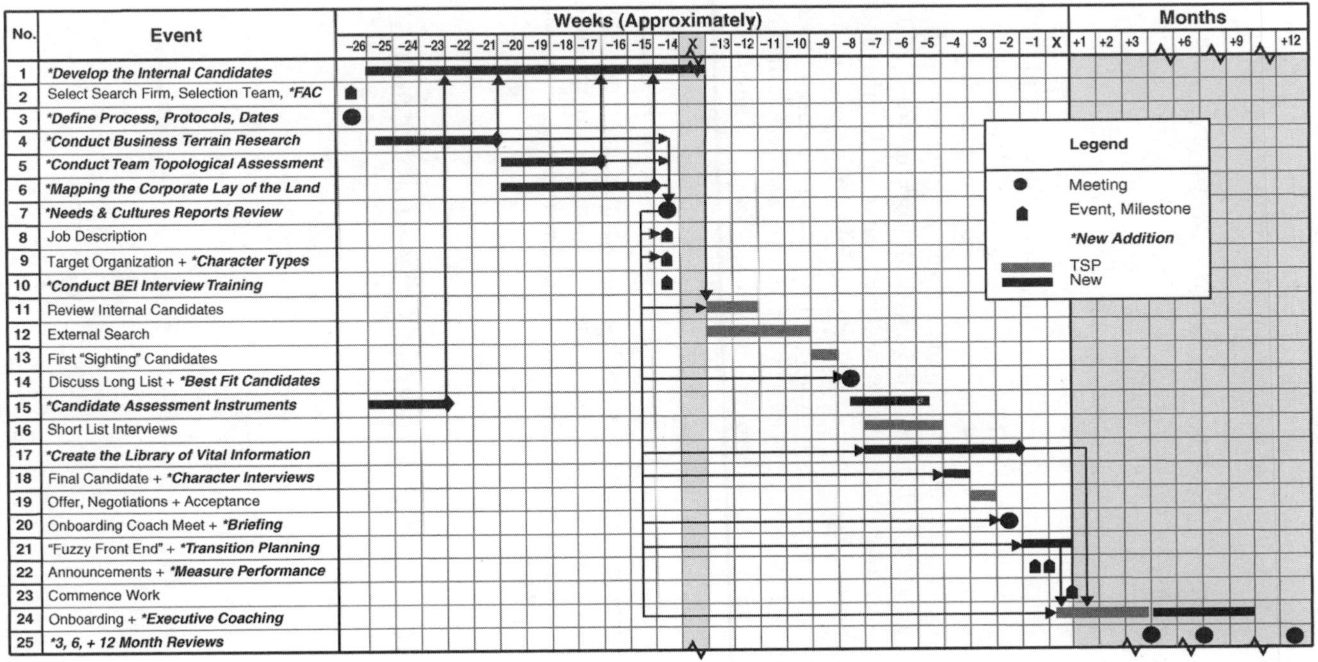

249

intended to show the relative phasing of events; they are not absolutes or even target times to be sought. Note too that the scale is also discontinuous to accommodate for periods of undeterminable duration required to develop internal candidates.

The steps in the Extended Leader Selection Process are virtually the same as those in the Accelerated Leader Selection Process described in Chapter 12, only executed in a different sequence. When Succession Planning is properly approached, there is sufficient lead time to complete all of the up-front research of the company's future needs and current cultures well in advance of when its output is needed. Consequently the work of the Forward Assessment Consultant (FAC) can precede other steps so the research findings can be fully integrated into the job description. The research data are also used in setting meaningful development goals for internal candidates. By completing the data gathering and analytical work up-front, the specific abilities, personality traits, energy level, and character that the right leader must possess to succeed in a particular cultural context will allow for the creation of a much sharper selection criteria and more focused process right from the outset. Consequently since only first-tier candidates will make it that far, the need for any second-round interviews can be eliminated from the extended process.

Besides its use in conjunction with CEO Succession Planning, the Extended Leader Selection Process is also recommended for use whenever there is sufficient advance notice of any senior executive departure: twenty-six or more weeks to complete the extended version (excluding development time of internal candidates), as compared to approximately sixteen weeks for the accelerated version.

Succession Planning Best Practices

The NACD Model

The 2006 Best Practices Study published by the NACD and Mercer Delta Consulting also identified ten best practices for boards to adopt when preparing for CEO Succession Planning.[36] These recommended practices are reproduced here as Table 13.1.

From Ideal to Real

Based upon the work we have done in developing the Extended and Accelerated Leader Selection Processes, an additional ten best practices have been

Table 13.1 Ten Best Practices for CEO Succession Planning
1. Plan three to five years out.
2. Ensure full board involvement.
3. Establish an open and ongoing dialogue and an annual review.
4. Develop an agreed-upon selection criteria.
5. Use formal assessment processes.
6. Interact with internal candidates.
7. Stage the succession but avoid horse races.
8. Develop internal candidates rather than recruit externally.
9. Have the outgoing CEO leave, or stay on as chair for a limited time.
10. Prepare a comprehensive emergency succession plan.
Source: National Association of Corporate Directors

identified. They are summarized in the following paragraphs and illustrated in Table 13.2 below:

1. **Begin Ongoing CEO Succession Planning Now.** Succession Planning is a journey, not a destination. Having a written Succession Plan

Table 13.2 The NEW Best Practices for CEO Succession Planning
1. Begin ongoing CEO Succession Planning now.
2. Grow internal talent by planning and monitoring progress.
3. Select the right Forward Assessment Consultant.
4. Establish the time frame for the process.
5. Aggressively manage the process.
6. Identify action-based capabilities and values-based character traits essential for success.
7. Fully integrate the executive recruiter into the process.
8. Incorporate Mapping tools and the Character Interview into the final interviews.
9. Seek feedback for continuous improvement.
10. Monitor the CEO's transition plan closely.

does not mean you have Succession Planning because factors affecting the plans are constantly in flux. Consequently, boards should have CEO succession as a topic of discussion on the board agenda at least two times per year. In some instances, having the current CEO present will be beneficial, and in other situations it will not. Once the process of Succession Planning becomes a routine part of board deliberations, its contentious nature will be greatly diminished. For this reason, after having replaced the CEO with a new leader, it is highly recommended that the topic of Succession Planning be on the board agenda within the new leader's first six months—well before it can be construed by anyone as anything other than normal board practice, and while it is clearly not related in any manner to current circumstances or performance.

2. **Grow Internal Talent by Planning and Monitoring Progress.** The longest lead time item in Succession Planning is developing the internal candidates. Grooming the right people can take years depending on a host of factors. Illustrating the level of precision, the scale in Figure 13.3 is shown to be discontinuous and of unknown duration ("X") at this juncture. Use the information gathered from the candidate assessment process (Step 15) and research of the company's needs and cultures (Steps 4, 5, and 6) to identify specific gaps in each internal candidate's background. Review their development needs with them and formulate specific assignments (full- or part-time) to provide needed experiences to close the development gap. The following are some specific practices to incorporate:

- Review the job description (Step 8) that is based on the research before each meeting with potential internal candidates. It is in comparison to these realities that candidates must be vetted, not some less specific or less relevant or subjective criteria that often comes from an interviewer's own past experiences.

- Conduct behavior-based interview training for all the directors involved in the selection process (see Chapter 9).

- Provide each candidate with an executive coach to work with him or her during the development period. The work should be related to the specific development needs of the individual.

- Ensure that "scorecards" identifying each individual's specific development needs are completed periodically by each internal candidate's current boss and reviewed with the head of the Selection Committee, the HR leader, the individual, and his or her executive coach every six months. Measuring progress in this fashion helps avoid surprises at the end of the process and maintains a more objective focus on what can become very personal agendas. Discuss each individual's "scorecard" and progress at the biannual board meetings, where time is devoted to the topic of Succession Planning.

3. **Select the Right Forward Assessment Consultant.** As you prepare for Succession Planning, select a Forward Assessment Consultant (FAC) who can serve as the board's special adviser throughout this process. (Refer to Chapter 10 for details on what to look for when making your selection.) Because the Forward Assessment Consultant will need to take on some of the work normally performed by the head of Human Resources in conducting other senior executive selection processes, the FAC should be experienced at managing projects of this nature of complexity, sensitivity, and confidentiality. More importantly the Forward Assessment Consultant must be capable of providing and coordinating the resources necessary to perform the Business Terrain Research, the Team Topography Assessment, and the quantitative research of the needs and cultures by Mapping the Corporate Lay of the Land in a timely fashion. The selected Forward Assessment Consultant must possess broad-based business experience at the CEO level and sufficient experience to serve as the new CEO's onboarding adviser when the time comes.

4. **Establish the Time Frame for the Process.** Ensure that time is adequately allotted to gather the needed factual data at critical points in the process and to develop the internal candidates based upon those findings. It is recommended that, at the outset, a qualitative needs and cultural assessment study (Business Terrain Research), a qualitative Team Topography Assessment, and an in-depth quantitative needs and cultures assessment (Mapping the Corporate Lay of the Land) be completed for benchmarking purposes and also for use in the event the current CEO encounters health or other problems requiring immediate action by the board during the interim. Depending upon how much time elapses between the completion of the initial research and when the external search is about to begin, it may be worthwhile to update the data to ensure proper calibration of the job criteria and the needed character traits for success in these particular cultures.

5. **Aggressively Manage the Process.** As the time approaches to begin interviewing outside candidates, the Forward Assessment Consultant's Project Leader can be utilized to drive the process, taking the coordination of schedules for all interviews out of the company's offices for greater security and to assure the anonymity of outside candidates. It is also easier for the Forward Assessment Consultant to manage board-level participants than the head of HR, who has an ongoing relationship with them. The following are some specific practices to incorporate:

- Have *all* interviewers block out two days for interviews on their calendars immediately at the start—a month or more in advance. Task the executive recruiter to fill these days with candidate interviews and then release unscheduled times from the reserved days back to each individual's calendar two weeks in advance.

- Prepare a description of the Leader Selection Process being used for the recruiter to review with all outside candidates at their first meeting. The Forward Assessment Consultant's Project Leader should review the same process description with each internal candidate as well. It is important that *all* candidates know what the major steps and milestones are and approximately when they are expected to occur. They should also know who to contact if they have any questions.

- Everyone on the Selection Team should be reminded that you are "selling" as well as "buying" right from day one and seek to establish a partnership relationship with all candidates as opposed to an arm's length or (worse yet) "professionally impersonal" one. You only have one chance to make a first impression on behalf of the company, and one of these people will, someday soon, be its new CEO.

- Share information about the process openly and keep candidates informed of their status proactively. Explain changes to timetables and be clear about what they can expect from your Selection Team throughout the process. Also be clear about what you expect from them as they navigate the process.

- Give each internal and external candidate the telephone number and contact information of the FAC's Administrative Specialist to be used as the central clearing house for questions and concerns that may arise on the part of the candidate. Assure them of a twenty-four-hour turnaround on all inquiries and questions.

6. **Identify Action-Based Capabilities and Values-Based Character Traits Essential for Success.** This is where an in-depth assessment of the executional and directional needs of the company is absolutely essential. Without knowing what *actions* are required to achieve the desired *results*, it is unlikely that an optimal match of abilities, personality, and energy needed for the job will be achieved. Avoid politically correct but distracting boilerplate generalizations to describe the traits of the ideal candidate as are typically found in so many CEO job specifications. Instead, focus on the *specific* background experiences and character traits that the right leader must possess to be successful in *this* particular situation. To do this effectively, the Selection Committee will need the research findings from both the qualitative and quantitative needs and cultures assessments. Besides the specific traits required for this particular situation, also look for the Universal Character Traits of Successful Leaders presented in Chapter 5 (Figure 5.1).

7. **Fully Integrate the Executive Recruiter into the Process.** Clearly define the role of the executive search professional chosen to source external candidates and to screen internal ones. Ensure that the findings from the research of needs and cultures are quickly communicated and thoroughly understood by the search executive(s) involved in the process (as well as everyone else on the Selection Committee). Provide your recruiter with the process description and other company materials to knowledgeably describe the journey ahead to outside candidates; the recruiters are not only your agents but your ambassadors as well. They are the proverbial "first impression you can only make once." Communicate openly and regularly with them, keeping them abreast of changes to dates and timetables as they occur. Be sure there are open communications between them and the Forward Assessment Consultant's Project Leader. Eliminate any economic incentives for them to favor recommending an external candidate over an internal one and/or a candidate discovered by them over one identified by any other source.

8. **Incorporate Mapping Tools and the Character Interview into the Final Interviews.** In addition to using the standard assessment tools as recommended in the NACD's list of best practices, also assess each final candidate's predisposed cultural expectations against those of the company to determine the best fit. Refer to the case of James and SDI, Inc. in Chapter 11 for an example of how this works by using the Culturemaps from Mapping the Corporate Lay of the Land. Explore the values of final candidates in Character Interviews (Chapter 9) to ensure adequate alignment with the candidate's values and those of the organization's key cultures. This interview is best accomplished by the individual to whom the new CEO will eventually report (such as the chairman or lead director).

9. **Seek Feedback for Continuous Improvement.** All candidates, internal and external, who come in contact with the Extended Leader Selection Process should be notified of the outcome of the process and, as described in Chapter 9, be asked to provide anonymous and confidential feedback about their experience, treatment, perceptions, and suggestions for future improvements. This feedback can best be obtained through the FAC Project Leader on behalf of the board.

10. **Monitor the CEO's Transition Plan Closely.** Because the FAC Project Leader has accumulated extensive knowledge of the company's true needs and cultures, as well as insights into the Executive Leadership Team's makeup and dynamics, it is highly recommended that she or he serve as the onboarding adviser for the new CEO. If an internal candidate is selected, the development coach who has worked with him or her may also make an excellent transition resource either as the onboarding adviser and/or the executive coach, providing their business background and acumen is sufficient to provide the full spectrum of

strategic, executional, personal, and political advice needed by the new CEO. It is critical that boards maintain the discipline of the three-, six-, and twelve-month reviews and that directors are made aware of the CEO's progress, as well as any issues or changes that may arise during the post-succession time frame.

Takeaways

This chapter has covered a number of key points for directors and senior executives involved in implementing a comprehensive CEO Succession Planning process. Some key points to bear in mind:

- Many significant changes have occurred over the past ten years that affect the nature of the CEO's job. Directors involved in, or preparing for, the development of CEO Succession Plans should be aware of these changes and how they potentially affect the interactions, roles, and responsibilities of the CEO, the board of directors, and their relationships with shareholders.
- Although Succession Planning is rapidly being recognized as the number one priority of boards today, only 40 to 50 percent have a credible Succession Plan in place.
- There are many plausible reasons that more boards have not yet implemented a CEO Succession Planning Process. Some of these are as follows:

  1. While highly recommended, the development of a Succession Plan is not a regulatory requirement.
  2. There is little unallocated time on board agendas for boards to undertake this important work.
  3. Succession Planning can become the source of an unpleasant confrontation between the Board and the CEO.
  4. Initiating succession planning may send inadvertent or inappropriate signals that could be disruptive.
  5. There is no specific accountability for Succession Planning at the committee level for which individual directors can be held accountable.
  6. Not all directors necessarily perceive "real value" in developing a CEO Succession Plan.
  7. The lack of experience with Succession Planning may discourage some directors from wanting to undertake it.

- The need for boards to develop substantive Succession Plans will continue to mount as business conditions and demographics put more and more pressure on the potential for CEO turnover. Besides, it is the right thing to do.

- As boards begin to undertake Succession Planning they should be cognizant that, historically, there have been very low levels of confidence placed in the credibility of Succession Plans by the HR executives who are privy to them. This suggests that there are deficiencies in the Traditional Selection Process, which is why this book has been written: to replace the flawed selection process used by most companies today with a better methodology for selecting the right leader.

- One of the most glaring deficiencies of the prevailing CEO Succession Planning processes is the lack of current, factual data about the needs and cultures of the organization into which the right leader must fit. Research that generates hard data about such "soft subjects" will improve the decisions that need to be made in selecting the right CEO for a particular situation.

- The new Extended Leader Selection Process is designed for Succession Planning purposes but can also be used for other senior positions whenever longer lead times exist. The Extended Leader Selection Process builds on the basic format recommended by the National Association of Corporate Directors (NACD) but provides more detailed steps to facilitate implementation by board members.

- Building on the ten best practices recommended by the NACD, the Leader Selection Process offers ten additional best practices that directors involved in Succession Planning can implement. As illustrated in Table 13.2 these are,

  1. Begin ongoing CEO Succession Planning now.
  2. Purposefully grow internal talent by planning and monitoring progress.
  3. Select the right Forward Assessment Consultant.
  4. Establish the time frame for the process.
  5. Aggressively manage the process.
  6. Identify action-based capabilities and values-based character traits essential for success.
  7. Fully integrate the executive recruiter into the process.
  8. Incorporate Mapping tools and the Character Interview into the final interviews.
  9. Seek feedback for continuous improvement.
  10. Monitor the CEO's transition plan closely.

Regardless of the reasons for having not yet developed meaningful CEO Succession Plans, boards are going to face more and more pressure to do so in the coming years. Given the current pressures, succession is an issue that will only get hotter in the future.

14

"You're Cleared in Hot"

This is not the end. It is not even the beginning of the end. But it is, perhaps, the end of the beginning.

—Winston Churchill

This book began with the premise that the cost of leadership failures is higher than most organizations can reasonably afford and that finding a process to avoid that problem is of great importance to all U.S. businesses. Drawing on years of experience working with corporations and C-Suite executives, we believe the most effective way to reduce the costs and risks of leadership failures plaguing business today is by selecting the right leaders in the first place. In this, our final chapter, we are going to "end this beginning" by:

- Recapping the main points of our thesis
- Addressing several FAQs (Frequently Asked Questions) about the work of FACs (Forward Assessment Consultants)
- Addressing three very "big pictures" we hope you will bear in mind about selecting executives who fit

The Journey in Retrospect

As we emphasized in Part One of the book, selecting a "right" leader requires an understanding of what needs to be done in terms of the executional (shorter-term) challenges facing the organization and what abilities and specific skill sets the leader must therefore possess. It also requires research into the true directional (longer-term) actions that must be addressed to deliver the expected future results. To be meaningful, these executional and directional needs must be expressed in terms of actions and not outcomes.

Using the Match-Fit Model as the underlying rationale for change, we also stressed in Part One the importance for the company to identify, measure, and describe the cultures at play in very specific terms. Only by understanding the powerful cultures that exist within an organization can those with the responsibility to select a leader choose the individual who best fits them. To determine fit, however, hirers must also understand the candidate's character. The Match-Fit Model we have developed explains the relationship between the critical aspects of the individual—abilities, personality, energy, and character—and those of the company—its needs and cultures.

Out of the Match-Fit Model evolved a selection process to improve the likelihood of selecting the right leader for a particular situation. In this book it is referred to as the new Leader Selection Process. The Leader Selection

Process incorporates the basic elements of the Traditional Selection Process (the process used by most companies today) in updated forms while adding to it four pieces of research administered by an outside Forward Assessment Consulting (FAC) Team.

This new process can be applied in two different fashions: The Accelerated Leader Selection Process is designed to work in situations where time is of the essence and the necessary Forward Assessment Consulting (FAC) work is undertaken simultaneously with the initial stages of screening candidates. The Extended Leader Selection Process approach better leverages the information that is gathered in the FAC research phase by completing it in advance of the initial screening activities. The Extended Leader Selection Process is recommended for situations where more lead time is available to the Selection Team, as is generally found in CEO Succession Planning.

At various times throughout this book we have used different metaphors and parables to help tell our story:

- We have frequently referred to the fact that when selecting the right "peg" (leader) to fit into the right "hole" (company), it helps to know the shape of the hole first. In the business context, the shape of the hole is determined by the needs and the cultures of the organization. We also pointed out that pegs that fit one hole extremely well rarely fit other holes—each with their own unique shape—nearly as well. Unlike wooden pegs, however, human pegs have a degree of malleability to improve their fit if they know what changes to make that will lead to success.

- When discussing the importance and power of cultures, we have drawn a parallel between the way in which a human body will accept or reject a perfectly well-transplanted organ based on its subtle chemical makeup, just as a culture will accept or reject an otherwise perfectly qualified new leader based on the alignment of his or her values to those of the organization.

- And we have likened leadership to a performing art and the leader to an actor—one who is constantly "onstage" and who, when starting out in a new leadership position, has been sent out onstage with no costumes, props, rehearsals, or script. The purpose of this analogy is to underscore the importance of providing post-selection support in the form of onboarding, executive coaching, and periodic reviews.

- When describing the work of the Forward Assessment Consultant (FAC) in the new Leader Selection Process, we have relied heavily on our military metaphor, comparing it to the function of the Forward Air Controller (FAC) working with the highly trained pilots of fast-moving and very powerful fighter aircraft (like CEOs and other top business leaders) in the ultimate of competitive settings: combat.

We hope that, through these parallels and the stories of various executive experiences, the key points will stay with you. We have also included "takeaways" as a quick reference for the points covered in each chapter.

But this is still all just the beginning. It is our hope that soon newer versions of the Leader Selection Process will emerge as others take the ideas, concepts, processes, and practices presented here and improve upon them, test them, refine them, and find better, even more effective ways to put them into use.

More About FAQs, FACs, and Other Facts

During the course of explaining the Match-Fit Model and the new Leader Selection Process to people over the years as Forward Assessment Consultants, we have encountered several frequently asked questions this book has not addressed. Some of the more relevant ones appear here.

Question: **Do the new Leader Selection Processes (the Accelerated Leader Selection Process and the Extended Leader Selection Process) also work when hiring executives and managers further down in the organization?**

Yes, they do. However, the cost-benefit equation adds up differently the further down in the organization you go. The good news is that once a comprehensive Map of the Corporate Lay of the Land has been completed, you can expect that:

- Its findings can serve as the basis for other selection processes with few, if any, changes.
- Because cultures do not change rapidly, the data regarding culture can be relied upon for a year or more before needing to be updated (unless, of course, a great number of significant changes at the top have occurred in the meantime).
- Once the basic Mapping questionnaire is developed, the ease of administering it or expanding its scope to a larger population is much greater than when it is first implemented.

Question: **The purpose of the new Leader Selection Process is to increase the likelihood that the selected leader will succeed. How would you measure "success" in this situation?**

Simply put, you will know the process works if the new leader is doing the right things (match) in the right ways (fit) to produce the right results. For many years professional services firms, including many of the major executive search companies, have attempted to find different measures of "success" of their CEO placements as a way of proving the efficacy of their work. Different measurements such as tenure, market capitalization increases, and stock price have all been considered, but to no avail. They have not worked because there are just too many variables beyond the control of the individual.

One of the nice things about the new Leader Selection Process is that it provides specific, tangible actions to be used as targets for the newly appointed leader. Because the Forward Assessment Research defines specific needs and priorities to be addressed (the "smoke" put on the target), they naturally become the standards of performance around which the organization, the boss, the board, and the new leader can all align. Defining what actions need to be accomplished to obtain the desired outcomes is key to measuring the success of a new leader in the Leader Selection Process.

Question: **Our company's CEO Succession Plan is working, and we are quite certain that our internal candidate is the right leader. In light of this, is it still necessary to do all the Forward Assessment Research, especially the culture-related elements?**

Consider this truism: "It's not what you don't know that gets you in trouble—it's what you don't know that you don't know that does you in." On that basis it can be argued that it is even *more* important when hiring an insider to conduct the research of culture. Outsiders are generally aware that they *do not know* the culture they are moving into and need to be attentive to its subtleties and to those "implicit guidelines" of behavior as well as to the explicit ones. Because insiders, on the other hand, are already a part of the culture, they often feel that they "know the ropes" and "how to get things done around here." Yet, as we have seen, powerful subcultures exist in every organization, and at least two of these subcultures—the new leader's team and the boss's team—will be new to the internal candidate. Any assumptions about the inner workings made by the internal candidate must be checked. Further, simply moving from one floor to another or from one building to another (let alone from one geographic location or division to another) can mean a dramatic change in culture. And depending on where the internal candidate is based, a move to a new country or region can add a whole additional level of complexity to the equation.

Internal candidates need facts not only to avoid pitfalls but to make decisions about the true executional and directional needs of the organization. Because they often lack the objectivity of someone coming from the outside, they may need the data the Forward Assessment Research will generate *more* than an outside candidate. Time is money, so, as with outside hires, newly appointed internal leaders need current data about important business issues to get off to a correctly directed start. By bringing all of the Forward Assessment Consulting tools to bear, both internal *and* outside appointees will benefit from access to candid, depoliticized, and honest input on which to build their transition plans. As a result they can begin to test those plans *before* they commence work rather than to have to start the data-gathering process *after* they have already begun working. Big decisions can be made more quickly and organizational alignment achieved more rapidly when the full FAC research is made available.

Question: **For a number of reasons (costs, lack of precedent, commitment to established ways, discomfort with change, and the like), I cannot get approval to adopt the *full* Leader Selection Process all at once. Is there some "mini-LSP" that I can adopt as a starting point for change that will produce at least *some* value beyond just the Traditional Selection Process?**

One of the interesting things I have noticed about the nature of change is that, "If nothing changes, nothing changes." So if what is preventing you from embracing the new process is a lack of the acceptance of the principles of the Match-Fit Model on which the Leader Selection Processes are built, then no amount of mini-steps will, sadly, get you where you want to go.

On the other hand, if what is holding you back stems from making a complete leap of faith to embrace the adoption of the Leader Selection Process all at once, then start with what you can. Most importantly, start.

The one caveat I would offer you in this situation, however, is (as the disclaimers on children's TV shows might say) "Do not attempt these feats at home without adult supervision." Meaning that, at a minimum, you need to get yourself even a one-person Forward Assessment Consultant to objectively gather and examine the facts you need about the needs and cultures of the organization. The person who gathers this information cannot be immersed in that culture or related to it. The individual must also be able to provide the assurance of third-party anonymity, or you will not get the candor and data that are so essential to the success of the process.

We would also encourage you to investigate some of the following ideas:

- Using the materials presented in Chapters 4 and 9, you can incorporate the basic assessment tools for both the candidates and the Executive Leadership Team who will report to him or her. (See Appendix A for more details regarding assessment tools.)
- In Chapter 10 you will find ample information about the six key areas to focus on when interviewing the ELT about executional and directional needs (the Business Terrain Research).
- The essence of the simplest of cultural Mapping initiatives can also be developed from the information that is provided in that chapter. (See Figure 10.1 for an example from one of our earlier Mapping processes that can serve as a template in this regard.)
- Appendix C contains a comprehensive list of items to request when assembling your own Field Guide of Vital Information.

While relatively simple tools, these "mini-steps" will work because, since starting out on our journey of discovery, we have employed each of these tools at one time or another. They are a start. Most importantly, keep pushing. The Accelerated Leader Selection Process and Extended Leader Selection Process work, and as people get some experience with them, they will sell themselves. Everybody likes success.

Question: **Can either of the two Leader Selection Process formats (the Accelerated Leader Selection Process presented in Chapter 12 or the Extended Leader Selection Process presented in Chapter 13) be used when the process must be kept secret so the incumbent is not aware it is underway?**

Have you ever heard the expression, "You're only as sick as your secrets"? Well, it happens to be true, and it is equally as true of organizations as it is of individuals. Perhaps even more so.

Since we have conducted Forward Assessment Research in other than situations involving the selection of a new leader (such as to assess needs and culture to ascertain what it would take to move a company to the next level of performance and excellence), we know it is possible to do this. However, before you look at ways to work around a "cloak and dagger" research scenario to gather the needed information about needs and cultures, I would encourage all those associated with the selection process to challenge one another with the questions: "Is secrecy *truly* essential in this situation? Why? Is the cost of secrecy really worth the alleged benefits?"

Rarely, in my estimation, is secrecy as important a requirement as it is made out to be. Usually a board wants to conduct a clandestine search so the sitting CEO (or another highly conspicuous senior executive) will not find out about it before the board is ready to replace him or her. They are concerned about the disruption that may occur. Tied to that concern is a fear of placing themselves in a position to be criticized by shareholders or the media for not having established an effective Succession Plan (or contingency Succession Plan). But announcing that the existing CEO has "left to pursue other interests" and in the same breath introducing a new appointee from the outside is hardly a demonstration of solid Succession Planning. Who do they think they are kidding? The day the change is announced, everyone knows that the search was undertaken in secret to cover up the fact that there was no internal choice ready.

A far more acceptable approach is to acknowledge a change is underway and undertake the Accelerated Leader Selection Process at the same time the search is announced. This two-pronged approach will maximize the value of the work and minimize the risk of selecting the wrong leader. If a former CEO needs to be brought out of retirement or an interim one appointed in the meantime, the disruptive effect of inadequate planning is far less than if a clandestine approach compromises the quality of the Selection Process.

Ask virtually any executive recruiter, and they will tell you that, in fact, the quality of the candidates they can recruit in a secret search when they cannot disclose vital industry and/or company information is significantly less than one conducted in the open. Not only is the quality affected, but, of course, a leak that results in someone finding out that the process is underway can be very costly. How would you like to have your CEO, the organization, and the shareholders learn of your plans to replace the CEO through a newspaper headline or a blog on the Internet? In our age of instantaneous communications, keeping a secret like a CEO search under wraps is almost impossible, and, for a public company, the risk of lawsuits and regulatory sanctions for not disclosing material information properly is very real. Talk about a way to undermine organizational trust!

Based on experience with Forward Assessment Consulting (FAC), we can also tell you that better research can be obtained when people know the real reason it is being undertaken, rather than if they think it is for some general purpose. If more boards and senior executives were willing to look at the risks and potential exposures they take by conducting research and executive searches in secrecy, we believe you would see significantly fewer failures resulting from these very contrived secret selection processes.

Question: **The Forward Assessment Consulting work introduces additional costs to the selection process that previously were not there. What is the cost-benefit justification (return on investment [ROI], payback, and such) of this added expense?**

The answer is, it's huge, but it all depends. If the Leader Selection Process helps select a different "right executive" than the one who was originally thought to be the right "heir apparent," then the payback is measured in tens of millions of dollars saved in the overall course of the next eighteen to thirty-six months. First, look at the figures in Table 1.1 where the estimated costs of leadership failures for large-, mid-, and small-cap companies are roughly $50 million, $20 million, and $12 million, respectively. Then consider the costs associated with terminating (on average) three of the new executive's direct reports, and then finding their replacements, and after having done so, going through the process *again* after terminating the "not-so-right" leader. Additional costs associated with lost market capitalization and stock volatility all need to be considered as well.

If the Leader Selection Process is undertaken and the executive selected is the same one who would have been selected had they not undertaken the Forward Assessment Research, then there are a couple of ways to look at the payback:

1. One is to consider the FAC's work as a key element in a prudent risk management program—an insurance policy, the premium of which, relative to the potential risks, is extremely low.

2. A second way of looking at the payback is based upon more tangible facts and hard currency. It has been reported that it takes a newly appointed CEO six months on average to reach breakeven.[1] New research by the Institute of Executive Development suggests that it is even longer for outside hires; 62 percent of respondents to their 2007–2008 survey stated that it took more than six months for them to reach productivity. For internal candidates 72 percent said that it took longer than three months to reach full productivity, and 28 percent said six months or longer was required.[2] Since the new leader is not necessarily trained in research, too much of his or her time is spent ferreting out what needs to be done, who are the keepers, what is the right way to organize the work, what priorities should be assigned, how this culture works, and the like. With the new Accelerated Leader Selection Process and Extended Leader Selection Process approaches, this work is all done for them *before* they arrive so they are truly able to begin contributing in a net positive way on the first day of work.

If we assume that the net, first-year total compensation for the new leader is X and he or she reaches productivity Y months sooner then the net savings is—well, you do the math. But do not forget to add in the net present value of every single decision the new leader makes during his or her first Y months that would have been made later without the information generated from the Forward Assessment Consulting work process.

So whether it is viewed as an inexpensive insurance policy to help manage risk or for its tangible payback, the Leader Selection Process is not difficult to justify on a financial basis because the stakes are so high.

Question: **What is the place of "gut feel" about one candidate being better suited than another in the new Leader Selection Process?**

To a large extent my answer to this question is simply, "Teach yourself to fly." A good pilot most definitely possesses a visceral "feel" for his or her plane. Without it the pilot is not much more than a passenger with controls. But pilots are taught repeatedly that, "When you're in the soup (bad weather), do *not* trust your senses—rely on the instruments or pay the consequences (which are usually of a fatal nature!).

Instruments provide data. They do not lie. When you cannot see where you are going, a phenomenon known as "spatial disorientation" can occur, and your senses can tell you that you are upside down when, in fact, you are not. Needless to say, if you are on final approach, either in an aircraft or in the process of selecting a new leader, and you do not stick with the facts, you will suffer the consequences.

Having said that, I will now temper my remarks with this one important stricture: The Accelerated Leader Selection Process and Extended Leader

Selection Process are not as precise as cockpit instruments. Aircraft instruments provide data for decision-making about indisputable physical principles, while the Leader Selection processes provide data about human factors—personality, character, and the cultures of people in groups. Humans are not ever 100 percent one way or another, so there are chances for error. As you pilot the process of selecting the right leader for your organization, use the data that has previously not been available in the Traditional Selection Process to narrow the range in which you ultimately turn to your "feel for the situation" to make the final decision. Keep your gut out of the decision until the last possible moment, and then, and only then, trust it implicitly. As we have said all along, the Leader Selection Process is intended to *help* those who have responsibility for selecting leaders do a better job. Ultimately, however, a decision must be made, and a decision made by humans about humans cannot be (and should not be) divorced from one of the most human of factors—intuition. Just keep it as a properly sized element of the decision, not the single most important one.

Question: **But what if there is dissension among the instincts of members of the Selection Team when all is said and done? What if you have two candidates, and half of the Selection Team feels strongly in favor of one, half feels equally as strongly in favor of the other, and the key decision maker has no overriding feeling one way or the other? Then what do you do?**

The answer is that you reach the decision through whatever process you would normally follow and then take comfort in the fact that "pegs are malleable." People will change when they have the information and the need to do so. By providing the selected leader the information about where his or her cultural predispositions differ significantly from those that exist in the organization, much of the battle will have already been won. Leaders like success, and given a choice between succeeding or failing, they will invariably make the better decision. Consequently the data provided in the FAC research and afforded to the new leader during the very first onboarding briefing will go a long way in overcoming the individual's initial lack of perfect compatibility with the cultural guidelines for behavior.

Final Perspectives

As we wrap up this initial leg of the journey toward a more advanced and effective process for selecting leaders, there are three key points that I feel need to be underscored. These points are essential, in my estimation, as a basis for *any* future work to be done to improve the effectiveness of the manner in which we select leaders:

1. **Every Leadership Job Is Becoming Increasingly Complex.** Without question, my first general management job in 1984 as the GM of outdoor products for Black & Decker was nowhere near as complex as that same job would be today. As depicted in Figure 14.1, there are so many initiatives, regulations, leadership principles, best practices, external priorities, and the like that must be considered today that did not exist even just a few years ago.

   Being a leader in today's world is an incredibly taxing and complex job. Finding the right leader should not be mistaken for finding the "perfect" leader under these conditions. The right leader needs the right abilities, personality, energy, and character to address the real needs of the organization and to fit its cultures. Beyond that, they must then be provided with the essential support to deal with the incredibly complex world in which he or she must create success. Those responsible for selecting the new leader must understand that the individual they are selecting will have to cope not only with *these* numerous challenges, but also with untold *others* that have not yet even appeared on the horizon.

2. **Culture Is the Next Frontier.** For far too many years, awareness of culture has hidden in the shadows of business life. Somehow the concept has escaped the rigors of examination to which virtually every other business process and concept has been submitted. As a result its power as a tool for transformation is almost completely untapped. Ask anyone who has done an acquisition, and invariably they will list among the top things that prompted the deal were "the people," "the organization," or "the leadership team," all of which are expressions of aspects of culture. But ask them how they valued these prize assets in their valuation models, and you will rarely get a meaningful answer.

   Unless business leaders collectively adopt the tools to measure, define, and communicate the true nature of culture—to create culture-maps to navigate their way through the "explicit, implicit, rational, irrational, and nonrational guides for behavior"—culture will forever remain the "soft stuff," as it has been labeled so far. This label is not only unwarranted, but it is detrimental to the best interests of corporate success. The importance of adopting, modifying, and continually improving the means by which culture is understood, measured, and shaped for success is essential for future productivity, efficiency, and growth. As Victoria Reese stated in an article several years ago:

   When recruiting, it is often easier to find a candidate with the right experience than one who would be a good cultural fit . . . companies should not be satisfied to watch qualified employees leave after twelve months, with

FIGURE 14.1 The Complex Leadership Situation

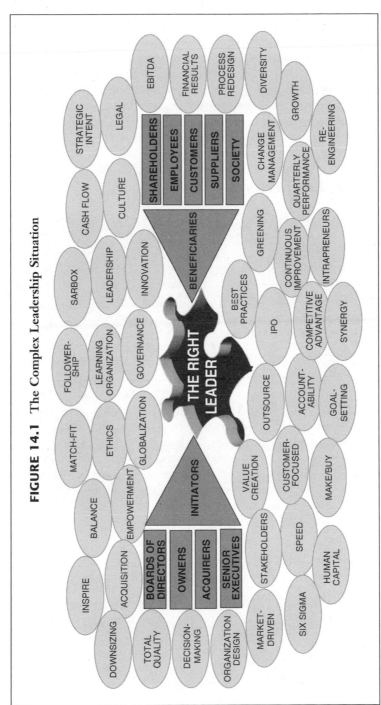

such comments as "He just wasn't a good fit here" or "He brought too much baggage from his previous employer" unless they have done everything they can up-front to educate the new manager about the culture.[3]

The new Leader Selection Process is a first step in providing more of "everything they can [do] up front to educate the new manager [leader] about the culture." But this is just the beginning.

3. It *Is* All About Trust

The Importance of Trust

It was not very long after I joined GardenWay in 1989 that it became apparent that we needed to integrate the recently acquired Bolens operation with the existing Troy-Bilt operation to maximize its potential value to the corporation. There were a host of strategic, as well as immediate, operating benefits to be derived from doing so correctly. It was easy enough to conceptualize how the pieces would potentially fit together, but selecting the optimal roles for the key managers and the size and constituency of their respective support organizations was daunting. While the people at the Troy, New York, facility were well-known to senior management due to its proximity and historical relationship with headquarters, the same was not true for the Bolens unit located hundreds of miles away in Port Washington, Wisconsin.

We knew the senior-level people there, well enough but we did not have much visibility into their support teams, which we believed held some very talented people whom we certainly did not want to lose. We hoped to retain and motivate them. In order to try to determine the best way to proceed, I decided to get to know the Port Washington facility in person. During my first visit, I walked the floor with the plant manager and introduced myself to everyone. I also made it a point to meet with all the managers.

Not satisfied until I knew enough, however, I returned the following week and every week thereafter for several months, staying at least two days per visit. I walked the floor daily, held ad hoc coffee and doughnut breaks, and conducted skip-level sessions. I sometimes took meals with managers and even had dinner with the town's mayor. My personal background as a graduate of a Midwestern college helped me to establish rapport and several lasting friendships. I made it a point to shift meeting

(continued)

venues from headquarters to Port Washington whenever it was possible to get more of the management team involved in the Bolens operations so I could benefit from their insights and impressions, too.

By April I felt we understood the culture well enough to implement a plan that considered not just the financial opportunities, but the people issues as well. So a small group from Troy flew out to Port Washington to hold open discussions with everyone whose job would possibly be affected by the changes we were contemplating. We talked about what we hoped to derive in the way of improved operating leverage and efficiencies, both short-term and long-term, and our rationale for why we were doing what we were doing. We showed them in a macro sense what the new, functional organization structure would probably look like, and we introduced them to the people who would head up each of the key areas. We talked about the jobs we thought would be necessary to make the new, consolidated operation a success. But that is as far as we went. That is as far as we could go. Before opening the meeting up to questions, we explained that until the newly appointed executives each had the chance to review his or her new role and responsibilities, we would not be able to establish the final number of jobs needed, let alone determine who was the best qualified to fill them. Until all the managers got together to talk about their people, we could not begin to make good decisions about who would be selected to stay with the company, where those jobs would be located, and which jobs would be changed or eliminated. We committed to hammer out the answers to these questions over the next thirty days and then return to show everyone the final picture and talk specifically with each one of them about where they fit into the future plan. I empathized with them, knowing what an uncertain time this was that we were entering, but I asked that they do their best to keep focused on the work at hand. Not too surprisingly, they did. This response confirmed my sense that I had come to understand the values and culture of the people—the real assets—we were working with here.

One month later, to the day, we returned to make the final restructuring announcements. As part of the communications team, we pulled in HR specialists from all over the company to go over each individual's situation, assigning specific responsibility for each person to one of them. We started the meeting by showing everyone the chart we had shown at the previous meeting, without the boxes indicating specific jobs. We then went over the process we had followed to arrive at our final decisions and revealed the organization chart showing the jobs to be filled but still without any names on it. Before we broke up, we told everyone what would happen over the course of the next several hours. At that time, the HR specialists began to meet with everyone who was

(continued)

affected and provide those who had new jobs with the details, and those who did not with their severance offer and timetables for change. Those who would be without jobs were spoken to first. Specific details regarding each individual's situation were provided to them, and then, after everyone had been spoken to, we reconvened to provide a copy of the final organization chart with the names of the selected people on it.

It was a very anxious day for many. Some of our employees had new, exciting job opportunities; some would be faced with accepting a lower-paying job in order to avoid a move; and still others were going to be informed of their termination date and associated benefits.

It was an extremely anxious day for me too, because I feared that even as hard as we had tried, someone might have been overlooked, or not treated properly, or not given the right information. I knew this was a very eventful day for the people and for the company. These were good people whose jobs and incomes were going to be affected. How we handled them would make a big difference in the trust relationship we had, not just with them, but with the other 500 employees who were not directly involved in this process but were part of that same corporate cultural unit. For that matter the eyes of all 2,500 people who made up the overall corporate cultural unit were on the new COO, too. And without their trust, I knew my tenure as president and chief operating officer would be in jeopardy. The Port Washington people who were selected to stay with the company were friends and neighbors of those who lost their jobs. How we treated them was extremely important to those who stayed. If not done properly (in their eyes), it would create a festering wound with nagging concerns: How will I be treated if it's my turn next? Are these new leaders to be trusted to do what's right? Is this the kind of company I really want to work for?

Once I felt comfortable that things were proceeding as planned, I left the building to go get some coffee and fresh air. A woman whom I did not know followed me out the door and hailed me as I approached my rental car. Standing in the parking lot as she came down the sidewalk, I thought, "Oh my gosh, here it comes—a person who's upset and unhappy with the way she has been treated for some reason. I wonder what could have gone wrong." I did not know her by name, but I recognized her from the meetings. I was fairly certain she was among those who had been told that their jobs had ended and that we had no options for future employment at this location to offer her.

As she approached me, she put out her hand and introduced herself, indicating that she was, indeed, one of those people who had been informed that her last day would be in two months. What she then said left me speechless. She said:

(continued)

This is the third time in less than a year that I have been let go. Last June, I lost the job I had had for nearly twenty years when the company I worked for was sold. Then, in December, the job I had started in August was eliminated due to downsizing. And now this. But the reason I wanted to speak with you, Mr. Stoddard, isn't about me and my particular situation—it's about them— those other people who lost their jobs today. I wanted to say "thank you" to you on their behalf. They're all upset and hurting right now, and it'll take a while before they get through this and can see it for what it is. They can't possibly see at the present time how well you and your team have handled it right from the very beginning, but I can. I know what it's like to be left in the dark and not know what changes like these will mean to me personally. I know what it's like in the pit of your stomach not to know what's going on or when you'll even receive an answer. These people are hurting because it's their first time through this, but maybe someday they'll realize how thoughtful and sensitive and forthright you and your team have been with them about this entire change. You've done things the right way—the way we'd hoped they'd be done. And for that, for them, I just wanted to say thank you.

As she turned and walked away, I realized fully for the first time just how important it is for a leader to be aligned with the values of their organization to be trusted and how important trust is to effectiveness. I had been lucky in this situation. My "read" of the Bolens culture had been correct thanks to the input I had received from many sources during the weeks leading up to the creation and implementation of our plan. The steps we had taken, which some on the executive team viewed as a bit of "overkill," had all been for good purpose. Standing in that Wisconsin parking lot, I realized that it is not so much what we do as leaders—anyone could have seen the advantages in the functional structure over the divisional one from either a strategic perspective or just for the short-term cost savings that were available. What mattered most was not *what* the decision was, but *how* we went about implementing it. *How* we go about doing the things we choose to do or are called upon to do is what makes a leader the *right* leader.

My experience that day helped to reinforce the importance of my values regarding open communication and the treatment of people with dignity and respect. But the experience also helped to affirm the values of the organization, its cultural essence, by demonstrating that its new operating leaders could be trusted to do what was right—right as seen through the eyes of the organization and measured against the standards of their culture—even when tough decisions are involved. In the following years we made many other changes, and one by one we continued to do not only the right things, but to do them right. We were not perfect, but our track record was pretty good. As trust was built, changes became easier to implement. To a large extent I believe that the reason we were able to make the necessary changes that led to a period of exceptional growth was because, from the very beginning, we had demonstrated through our actions that there was alignment between the values of the company's leaders and those of its predominant cultures.

My Takeaway from That Experience Was This:

*From the alignment of the leader's values
(character) with those of the organization (culture)
comes trust.
From trust comes the willingness to follow.
From followership comes the permission to
lead.
From leadership comes success.
Trust, then, is at the very core of success.*

Ostensibly, the purpose of the new Leader Selection Process is to help those responsible for selecting leaders do a better job by giving them the information to choose those whose abilities, personality and energy match up well against the real needs of the organization and whose characters are well aligned with the prevailing cultures through which they must deliver results. In reality it is as much about helping hirers select leaders who are trustworthy in the eyes of the people they must lead and who possess the other necessary traits to do the job. The "right leader" is always a trusted leader.

One Final Flyby

In the closing of the Preface I wrote, "let me simply conclude with a statement that will make much more sense once you have read the book: 'Hit my smoke . . . you're cleared in hot.'" By now I hope that the "hit my smoke" portion of that phrase makes sense to you. So let me give you the significance of the remainder:

When forward air controllers gave their final authorization for the fighters to initiate their attack, they would say, "You're cleared in hot." It was their authorization to do what they were trained to do. The FACs did not tell them what to do or how to do it. In effect, having illuminated the targets and informed them of the situation they faced, they simply gave them permission to take the information they had been given and put it to best use on the basis of their knowledge, skills, and abilities, all with the phrase, "You're cleared in hot." The pilots then went about doing what they had been brought in to do— protect the people who were counting on them.

So, I will close with that same phrase to you. You now know everything you need to know about how to change the selection process to find the right leader who fits your situation best. It is now up to you to make it happen. "So, hit my smoke . . . you're cleared in hot."

Notes

FOREWORD

[1] The following is a list of trademarks belonging to Crenshaw Associates:

Business Terrain Research®
Culturemap®
Field Guide of Vital Information™
Forward Assessment Consulting®
Library of Vital Information™
Team Topography™
Topographical Mapping and Bridging®
Topographical Bridging®
Mapping the Corporate Lay of the Land®
Senior Executive Dynamics®
The Corporate Lay of the Land®
The Match-Fit-Model™

We have not labeled each mark in the text of this book to make it easier for the reader to read. However, it is the intention of the authors and of Crenshaw Associates to protect these and all our copyrights, marks, and intellectual property to the fullest extent possible under the law.

PREFACE

[1] Karlsson, Neilson, and Webster, "The Performance Paradox," 4.

[2] Lucier, Wheeler, and Habbel, "The Era of the Inclusive Leader," 47.

[3] Bradt, Check, and Pedraza, *The New Leader's 100-Day Action Plan*, 1.

[4] "Nike, Inc. Appoints William D. Perez President, Chief Executive Officer, and Director Effective December 28, 2004," http://www.Nikebiz.com.

[5] "Nike, Inc. Names Mark Parker CEO, William D. Perez Resigns," http://www .Nikebiz.com.

[6] Holmes, "Nike's CEO Gets the Boot."

[7] Barbaro and Dash, "Another Outsider Falls Casualty to Nike's Insider Culture."

CHAPTER 1

[1] Karlsonn, Neilson and Webster, "CEO Succession 2007: The Performance Paradox, 4–5.

[2] Challenger, Gray, & Christmas, "370 CEO Departures in First Quarter," 1. Data from this source was used by the author to calculate the averages contained in the text.

[3] Ciampa and Watkins, *Right from the Start*, 4.

[4] Bradt, Check, and Pedraza, *The New Leader's 100-Day Action Plan*, 1.

[5] Lucier, Wheeler, and Habbel, "CEO Succession 2006: The Era of the Inclusive Leader," 47. More recent data in Karlsonn, Neilson, and Webster, "CEO Succession 2007: The Performance Paradox" suggests the role of performance-related CEO terminations has declined of late.

[6] Booz Allen Hamilton, "Global CEO Turnover Set New Record in 2005." If performance (or lack thereof) is the key driver of CEO departures, however, this phenomenon can be understood in light of the short time frames afforded these top leaders to deliver results or be replaced. This study by Booz Allen Hamilton indicates that outside CEOs perform better than insiders during the first years of their tenures, while insiders deliver higher returns to shareholders during their later years on the job. Given the greatly shortened tenure of a CEO these days, it appears that internal ascendants who get off to a slow start are axed before their longer-term contributions ever reach fruition. Outside hires, on the other hand, who appear to bring more objectivity and willingness to slaughter sacred cows, tend to buy more time initially.

[7] Charan, "Ending the CEO Succession Crisis," 74.

[8] Lucier, Kocourek, and Habbel, "The Crest of the Wave," 8.

[9] Opinion Research Corporation, "Putting Customers First," 61.

[10] Lucier, Spiegal, and Schuyt, "Why CEOs Fail," 9.

[11] Opinion Research Corporation, "Putting Customers First," 61.

[12] Murray, *Revolt in the Boardroom*, xi.

[13] Karlsonn, Neilson, and Webster, "CEO Succession 2007: The Performance Paradox," 4.

[14] Epsen Fuller/IMD, "Global Survey Results 2008: The Changing Face at the Top." 5.

[15] Paul Hodgson, e-mail message to author, June 23, 2008.

[16] According to the following two sources, Nike also agreed to buy his house for $3.6 million (Holmes, "Nike CEO Gets the Boot"), in addition to covering the remodeling and furnishing costs of it and to repaying him for $150,000 for club

memberships (Barbaro and Dash, "Another Outsider Falls Casualty to Nike's Insider Culture"). All told, cash payments to Bill Perez during his stay at Nike came out to a little bit more than $1 million a month on top of the $117,000 monthly salary he was receiving.

[17] "Robert L. Nardelli," http://en.wikipedia.org/wiki/Robert_Nardelli.

[18] "Gary Forsee's Lavish Exit Package," *Business Week* (October 10, 2006); Donlon, "Time Out Between Nardelli Meltdowns," Chief Executive (January 1, 2007); "Grasso Ordered to Return NYSE Pay," *NPR Morning Edition* (October 20, 2006).

[19] The larger severance amounts that are most often reported contain the value of the gain on stock options due to the accelerated vesting that usually occurs upon termination. While large, the "cost" of these gains is borne by the market and not the company nor the shareholders necessarily. The other factor inflating large severance payments is that they are not "severance" payments at all but "hiring payments" deferred until (if) something goes wrong. These guarantees were given to the executives by their previous employer usually to keep them in place during a transition, as was the case with Bob Nardelli. In order to lure him away from GE, Home Depot had to match the benefit in their hiring offer although they did not need to recognize the potential liability it created until he was fired.

[20] Paul Hodgson, http://www.thecorporatelibrary.com.

[21] Data courtesy of Capital IQ a division of Standard and Poors (http://www.capitaliq.com).

[22] Watkins, *The First 90 Days*, 2–3.

[23] Coyne and Coyne, "Surviving Your New CEO," 64.

[24] Lucier, Wheeler, and Habbel, "The Era of the Inclusive Leader," 47. These stock price-related findings provide more insight into the performance of the Nike stock at the time the Perez departure was announced than simply that "the Street having taken the development in stride" as reported in *Business Week* (Holmes, "Nike's CEO Gets the Boot"). The drop in the Nike common share of only an "immediate 1 percent (75 cents)" can be better attributed to the fact that Perez was succeeded by Mark Parker, a long-time Nike insider that mitigated the otherwise negative impact that the unexpected removal of the CEO of a well-performing company would otherwise have had. As reported by Holmes, Nike had "been enjoying strong gains in the U.S. and elsewhere and posted a 15 percent jump in the most recent quarter's profits."

[25] Mendels, "The Real Cost of Firing a CEO," 41.

[26] Norton, "CEO Departures at an All-Time High."

[27] Smart, *Topgrading*, 44–51, 540–543.

[28] On page 50 of the earlier edition of *Topgrading* (1999) Smart provided cost data for executives earning $100,000–$250,000 ($168,000 average), which we used on the basis that it was more representative of the impact that a CEO would have than that of lower paid managers reported in the 2005 edition. To develop Table 1.1 we began by taking each line item Smart had quantified through Mursau's interviews and calculated what percentage each one represented of the sum of the costs for mis-hires. We replaced Smart's severance figures with those based upon Hodgson's findings

(3X for CEOs and 2X for other top executives) as reported in this chapter and, also as discussed in the text, we reduced the severance multiplier for CEOs of mid-cap and smaller firms to 2X and 1X, salary respectively, to be conservative and to be more in alignment with our experience at Crenshaw assisting executives as they are leaving jobs and negotiating packages at new ones. We also calculated the "Cost to Hire" based on a 33 percent contingency search fee and added an amount equal to 50 percent of the recruitment fees to cover the sign-on bonuses, relocation expenses, cars, club fees, and other up-front expenses usually incurred for CEOs that are not a proportional part of a lower level manager's cost-to-hire picture. The only place we otherwise deviated from the Smart/Mursau research values provided by Smart was in the area of "Disruption Costs." We did this for two reasons: 1) Smart indicates in the 2005 edition that, "The biggest understated cost is the cost of disruption. More than half the respondents registered the cost at $0. When asked why, they said that assigning a dollar value to the costs was too difficult, too subjective. Almost all respondents, however, indicated that "they believe costs associated with disrupting the workplace to be huge" (46–47). We know from other research presented in this chapter (Coyne and Coyne, "Surviving Your New CEO") that, on average, 25 percent of executives will be involuntarily terminated upon the arrival of a new CEO. Consequently, we raised the estimate of disruption costs from 6 percent of Mistakes and Failures to 25 percent. Bear in mind that Table 1.1 does *not* reflect the value of stock options or the negative impacts to shareholder value, market capitalization, or stock volatility, all of which can be quite significant. Nor does it consider any of the future costs associated with the bad decisions made by the CEO during his or her eighteen months on the job.

[29] Koepp, "Fortune 500: America's Largest Corporations," 235. These calculations were made by using the mean size for the large-cap group due to the wide spread in the range (from $4.5 billion to $351.1 billion) and the median for the other two segments where revenue and profit information was not available. Annual average profits were assumed to occur equally throughout the year for all segments in converting the annual profit contributions to eighteen months for comparison to the cost data for CEO failures. Since the direct costs are deductible business expenses we assumed all segments had the same (35 percent) corporate tax rate, which was applied before calculating the percentages in the text.

[30] Sonnenfeld and Ward, *Firing Back*, 137.

[31] The Traditional Selection Process Gantt Chart was created with the input, critique, and direction of six very senior HR leaders who, dubbed as our "HR Advisory Council," unselfishly volunteered their time, thoughts, and experiences to the creation of *The Right Leader*.

[32] Barbaro and Dash, "Another Outsider Falls Casualty to Nike's Insider Culture."

CHAPTER 2

[1] Historically, some people have used the two terms, "match" and "fit," interchangeably. We will define and use the terms much more specifically in this book.

[2] Lucier, Kocourek, and Habbel, "The Crest of The Wave," 8.

[3] Loehr and Schwartz, *The Power of Full Engagement*, 4.

[4] Ibid., 5.

[5] Collins, *Good to Great*, 13.

[6] Covey, *The 7 Habits of Highly Effective People*, 34 and 188.

[7] "Resume Trouble," *The Wall Street Journal*; "Short Tenure: O'Leary Out at Notre Dame after One Week," http://www.si.com.

[8] "Bush Administration Stepping Up Obscenity Precautions," *USA Today*.

[9] Frequently, solutions to these executional needs are already under way before the selection process ends, in which case the new leader must be able to embrace them and enhance them to ensure they are properly implemented. Sometimes, however, key executional initiatives have not been undertaken and must be put in place, even at the expense of other initiatives already under way. Sometimes the new leader must abandon some popular policies, programs, or practices and put new ones in their place. These changes are far riskier and will often require that the selected leader possess a different set of abilities and operating style than if fewer changes are needed to reach short-term objectives of a critical nature.

[10] A possible exception affects leaders of organizations that are more homogeneous, like trade unions and governmental bodies.

CHAPTER 3

[1] Merriam-Webster, ed., *Merriam-Webster's Collegiate Dictionary, 11th Revised Edition*, 44.

[2] Strack, Baier, and Fahlander, "Hiring and Keeping the Best People," 2–3.

[3] Spencer and Spencer, *Competence at Work*, 117–18.

[4] Lucht, *Rites of Passage at $100,000 to $1 Million+*, 376–404.

[5] Smart, *Topgrading*, 486–501.

[6] Hunt, *Hiring Success*, 54.

[7] Ibid., 54.

[8] Hoevemeyer, *High Impact Interview Questions*, 11–12.

[9] Information concerning stress interviews can be found in many sources including: "Types of Interviews," http://en.wikipedia/job_intervew#types_of interview; Lucht, *Rites of Passage at $100,000 to $1 Million+*, 395–396.

[10] Sources for behavioral-based interviews include: Hoevemeyer, *High Impact Interview Questions*, 19, 36–38 (available at http://books.google.com); "Types of Interviews," http//en.wikipedia/job_intervew#types_of interview; and Spencer and Spencer, *Competence at Work*, 117–124.

[11] Hoevemeyer, *High Impact Interview Questions*, 11–12.

[12] Ibid., 19.

[13] Spencer and Spencer, *Competence at Work*, 117.

[14] Hamel and Prahalad, *Competing for the Future*.

[15] Spencer and Spencer, *Competence at Work*, 124.

[16] Goleman, *Emotional Intelligence*.

[17] Lynn, *The EQ Interview*, 8–9.

[18] Strack, Baier, and Fahlander, "Hiring and Keeping the Best People," 23–24.

[19] Hunt, *Hiring Success*, 434–44.

[20] Mornell, *Hiring Smart!*, 123.

[21] Alan Renne, Russell Reynolds Associates, phone conversation (June 26, 2008).

[22] DuBois, "A Test-Dominated Society: China 1115 B.C. 1905 A.D."

[23] Maddux, *Quality Interviewing*, 41–42.

[24] Broadley, *Your Natural Gifts*, 13–19.

[25] Ibid.

[26] StrengthsFinder® is a registered trademark of the Gallup Organization.

[27] Buckingham and Clifton, *NOW, Discover Your Strengths*, 5–29.

[28] Maddux, *Quality Interviewing*, 41–42.

[29] The list of questions never to be asked in a job interview were compiled from: Renckly, *Human Resources*, 86–87; Strack, Baier, and Fahlander, "Hiring and Keeping the Best People," 21; and Waldrop, *The Everything Human Resource Management Book*, 21. Depending upon ever-changing state and other jurisdictions law, the authors are not qualified to offer legal advice and do not represent any remarks made in this book as constituting to that effect. Hirers are encouraged to seek proper advice from their own qualified counsel.

CHAPTER 4

[1] Finkelstein, *Why Smart Executives Fail*, 213–237.

[2] Dotlitch and Cairo, *Why CEOs Fail*, xxvii.

[3] "Leadership IQ Study: Why New Hires Fail," http://leadershipiq.com/news.

[4] American Psychological Association, http://psychologymatters.apa.org.

[5] Merriam-Webster, ed., *Merriam-Webster's Collegiate Dictionary, 11th Revised Edition*, 878.

[6] Wikipedia, http://en.wikipedia.org/wiki/personality_traits.

[7] Ram Charan, Presentation to the Directorship Institute (December 12, 2007).

[8] Wikipedia, http://en.wikipedia.org/wiki/personality_traits. The Openness factor is referred to by some in the field as "Intellect," which for the sake of the New Match-Fit Model we categorize as belonging in the abilities bucket, not the personality one. This is the reason that we encourage the reader to not get tangled up in the specific jargon at the risk of losing sight of the overall purpose and significance of the Model in the first place. It really does not matter what a particular trait is called or where in what bucket it is characterized as belonging for the broad concept of the New Match-Fit Model to ring true.

[9] Kaihla, "The CEO's Secret Handbook," 69.

[10] Loehr and Schwartz, *The Power of Full Engagement*, 5.

[11] Campbell, Baites, Martin, and Meddings, "The Stress of Leadership," 12.

[12] Armstrong, "Comments on Leadership: 2008," e-mail correspondence (July 11, 2008).

CHAPTER 5

[1] Because of the complex and ever-changing nature of the legal context in any given state or other legal jurisdiction, it is extremely important that hirers be well-advised of those specific areas where they can and cannot tread during the course of interviewing or discussing job candidates, whether internal or external. The authors are not qualified to offer legal advice in this area and do not represent any remarks made in this book as constituting to that effect. Hirers are encouraged to seek proper advice from their own qualified legal counsel.

[2] Merriam-Webster, ed., *Merriam-Webster's Collegiate Dictionary, 11th Revised Edition*, 227.

[3] Hall and Wagie, "The U.S. Air Force Academy's Cutting-Edge Character Development Program," 35–39.

[4] Wikipedia, http://www.wikipedia.org/wiki/moral_character.

[5] Klann, *Building Character*, 7.

[6] Ferguson, "Moral and Character Development," http://chiron.valdosta.edu/whuitt/col/morchr/morchr.html.

[7] Bossidy, Charan, and Burck, *Execution*, 128.

[8] Urdang, ed., *American Century Dictionary*, 184.

[9] Merriam-Webster, ed., *Merriam-Webster's Collegiate Dictionary, 11th Revised Edition*, 1317.

[10] Peterson and Seligman, Character Strengths and Virtues.

[11] Lee, *The Power Principle*, 12.

[12] Klann, *Building Character*, 21–47.

[13] Kidder, *Moral Courage*, 47.

[14] Collins, *Good to Great*, 17–48.

[15] Urdang, ed., *American Century Dictionary*, 72.

[16] King Jr., *"The Purpose of Education."*

[17] http://www.bsa.com.

[18] http://www.gsusa.com.

[19] Klann, *Building Character*, 85.

[20] Collins, "Level 5 leadership," 27–28. Jim Collins's position as to whether great leaders are born or bred is shared by the authors.

[21] Bennis, *On Becoming A Leader*.

[22] Klann, *Building Character*, 3.

[23] Mourkogiannis, *Purpose*, 206.

[24] Barrett, *Liberating the Corporate Soul*, 147.

[25] Drucker, "Managing Oneself," 1.

[26] Galford and Drapeau, "The Enemies of Trust," 3.

[27] Bennis, *On Becoming A Leader*, 45.

[28] Galford and Drapeau, "The Enemies of Trust," 1.

[29] Hock, *Birth of the Chaordic Age*, 6.

[30] Finkelstein, *Why Smart Executives Fail.*

[31] Booz Allen Hamilton, "Measuring and Analyzing Corporate Values During Major Transformations," 5.

CHAPTER 6

[1] Lucier, Schuyt, and Tse, "CEO Succession 2004: The World's Most Prominent Temp Workers," 3.

[2] Leadership IQ Study, "Management, Inaction Among the Real Reasons Why CEOs Get Fired," http://www.leadershipiq.com/news/.

[3] Right Management Consultants, "Research: Building Relationships is Key to New Leader Survival, Success," 1.

[4] Bossidy and Charan, *Execution*, 22.

[5] This is something we learned from a company with whom we developed a strategic alliance, Genesys Solutions, LLC, of Radnor, PA.

[6] This highlights one of the fundamental problems with the Traditional Selection Process—those who are doing the hiring really do not *know* what needs to be done, so they hire to the wrong profile. The situation is even worse when the hirers *think* they know what and how to fix a problem based entirely on their perception of the problem and their own, often limited, experiences elsewhere.

[7] Burson-Marsteller, http://www.ceogo.com.

[8] Bossidy and Charan, *Execution*, 19.

CHAPTER 7

[1] Don Valdes, Ph.D., Sociology 101 class notes, Denison University (February 14, 1963).

[2] Goodes, "Transforming the Culture of a Global Enterprise . . . One Employee at a Time," 189–198.

[3] Deal and Kennedy, *Corporate Cultures*, 14.

[4] Goffee and Jones, "What Holds the Modern Company Together?"

[5] Deal and Kennedy, *Corporate Cultures*, 21.

[6] Ibid., 15.

[7] Schein, *Organizational Culture and Leadership*, 26.

[8] Deal and Kennedy, *Corporate Cultures*, 15–16.

[9] Chatman and Cha, "Leading by Leveraging Culture," 23.

[10] Collins and Portas, *Built to Last*, 8.

[11] Schein, *Organizational Culture and Leadership*, 15.

[12] Dauphinas and Price. *Straight from the CEO*, referring to Peters and Waterman Jr., *In Search of Excellence*, 183.

[13] Peters and Waterman, Jr., *In Search of Excellence*, 103.

[14] Bains, *Meaning Inc.*, 167.

[15] Barrett, *Liberating the Corporate Soul*, 16.

[16] Zweifel, *Culture Clash*, 51.

[17] Chatman and Cha, "Leading by Leveraging Culture," 23.

[18] Schein, *Organizational Culture and Leadership*, 36–37.

[19] Ibid., 246.

[20] Booz Allen Hamilton, "Measuring and Analyzing Corporate Values During Major Transformations," 1; Covey, *The Speed of Trust*, 120.

[21] Colvin, "How Top Companies Breed Stars."

[22] Bossidy and Charan, *Execution*, 150–152.

[23] Chatman and Cha, "Leading by Leveraging Culture," 23.

[24] Ibid., 32.

[25] National Defense University, "Strategic Leadership and Decision Making."

[26] Booz Allen Hamilton, "Measuring and Analyzing Corporate Value During Major Transformations," 3.

[27] Barrett, *Liberating the Corporate Soul*, 74–76.

[28] Core assumptions are more difficult to get at and, frankly, do not pass a reasonable cost-benefit analysis to warrant going after as an element of a senior-level selection processes. All of these and other data-driven approaches to measuring culture are but early steps of an overdue journey toward the eventual acceptance of a more precise, standardized set of tools, methodologies, and vocabulary that can be used to measure the strength of key elements of corporate cultures and to describe those findings in meaningful ways so those same cultural elements can be taught, learned, and thereby managed in the cultures of business organizations. And, of course, to help select the right leader who fits the culture to bring about the changes needed for future success.

[29] Another reason why the measurement, description, and communication of culture is so essential today is that the manner in which people experience the same culture of an organization can vary. The vocabulary used to describe the culture of business organizations consistently has not yet been broadly established and accepted. Consequently, two people who experience a culture in the same way may describe it differently, or the converse; individuals may use the same words to describe very different aspects of the same or different cultures. This makes the need for a broader-based, more standardized approach to describing culture even more essential. Again, this is one area that we hope this book will help.

As the head of General Electric's Canadian affiliate for major appliances, I was fortunate to have been at the Boca Raton meeting in January of 1997 when Jack Welch introduced Six Sigma to the 400 or so top leaders of the company from around the world. It was truly an impressive series of presentations, and there was no mistaking that each and every person in the audience was expected to not only understand this new concept, but to immediately become a disciple of it, carrying the process with them back to their various business units for immediate implementation. Six Sigma is a disciplined, data-driven approach and methodology for eliminating defects in any process—from manufacturing to transactional, and from product to service (Schein, *Organizational Culture and Leadership*, 70–84). The most basic Six Sigma process involves five fundamental steps referred to as DMAIC—Define,

Measure, Analyze, Improve, and Control (Booz Allen Hamilton, "Measuring and Analyzing Corporate Values During Major Transformations," 5). While Six Sigma has been criticized rightfully for having some shortcomings and for not being the "end-all, bet-all" approach as some may have regarded it, it has brought about a new sense of measurement to the workplace.

With "measurement" at the heart of the Six Sigma process, I have found it incredible that some trained "Black-Belts" or "Champions" who are now in very senior leadership positions and who would demand the rigorous measurement of some "soft areas" of a business like those dealing with highly subjective customer perceptions such as the "the feel of quality when I touch it" or the "the sound of quality when the door closes" would continue to turn their backs on the application of similar measurement techniques to another "soft area"—that of culture. When shown that culture can be measured and therefore defined and taught, it can, then, be managed. And managing culture can have greater benefit to an organization than all the billions of cost savings generated by Six Sigma techniques because, when you get right down to it, ". . . a strong culture has almost always been the driving force behind continuing success in American business"(Goodes, *Straight from the CEO*, 191).

[30] National Defense University, "Strategic Leadership and Decision Making."

[31] Schein, *Organizational Culture and Leadership*, 15–16.

[32] Ibid., 274–278.

[33] National Defense University, "Strategic Leadership and Decision Making."

[34] Bower, "Solve the Succession Crisis by Growing Inside-Outside Leaders," 2.

[35] Lucier, Schuyt, and Handa, "CEO Succession 2003: The Perils of 'Good' Governance," 14.

[36] Goldsmith and Reiter, *What Got You Here Won't Get You There*, 8.

[37] Groysberg and Snock, "The Pine Street Initiative at Goldman Sachs," 3.

[38] Covey, with Merrill, *The Speed of Trust*, 5.

[30] Barrett, *Liberating the Corporate Soul*, 144.

[40] Schein, *Organizational Culture and Leadership*, 23.

[41] Clemons and Santamaria, "Maneuver Warfare," 58.

CHAPTER 8

[1] Much of the information regarding the mission and the role of Forward Air Controllers in Southeast Asia came from general knowledge accumulated over the years, refined and focused by my friend, Lt. Col. Michael "Scoop" Jackson, USAF (Ret.), probably the only FAC pilot to ever have an SA-2 SAM missile shot at him while flying a Cessna O-2 over the Demilitarized Zone in 1972. His insightful, touching, and humorous recounting of his experiences as a FAC can be found in his first book, *Naked in DaNang: A Forward Air Controller in Vietnam*. Additional information used in this chapter was obtained from various Web sites found under "Vietnam Conflict," "USAF Forward Air Controllers," and "Forward Air Controllers Association." One special source that contains the annotated record of radio transmissions from the Battle of Hua Cu where the quote at the beginning of this chapter was taken is found at http://www.static.cc.gatech.edu/~tpilsch/AirOps/

index.html. If you have a further interest in learning more about the courageous aviators who flew these incredibly harrowing missions in SEA, I would also recommend, *Sock It to 'Em, Baby: Forward Air Controller in Vietnam* by Garry Cooper and Robert Hiller, *DaNang Diary: A Forward Air Controller's Gunsight View of Combat in Vietnam* by Tom Yarborough, *A Certain Brotherhood* by Jimmie H. Butler, and *Bury Us Upside Down: The Misty Pilots and the Secret Battle for the Ho Chi Minh Trail* by Rick Newman and Don Shepperd.

[2] Forward Air Controllers assigned to support Free World Forces (the ARVN [Army of the Republic of Vietnam], and the ROK [Republic of Korea]) and those who served as sector FACs with specific geographic responsibility were not required to have previously had experience in fighter aircraft. All FACs, however, received special training at the USAF Air-Ground Operations School at Hurlburt Field in Florida, the Survival, Escape, and Evasion School at Fairchild AFB in Washington, and Jungle Survival School at Clark AFB in the Philippines. In addition to the Air Force Forward Air Controllers, the Marines had their own FACs who worked with Navy and Marine assets on the ground.

[3] The Cessna 0-1 "Bird Dog" was replaced by the two-engine Cessna O-2 "Skymaster," both of which served their mission well when the threat consisted primarily of small arms and light machine guns. Later in the war when the enemy began to possess larger caliber machine guns and man-portable surface-to-air missiles, the North American OV-10 "Bronco" became the Forward Air Controller's aircraft of choice because of its higher speed. In high threat areas of Laos and north of the Demilitarized Zone, "Fast FACs" flying two-seat models of the F-100 Super Sabres (call sign, "Misty") and later the F-4 Phantom II (call sign "Wolf") were used to interdict trucks and targets of opportunity along the Ho Chi Minh Trail.

[4] We feel it is important to avoid calling it the "New Selection Process" or the "Modern Selection Process" because we recognize (and hope!) that this is just the first of many improvements and refinements that will be made by different contributors over the coming years. Hopefully, this is just the first generation of the Leadership Selection Process of the future.

CHAPTER 9

[1] Lucier, Schuyt, and Tse, "CEO Succession 2004: The World's Most Prominent Temp Workers," 1.

[2] One of the best textbooks we know covering the basics of project management is Kim Heldman's *Project Management JumpStart.*[TM] 2nd Edition.

[3] Spencer and Spencer, *Competence at Work*, 117–121.

[4] Sonnenfeld and Ward, *Firing Back*, 2.

[5] Wikipedia, http://www.wikipedia.org/wiki/personnel_selection.

[6] Gary Hayes, Interview (June 15, 2008).

[7] Hunt, *Hiring Success*, 119–120.

[8] Wikipedia, http//en.wikipedia.org/wik/Big_Five_personality_traits.

[9] Wikipedia, http//en.wikipedia.org/wiki/Personality_test.

[10] Meyers-Briggs, Myers-Briggs Type Indicator® (MBTI®) instrument, http://www.meyers-briggs.com, and company literature.

[11] Ibid.

[12] 16-Personality Factor Test, http://www.ipat.com.

[13] Hogan Assessments, http//www.hoganassessments.com.

[14] Ibid.

[15] SHL'S Occupational Personality Questionnaire, http://www.shl.com.

[16] Personality Research Form—Form E (PRF), http://www.sigmaassessmentsystems.com.

[17] Kerry Sulkowicz, M.D., Interview (June 6, 2008).

[18] Loehr and Schwartz, *The Power of Full Engagement*, 165–171.

[19] Collins, *Good to Great*; Covey, *The 7 Habits of Highly Effective People*; and Groppel, *The Corporate Athlete*.

[20] Hogan Assessments, http//www.hoganassessments.com.

[21] Barrett, *Liberating the Corporate Soul*.

CHAPTER 10

[1] McCool, *Deciding Who Leads*, 95. Indicates, "But the best decisions about leadership are made with input from those who will report to the new leader because workers often have much to say about what they've witnessed, how they feel about where the organization is heading, and which inside candidates have earned their respect."

[2] Coyne and Coyne, "Surviving Your New CEO," 64.

CHAPTER 12

[1] For additional insight into Mapping the Corporate Lay of the Land, go to www.therightleader.com to see a video overview, sample questions, and examples of the kinds of analytical reports that are generated in conjunction with this work.

[2] Ciampa and Watkins, *Right from the Start*, 29. These authors cite the term as being "borrowed from new-product development in high-tech manufacturing" where it refers to the essential thinking, talking, experimenting, and recording of ideas and concepts that occurs before a project is ever accepted and before the tracking of cost ever begins.

[3] Ibid, 30.

[4] Armstrong, "Comments on Leadership 2008," e-mail correspondence (July 11, 2008).

[5] Ciampa, *Taking Advice*, 82.

CHAPTER 13

[1] Ram Charan, Presentation to the Directorship Institute (December 12, 2007).

[2] Melican, http://www.proxygovernance.com/content/pgi/content/pgi_press_news.

[3] Ciampa and Watkins, *Right from the Start*, 4; and Bradt, Check, and Pedraza, *The New Leader's 100-Day Action Plan*, 1.

[4] Karlsonn, Neilson, and Webster, "CEO Succession 2007: The Performance Paradox," 4; and Lucier, Wheeler, and Habbel, "The Era of the Inclusive Leader, 5." In the latter, Lucier, Wheeler, and Habbel report average CEO tenure in the United States to be 7.8 years, versus less than 5 years as reported in the former. While there appear to be differences in the absolute number of years of tenure for CEOs between the two sources, the fact that the average number of years for a CEO to hold that position has dropped dramatically is indisputable. For the next several years, the calculation of "average years in office" of CEOs will continue to drop, simply as a result of lower turnover years of the late 1990s and early 2000s being replaced by higher turnover years of the mid to late 2000s.

[5] Murray, *Revolt in the Boardroom*, x.

[6] Lucier, Wheeler, and Habbel. "The Era of the Inclusive Leader," 3.

[7] Ibid., 11.

[8] Several sources including: Colvin, "Wanted: CEO of Major Corporation;" Murray, *Revolt in the Boardroom*; Graybow, "New Year Sees Shake-Ups in Corporate America;" and Kirdahy, "Bye-Bye Boss."

[9] Kirdahy, "Bye-Bye Boss."

[10] Gandossy and Sonnenfeld, *Leadership and Governance from the Inside Out*, xii–xv. By my estimation, these six companies accounted for less than 1/10 of 1 percent of the market cap of the New York Stock Exchange at the time their wrongdoings came to light. Nevertheless, for the next several years, the same six companies were mentioned repeatedly in all sorts of media, Often with the implication that their behavior ws representative of untold other corporations on a routine basis.

[11] Montgomery and Kaufman, "The Board's Missing Link," 88.

[12] Ibid.

[13] Bower, The Board Book, 21.

[14] Charan, "Ending the CEO Succession Crisis," 74.

[15] Wiersema, "Holes at the Top: Why CEO Firings Backfire," 77.

[16] National Association of Corporate Directors, "Succession Planning," 20.

[17] RHR International, "Is a Smooth Transition in CEO Leadership Expected?" Slide Handout from the Directorship Search Group Conference (2005).

[18] Corporate Leadership Council, https://www.clc.executiveboard.com/Public/CurrentResearch.

[19] National Association of Corporate Directors, "Succession Planning," 17.

[20] Bower, "Solve the Succession Crisis by Growing Inside-Out Leaders," 91.

[21] Epsen Fuller/IMD, "Global Survey Results 2008: The Chancing Face at the Top," 5.

[22] Karlsonn, Neilson, and Webster, "CEO Succession 2007: The Performance Paradox," 4.

[23] NYSE Rule 303A.09.

[24] National Association of Corporate Directors with Mercer Delta Consulting LLC, "The Role of The Board in Succession Planning."

[25] Charan, "Ending the CEO Succession Crisis," 93.

[26] Epsen Fuller/IMD, "Global Survey Results 2008: The Chancing Face at the Top," 7.

[27] Lucier, Wheeler, and Habbel, "The Era of the Inclusive Leader," 11–12.

[28] Ibid.

[29] Ibid.

[30] Ibid.

[31] Lucier, Schuyt, Handa. "CEO Succession 2003: The Perils of 'Good' Governance," 14.

[32] Charan, "Ending the CEO Succession Crisis," 74.

[33] Ibid., 76.

[34] Landsburg, "In Search of Excellence in CEO Succession: The Seven Habits of Highly Effective Boards," 1.

[35] National Association of Corporate Directors, in collaboration with Mercer Delta Consulting, LLC., "The Role of the Board in CEO Succession."

[36] Ibid., 1–17.

CHAPTER 14

[1] Watkins, The First 90 Days, 3.

[2] The Institute of Executive Development, "Executive Transitions Market Study Summary Report: 2008," 3.

[3] Reese, "Maximizing Your Retention and Productivity with On-Boarding," 24.

Appendix A

LEADER ASSESSMENT INSTRUMENTS

Leader Assessment Instruments

The following are some of the more commonly used tools for assessing a senior executive candidate's abilities, personality and energy, and character. This list is not exhaustive nor does inclusion in it imply any endorsement on the part of the authors, nor do we attest to the accuracy or validity of any tests included in the list. It is provided as a helpful reference for use by hirers interested in becoming more familiar with these kinds of testing vehicles.

Instrument Name	Abilities	Personality & Energy	Character	Source
16PF		X	X	http://www.ipat.com
ASSESS Systems			X	http://www.bigby.com
Benchmarks by The Center for Creative Leadership	X			http://www.ccl.org
Career Assessment Inventory (CAI)	X	X		http://www.pearsonassessments.com
California Psychological Inventory™ (CPI™ 434 Long Form)		X	X	http://www.cpp.com
California Psychological Inventory™ (CPI 260® Short Form)		X	X	http://www.cpp.com
Campbell™ Interest and Skill Survey (CISS®)	X			http://www.pearsonassessments.com
Campbell™ Leadership Index (CLI®)	X		X	http://www.ccl.org/leadership/index.aspx
CentACS's Workplace Big Five		X		http://centacs.com
Comprehensive Personality Profile® (CPP®)		X		http://wonderlic.com
DiSC®		X	X	http://www.discprofile.com
Emotional Competency Inventory (ECI)		X	X	http://www.haygroup.com
Extended DISC®		X		http://www.extendeddisc.com

(continued)

Instrument Name	Abilities	Personality & Energy	Character	Source
Fundamental Interpersonal Relations Orientation–Behavior™ (FIRO-B®)		X		http://www.cpp.com
Guilford-Zimmerman Temperament Survey (GZTS)		X		http://www.pearsonassessments.com
Hogan Development Survey (HDS)		X		http://www.hoganassessments.com
Hogan Personality Inventory (HPI)		X		http://www.hoganassessments.com
Hogan Business Reasoning Inventory (HBRI)	X			http://www.hoganassessments.com
Hogan's Motives, Values, Preferences Inventory (MVPI)			X	http://www.hoganassessments.com
Johnson O'Connor Research Foundation, Inc. Aptitude Test	X			http://www.jocrf.org
Lominger's LEADERSHIP ARCHITECT® Cards	X			http://www.lomingcr.com
Multidimensional Aptitude Battery-II (MAB-II)	X			http://www.sigmaassessmentsystems.com
Myers-Briggs Type Indicator® (MBTI®)		X		http://www.myersbriggs.org
NEO Personality Inventory-Revised (NEO PI-R)		X	X	http://www.sigmaassessmentsystems.com
PDI's Global Personality Inventory		X		http://www.personneldecisions.com
PDI's PROFILOR® Developmental Assessments	X			http://www.personneldecisions.com
Personality Research Form—Form E (PRF)		X	X	http://www.sigmaassessmentsystems.com
Raven's Progressive Matrices	X			http://harcourtassessment.com

(*continued*)

Instrument Name	Abilities	Personality & Energy	Character	Source
SHL's Critical Thinking Test (CTT)	X			http://www.shl.com
SHL's Occupational Personality Questionnaire (OPQ32)		X		http://www.shl.com
StrengthsFinder™	X			https://www.strengthsfinder.com
Watson-Glaser Critical Thinking Appraisal® (WGCTA)	X			http://harcourtassessment.com
Wesman Personnel Classification Test	X			http://harcourtassessment.com
Wonderlic Personnel Test (WPT)	X			http://www.wonderlic.com

Appendix B

CROSS-CULTURAL VIRTUES

APPENDIX B Cross-Cultural Virtues							
Virtues	Greek (a)	Roman (b)	Judaism (c)	Christianity (d)	Islam (e)	Buddhism (f)	Chinese Morality (g)	ψal Universal (h)
Altruistic Joy						X		
Compassion						X		
Contentment					X			
Courage	X				X		X	X
Courtesy					X			
Dignity		X			X			
Discipline		X			X			
Dutifulness		X						
Endurance							X	
Equality			X					
Equanimity						X		
Faith			X		X			
Firmness					X			
Fortitude			X	X				
Frankness					X			
Frugality		X			X			

(*continued*)

Virtues	Greek (a)	Roman (b)	Judaism (c)	Christianity (d)	Islam (e)	Buddhism (f)	Chinese Morality (g)	ψal Universal (h)
APPENDIX B Cross-Cultural Virtues								
Generosity					X			
Good Speech					X			
Gratitude					X			
Gravity		X						
Honesty					X			
Hope			X	X	X			
Humanity		X						X
Humility					X		X	
Humor		X						
Industriousness		X						
Justice	X	X	X	X	X			X
Love (Charity)			X	X				
Loving-Kindness					X	X		
Loyalty					X		X	
Mercy		X	X		X			
Moderation	X				X			

(continued)

APPENDIX B Cross-Cultural Virtues							
Virtues	Greek (a)	Roman (b)	Judaism (c)	Christianity (d)	Islam (e)	Buddhism (f)	Chinese Morality (g)	ψal Universal (h)
Patience					X		X	
Perseverance		X			X		X	
Proper Pride					X			
Prudence		X		X				
Purity					X			
Repentance					X		X	
Respect for Nature			X					
Respectability		X						
Responsibility					X			
Right Actions						X		
Right Effort						X		
Right Livelihood						X		
Right Meditation						X		
Right Mindfulness						X		
Right Speech						X		
Right Values						X		

(continued)

Virtues	Greek (a)	Roman (b)	Judaism (c)	Christianity (d)	Islam (e)	Buddhism (f)	Chinese Morality (g)	ψal Universal (h)
APPENDIX B Cross-Cultural Virtues								
Right Viewpoint						X		
Righteousness					X		X	
Self-Restraint		X			X			
Sincerity					X			
Spiritual Authority		X						
Study & Prayer			X					
Temperance			X	X				X
Tenacity		X						
Tolerance					X			
Transcendence								X
Trust							X	
Trustworthiness					X			
Truthfulness		X	X					
Unity					X			
Wholesomeness		X						
Will							X	

(*continued*)

APPENDIX B Cross-Cultural Virtues								
Virtues	Greek (a)	Roman (b)	Judaism (c)	Christianity (d)	Islam (e)	Buddhism (f)	Chinese Morality (g)	ψal Universal (h)
Wisdom	X				X			X

Sources: (a) http://en.wikipedia.org/wiki/Virtue

(b) http://en.wikipedia.org/wiki/Virtue

(c) http://www.essortment.com and http://www.jewishencyclopedia.com

(d) http://www.changingminds.org

(e) http://www.meccacentric.com

(f) http://en.wikipedia.org/wiki/Virtue

(g) http://en.wikipedia.org/wiki/Virtue

(h) Peterson and Seligman (2004)

Appendix C

FIELD GUIDE OF VITAL INFORMATION REQUEST LIST

1. **Board and Shareholder Information**

   a. Stock Information
      i. List of Analysts who follow the company
      ii. Analysts' Reports— most recent, previous year
   b. Shareholders
      i. List of Major Investors—percentage, changes
      ii. Stock quotes—historical comparison charts
   c. Board of Directors
      i. Profile of Board Members
         1. Background, contact info, relationships between Directors, etc.
      ii. Board Minutes (past 12 months)
   d. Equity positions—Directors and key executives
      i. Shares owned
      ii. Stock options summary

2. **Enterprise-Wide Information**

   a. Corporate Calendar
      i. Board, Committee, and Annual Shareholder meetings
      ii. Executive Committee meetings
      iii. Marketing and Sales conferences, shows, key customer meetings
      iv. Product Development reviews
      v. Operations and Strategic Planning due dates
      vi. Sales, Inventory, Production Meetings
      vii. Financial closing dates
      viii. Analyst calls
      ix. HR event dates (succession planning, headcount reviews, salary planning)
         1. Corporate and religious holidays
         2. Plant Shutdowns
         3. Community Events
   b. Strategic Plan
      i. Previous strategic consulting reviews, reports

3. **Human Resources**

   a. Mission Statement
   b. HR Policies, Employee Handbook
   c. Organizational chart and headcount plan
   d. Strategic Talent Management Report

(continued)

     i. High Potential, rising stars, key contributors—name, job, profile

     ii. Key contributor compensation history

  e. Performance Management System review (merit reviews)

  f. Attitude/workforce engagement surveys

  g. Diversity report

4. Financial Information

  a. Most recent Annual Report, Proxy, 10K, 10Q and earnings announcements

  b. Audit reports and findings (if any)

  c. Income Statement and Balance Sheet

  d. CFO Dashboard

     i. Cash flow

     ii. Monthly and Quarterly Financial and Operational reports

     iii. Receivables aging

  e. Capital spending plan and history

  f. Bank plan

     i. List of Creditors—amounts, terms, rates

     ii. Summary of any covenant issues

5. Operations Information

  a. Daily Dashboard

     i. Sales—actual and variance vs. plan

     ii. Inventory status

     iii. Cost reduction initiatives

     iv. Key marketing programs

  b. List and description of top 20 supplier contracts, contacts, CEOs

6. Marketing and Sales Information

  a. Annual marketing strategy/plan

     i. Media campaigns

     ii. Ad agency contacts

     iii. Advertising tracking reports

  b. Product catalogs

  c. Sales channel plans for current year

  d. Territory and Salesperson recap

     i. Territory sales recap (last year, YTD)

  e. List and description of top 20 customer contracts, contacts, CEOs

  f. Key Account summaries

(continued)

7. Product
   a. Product research and market research (past 12 months)
   b. Product development process description and pipeline status
   c. Product safety
   d. R&D spending history

8. Manufacturing and Sourcing
   a. Inventory turnover history, current plan, YTD run rates
   b. Facilities list
      i. Safety reports by site
      ii. OSHA reports
      iii. Plan metrics, tracking reports
   c. Map, contact at sites
   d. Key suppliers—contacts, history of relationships

9. Legal/Risk/IT
   a. List and description of legal issues—spending, history
   b. Current risk assessment
      i. Strategic, financial, operational, product
   c. IT review

Bibliography

16-Personality Factor Test, http://www.ipat.com.

Alcoholics Anonymous World Services, Inc. *Twelve Steps and Twelve Traditions*. New York: Hazelden, 1986.

American Psychological Association. Available at http://psychologymatters.apa.org.

Anastasi, Anne. *Psychological Testing*, (5th ed.). New York: Macmillan, 1982.

Bains, Gurnek. *Meaning Inc.: The Blueprint for Business Success in the 21st Century*. London: Profile Books Ltd, 2007.

Barbaro, Michael , and Eric Dash. "Another Outsider Falls Casualty to Nike's Insider Culture." *New York Times*, (January 24, 2006.).

Barrett, Richard. *Building a Value-Driven Organization: A Whole System Approach to Cultural Transformation*. Oxford, UK: Butterworth-Heinemann, 2006.

———. *Liberating the Corporate Soul: Building a Visionary Organization*. Oxford, UK: Butterworth-Heinemann, 1998.

Bennis, Warren. *On Becoming A Leader: The Leadership Classic—Updated And Expanded*. New York: Perseus, 2003.

Bernick, Carol Lavin. "When Your Culture Needs a Makeover." *Harvard Business Review* 79 (June 2001): 5–11.

Betof, Edward, and Frederic Harwood. *Just Promoted! How to Survive and Thrive in Your First 12 Months as a Manager*. New York: McGraw-Hill, 1992.

Blaine, Lee. *The Power Principle: Influence with Honor*. New York: Free Press, 1998.

Booz Allen Hamilton. "CEO Turnover in 2002: Trends, Causes, and Lessons Learned." *Booz Allen Hamilton, Inc.*, 2002.

———. "Global CEO Turnover Set New Record in 2005." *Booz Allen Hamilton Press Release*, (May 18, 2006.).

———. "Measuring and Analyzing Corporate Values During Major Transformations." *Booz Allen Hamilton, Inc. Research Reports*, (June 16, 2004.).

Bossidy, Larry, and Ram Charan, with Charles Burck. *Execution: The Discipline of Getting Things Done.* New York: Crown Publishers, 2002.

Bowen, William G. *The Board Book: An Insider's Guide for Directors and Trustees.* New York, NY: W.W. Norton, 2008.

Bower, Joseph L."Solve the Succession Crisis by Growing Inside-Outside Leaders." *Harvard Business Review* (November 2007).

Boy Scouts of America. www.bsa.com.

Bradt, George B., Jayme A. Check, and Jorge Pedraza. *The New Leader's 100-Day Action Plan: How to Take Charge, Build Your Team, and Get Immediate Results.* Hoboken, NJ: Wiley, 2006.

Brassard, Michael, and Diane Ritter. *GE Capital Services Memory Jogger*™ *II: A Pocket Guide of Tool for Quality.* Methuen, MA: GOAL/QPC, 1994.

Broadley, Margaret E. *Your Natural Gifts: How to Recognize and Develop Them for Success and Self-Fulfillment.* McLean, VA: EPM Publications, Inc., 1991.

Buckingham, Marcus. "What Great Managers Do." *Harvard Business Review* (March 1, 2005).

Buckingham, Marcus, and Donald O. Clifton. *NOW, Discover Your Strengths.* New York: The Free Press, 2001.

Buckingham, Marcus, and Curt Coffman. *First, Break All the Rules: What the World's Greatest Managers Do Differently.* New York: Simon & Schuster, 1999.

Burson-Marsteller. "2005 Year-End CEO Succession Tracking Survey," http://www. accessmylibrary.com.

"Bush Administration Stepping Up Obscenity Precautions," *USA Today* (May 4, 2003).

Butler, Jimmie H. *A Certain Brotherhood.* Lancaster, PA: Stealth Press, 2002.

Campbell, Michael, Jessica Innis Baites, André Martin, and Kyle Meddings. "The Stress of Leadership." Center for Creative Leadership (CCL) Research White Paper, 2007.

CEOGO. Burson-Marsteller, www.ceogo.com

Challenger, Gray, & Christmas. "370 CEO Departures in First Quarter." *Challenger, Gray, & Christmas Press Release*, (April 7, 2008.)

Charan, Ram. "Conquering a Culture of Indecision." *Harvard Business Review* 79 (April 2001): 74–82.

———. "Ending the CEO Succession Crisis." *Harvard Business Review* 83 (February 2005): 72–81.

———. "Home Depot's Blueprint for Culture Change." *Harvard Business Review* 84 (April 2006): 60–70.

Charan, Ram, Stephen Drotter, and James Noel. *The Leadership Pipeline: How to Build the Leadership Powered Company.* San Francisco: Jossey-Bass, 2001.

Chatman, Jennifer A., and Sandra Eunyoung Cha. "Leading by Leveraging Culture." *California Management Review* 45 (Summer 2003): 20–34.

Ciampa, Dan. *Taking Advice: How Leaders Get Good Counsel and Use it Wisely.* Boston: Harvard Business School Press, 2006.

Ciampa, Dan, and Michael Watkins. *Right from the Start: Taking Charge in a New Leadership Role*. Boston: Harvard Business School Press, 1999.

Citrin, James M., and Richard A. Smith. *The Five Patterns of Extraordinary Careers*. New York: Crown, 2003.

Clemons, Eric K., and Jason A. Santamaria. "Maneuver Warfare: Can Modern Military Strategy Lead You to Victory?" *Harvard Business Review* (April 2002).

Collins, James C. *Good to Great: Why Some Companies Make the Leap and Others Don't*. New York: HarperCollins, 2001.

———. "Level 5 Leadership: The Triumph of Humility and Fierce Resolve." *Harvard Business Review OnPoint* 79 (January 2001): 18–28.

Collins, James C., and Jerry I. Porras. *Built to Last: Successful Habits of Visionary Companies*. New York: HarperCollins, 1994.

Colvin, Geoff. "How Top Companies Breed Stars." *Fortune*, (September 20, 2007.)

———. "Wanted: CEO of Major Corporation:" *Fortune*, (November 5, 2007.)

Cooper, Garry, and Robert Hiller. *Sock It to 'Em Baby: Forward Air Controller in Vietnam*. St. Leonards NSW, Australia: Allen and Unwin, 2006.

Covey, Stephen R. *Principle Centered Leadership*. New York: Simon & Schuster, 1991.

———. *The 7 Habits of Highly Effective People: Restoring the Character Ethic*. New York: Simon & Schuster, 1989.

Covey, Stephen M.R., with Rebecca R. Merrill. *The Speed of Trust: The One Thing That Changes Everything*. New York: Free Press, 2006.

Coyne, Kevin P., and Edward J. Coyne Sr. "Surviving Your New CEO." *Harvard Business Review* 85 (May 2007): 62–69.

Dalton, Catherine M. "Executive Focus: Values, Relationships, and Organizational Culture: Principled Leadership at Brightpoint, Inc." *Business Horizons* (January 2005).

Dauphinas, William G., and Colin Price. *Straight from the CEO: The World's Top Business Leaders Reveal Ideas That Every Manager Can Use*. New York: Simon & Schuster, 1998.

Deal, Terrance E., and Allan A. Kennedy. *Corporate Cultures*. New York: Basic Books, 1982.

———. *Corporate Cultures: The Rites and Rituals of Corporate Life*. Cambridge, MA: Perseus Book Group LLC, 2000.

DeSmet, Aaron, Mark Loch, and Bill Schaninger. "The Link Between Profits and Organizational Performance" *The McKinsey Quarterly* 3 (August 2007).

Donlon, J. P. "Time Out Between Nardelli Meltdowns." *Chief Executive*, (January 9, 2007). http://www.chiefexecutive.net.

Dotlich, David L., and Peter C. Cairo. *Why CEOs Fail: The 11 Behaviors That Can Derail Your Climb to the Top—and How To Manage Them*. San Francisco: Jossey-Bass, 2003.

Drucker, Peter F. "Managing Oneself." *Harvard Business Review* (March–April 1999).

DuBois, Philip. "A Test-Dominated Society: China 1115 B.C.–1905 A.D." In *Readings in Psychological Tests and Measurements*, ed. N. I. Barnette Jr. Baltimore: The Williams & Wilkins Company, 1964.

Epsen Fuller/IMD. "Global Survey Results 2008: The Changing Face at the Top." Morristown, NJ: Epsen Fuller, 2008.

Ferguson, Reginald. "Moral and Character Development." http://chiron.valdosta. edu/whuitt/col/morchr/morchr.html, 2004.

Finkelstein, Sydney. *Why Smart Executives Fail: and What You Can Learn from Their Mistakes*. New York: Portfolio, 2003.

Fischer, Peter. *The New Boss: How to Survive the First 100 Days*. London: Kogan Page Limited, 2007.

Fisher, Anne. "Don't Blow Your New Job." *Fortune*, June 22, 1998.

Fry, Ron. *Ask the Right Questions, Hire the Best People* (Revised ed.). Franklin Lakes, NJ: Book-Mart Press, 2006.

Gabarro, John J. *The Dynamics of Taking Charge*. Boston, MA: Harvard Business School Press, 1987.

Galford, Robert, and Anne Seibold Drapeau. "The Enemies of Trust." *Harvard Business Review* 81 (February 2003): 88–95.

Gandossy, Robert, and Jeffery Sonnenfeld. *Leadership and Governance from the Inside Out*. Hoboken, NJ: Wiley, 2004.

"Gary Forsee's Lavish Exit Package," *Business Week* (October 10, 2006).

Girl Scouts of America. www.gsusa.com.

Goffee, Rob, and Gareth Jones. "What Holds the Modern Company Together?" *Harvard Business Review* (January 20, 1999).

Goldsmith, Marshall, and Mark Reiter. *What Got You Here Won't Get You There: How Successful People Become Even More Successful!* New York: Hyperion, 2007.

Goleman, Daniel. *Emotional Intelligence: Why It Can Matter More Than IQ*. New York: Bantam Books, 1997.

Goodes, Melvin R. "Transforming the Culture of a Global Enterprise . . . One Employee at a Time." In *Straight From The CEO: The World's Top Business Leaders Reveal Ideas That Every Manager Can Use*, ed. William G. Dauphinas and Collin Price, 189–198. New York: Simon & Schuster, 1998.

"Grasso Ordered to Return NYSE Pay," NPR Morning Edition (October 20, 2006).

Graybow, Martha. "New Year Sees Shake-Ups in Corporate America." Reuters (January 9, 2008). http://www.baselinemag.com.

Groppel, Jack, and Bob Andelman. *The Corporate Athlete: How to Achieve Maximal Performance in Business and Life*. New York: Wiley, 1998.

Groysberg, Boris, and Scott Snook. "The Pine Street Initiative at Goldman Sachs." *Harvard Business Review* (November 14, 2006).

Hall, Maj. Brian F., and Col. David A. Wagie. "The U.S. Air Force Academy's Cutting-Edge Character Development Program." *Airpower Journal 10* (Summer 1996):35–39.

Hamel, Gary, and C. K. Prahalad. *Competing for the Future*. Boston: Harvard Business School Press, 1997.

Harris, Philip R. *The New Work Culture*. Amherst, MA: HRD Press, 1998.

Heldman, Kim. *Project Management JumpStart*: 2nd ed. San Francisco: Jossey-Bass, 2005.

Hempel, Jessie. "Why the Boss Really Had to Say Goodbye." *Business Week*, (July 4, 2005).

Hesselbein, Frances, Marshall Goldsmith, and Richard Beckhard. *The Organization of the Future*. San Francisco, CA: Jossey-Bass, 1997.

Hock, Dee. *Birth of the Chaordic Age*. San Francisco, CA: Berrett-Koehler Publishers, Inc., 1999.

Hodgson, Paul.wwwthecorporatelibrary (June 23, 2008).

Hoevemeyer, Victoria A. *High-Impact Interview Questions: 701 Behavior-Based Questions to Find the Right Person for Every Job*. New York: AMACOM, 2006.

Hogan Assessments. http//www.hoganassessments.com.

Holmes, Stanley. "Nike's CEO Gets the Boot." *Business Week* (January 24, 2006).

Hunt, Steven. *Hiring Success: The Art and Science of Staffing Assessment and Employee Selection*. San Francisco: Pfeiffer, 2007.

The Institute of Executive Development. "Executive Transitions Market Study Summary Report: 2008." http://www.execsight.com.

Jackson, Mike, and Tara Dixon-Engel. *Naked in Da Nang: A Forward Air Controller in Vietnam*. St. Paul, MN: Zenith Press, 2004.

Kaihla, Paul. "The CEO's Secret Handbook" *Business 2.0*, 6 (July 2005).

Karlsson, Per-Ola, Gary L. Neilson, and Juan Carlos Webster. "CEO Succession 2007: The Performance Paradox" *Strategy + Business* 51 (Summer 2007): 1–12.

Kidder, Rushworth M. *Moral Courage: Taking Action When Your Values Are Put to the Test*. New York: HarperCollins Publishers, 2005.

King, Jr., Martin Luther. "The Purpose of Education." In *The Papers of Martin Luther King, Jr., Volume I: Called to Serve, January 1929–June 1951*. Atlanta, GA: The King Center, 1985.

Kirdahy, Matthew. "Bye-Bye Boss." *Forbes* (December 18, 2007). http://www.forbes.com.

Klann, Gene. *Building Character: Strengthening the Heart of Good Leadership*. San Francisco: Jossey-Bass, 2006.

Koepp, Steve, ed. "Fortune 500: America's Largest Corporations." *Fortune* (May 5, 2008), 225–235.

Kotter, John P., and James L. Heskett. *Corporate Culture and Performance*. New York: The Free Press, 1992.

Lafferty, J. Clayton. *LSI-1: Life Styles Inventory Guide Book*. Chicago: Human Synergistics International, 2004.

Landsburg, Max. "In Search of Excellence in CEO Succession: The Seven Habits of Highly Effective Boards." *Heidrick and Struggles*, 2006.

"Leadership Fundamentals: Chart Your Course to Great Leadership." *Harvard Business Review Article Collection*. Boston: Harvard Business School Publishing Corporation, 2006.

"Leadership IQ Study: Why New Hires Fail." *Leadership IQ Press Release* (September 20, 2005).

"Leadership IQ Study: Mismanagement, Inaction Among the Real Reasons Why CEOs Get Fired." *Leadership IQ Press Release* (June 20, 2005).

Lee, Blaine. *The Power Principle: Influence with Honor*. New York: Simon & Schuster, 1997.

Leslie, Jean Brittain, Maxine Dalton, Christopher Ernst, and Jennifer Deal. *Managerial Effectiveness in a Global Context*. Greensboro, NC: CCL Press, 2002.

Loehr, Jim, and Tony Schwartz. *The Power of Full Engagement: Managing Energy, Not Time, Is the Key to High Performance and Personal Renewal*. New York: Free Press, 2003.

Lucht, John. *Rites of Passage at $100,000 to $1 Million+: Your Insider's Lifetime Guide to Executive Job-Changing and Faster Career Progress*. New York: The Viceroy Press, Inc., 2004.

Lucier, Chuck, Paul Kocourek, and Rolf Habbel. "CEO Succession 2005: The Crest of the Wave." *Strategy + Business* 43 (Summer 2006).

Lucier, Chuck, Rob Schuyt, Junichi Handa. "CEO Succession 2003: The Perils of 'Good' Governance." *Strategy + Business* 35 (Summer 2004).

Lucier, Chuck, Rob Schuyt, and Edward Tse. "CEO Succession 2004: The World's Most Prominent Temp Workers." *Strategy + Business* 39 (Summer 2005).

Lucier, Chuck, Eric Spiegel, and Rob Schuyt. "Why CEOs Fail: The Causes and Consequences of Turnover at the Top." *Strategy + Business* 28 (Third Quarter 2002).

Lucier, Chuck, Steven Wheeler, and Rolf Habbel. "CEO Succession 2006: The Era of the Inclusive Leader." *Strategy + Business* 47 (Summer 2007).

Lynn, Adele B. *The EQ Interview: Finding Employees with High Emotional Intelligence*. New York: AMACOM, 2008.

Maddux, Robert B. *Quality Interviewing: Third Edition*. Menlo Park, CA: Crisp Publication Inc., 1994.

Martin, André. "The Changing Nature of Leadership: A CCL Research White Paper." Greensboro, NC: Center for Creative Leadership, 2007. 1–23.

McCool, Joseph Daniel. *Deciding Who Leads: How Executive Recruiters Drive, Direct & Disrupt the Global Search for Leadership Talent*. Mountain View, CA: Davies-Black Publishing, 2008.

McDonnell, Patrick M. *Everybody Wants To Go To Heaven*. Colorado Springs: Sunrise Publishing, 2002.

Melican, James P. http://www.proxygovernance.com/content/pgi/content/pgi_press_news.shtml

Mendels, Pamela. "The Real Cost of Firing a CEO." *Chief Executive* 177 (April 2002): 40–45.

Merriam-Webster, ed. *Webster's New World Dictionary, 2nd ed*. New York: Prentice Hall Press, 1986.

Merriam-Webster, ed. *Merriam-Webster's Collegiate Dictionary, 11th Revised Edition*. Springfield, MA: Merriam-Webster, 2003.

Montgomery, Cynthia A., and Rhonda Kaufman. "The Board's Missing Link." *Harvard Business Review* 81 (March 2003): 86–93.

Mornell, Pierre. *Hiring Smart!* Berkeley, CA: Ten Speed Press, 1998.

Morrison Terri, and Wayne A. Conaway. *Kiss, Bow, or Shake Hands* (2nd ed.). Avon, MA: Adams Media, 2006.

Mourkogiannis, Nikos. *Purpose: The Starting Point of Great Companies.* New York: Palgrave Macmillan, 2006.

Munck, Bill, Robert Kegan, Lisa Laskow Lahe, Debra E. Meyerson, Donald Sull, Katherine M. Hudson, and Paul F. Levy. *Harvard Business Review on Culture and Change.* Boston, MA: Harvard Business School Publishing Corporation, 2002.

Murray, Alan. *Revolt in the Boardroom: The Rules of Power in Corporate America.* New York: HarperCollins, 2007.

Myers-Briggs. Myers-Briggs Type Indicator® (MBTI®) instrument. http://www.myers-briggs.com.

Nash, Laura, and Howard Stevenson. *Just Enough: Tools for Creating Success in Your Work and Life.* Hoboken, NJ: Wiley, 2004. National Association of Corporate Directors. "Succession Planning." Boardroom Briefing, (November, 2004).

National association of Corporate Directors. "Succession Planning." Best Practices Study NACD, 2004.

National Association of Corporate Directors, in collaboration with Mercer Delta Consulting, LLC. "The Role of the Board in CEO Succession." Best Practices Study. NACD, 2006.

National Defense University. "Strategic Leadership and Decision Making." In *Organizational Culture* 16. St. Louis: National Defense University Press, 1999. Available at http://www.au.af.mil/au/awc/awcgate/ndu/strat-ldr-dm.

Neff, Thomas J., and James M. Citrin. *You're in Charge—Now What?: The 8 Point Plan.* New York: Crown, 2005.

Neff, Thomas J., and James M. Citrin, with Paul B. Brown. *Lessons from the Top: The 50 Most Successful Business Leaders in America—and What You Can Learn From Them.* New York: Doubleday, 1999.

Newman, Rick, and Don Shepperd. *Bury Us Upside Down: The Misty Pilots and the Secret Battle for the Ho Chi Minh Trail.* New York: Presidio Press, 2007.

"Nike Inc. Appoints William D. Perez President, Chief Executive Officer, and Director Effective December 28, 2004." http://www.Nikebiz.com (November 18, 2004).

"Nike Inc. Names Mark Parker CEO, William D. Perez Resigns." http://www.Nikebiz.com (January 23, 2006).

Norton, Jennifer. "CEO Departures at All-Time High." http://www.ceogo.com (November 2005).

Opinion Research Corporation. "Putting Customers First." *Opinion Research Corporation.* New York Stock Exchange (NYSE) CEO Report, 2008.

Penn, Mark J., and Kinney Zalesne. *Microtrends: The Small Forces Behind Tomorrow's Big Changes.* New York: Twelve-Hachette Book Group USA, 2007.

Personality Research Form—Form E (PRF), http://www.sigmaassessmentsystems.com.

Peters, Thomas J., and Robert H. Waterman Jr. *In Search of Excellence: Lessons from America's Best-Run Companies*. New York: Harper and Row Publishers, 1982.

Peterson, Christopher, and Martin E.P. Seligman. *Character Strengths and Virtues: A Handbook and Classification*. New York: Oxford University Press & American Psychological Association, 2004.

Reese, Victoria. "Maximizing Your Retention and Productivity with On-Boarding." 2005. http://www.heidrich.com.

Renckly, Richard G. *Human Resources* (2nd ed.). Hauppauge, NY: Barron's Educational Series, Inc., 2004.

"Résumé Trouble," *The Wall Street Journal*" (March 3, 2006).

Right Management Consultants. "Research: Building Relationships is Key to New Leader Survival, Success." *Communique* (May 10, 2005).

Riso, Don Richard, and Russ Hudson. *Personality Types: Using the Enneagram for Self-Discovery*. New York: Houghton Mifflin Company, 1996.

"Robert L. Nardelli," http://en.wikipedia.org/wiki/Robert_Nardelli.

Schein, Edgar H. *Organizational Culture and Leadership* (3rd ed.). San Francisco, CA: Jossey-Bass, 2004.

Seligman, Martin. *Authentic Happiness: Using the New Positive Psychology to Realize Your Potential for Lasting Fulfillment*. New York: Free Press, 2004.

SHL'S Occupational Personality Questionnaire, http://www.shl.com.

"Short Tenure: O'Leary Out at Notre Dame after One Week," *Sports Illustrated*, December 14, 2001. http://www.si.com.

Smart, Bradford D. *Topgrading: How Leading Companies Win by Hiring, Coaching, and Keeping the Best People*. New York: Penguin Group, 2005.

Sonnenfeld, Jeffrey, and Andrew Ward. *Firing Back: How Great Leaders Rebound After Career Disasters*. Boston, MA: Harvard Business School Press, 2007.

Spencer, Jr., Lyle M., and Signe M. Spencer. *Competence at Work: Models for Superior Performance*. Hoboken, NJ: Wiley, 1993.

Spencer Stuart. "Cornerstone of the Board: The New Steps Of Director Search." (October 2004). http://www.spencerstuart.com/practices/boards/publications/788/.

Stoddard, Nat, and Claire Wyckoff. "Succession Planning—A Higher Order of Thinking," *Directorship* (October–November, 2008).

———. "Identifying and Understanding Corporate Culture for Success in Leadership" *MWorld* (Winter 2008).

———. "The Importance of Understanding Corporate Culture for Leadership Success," *Leadership Excellence* (February 2009).

———. "Playing by the Numbers—Reducing the Costs of Leadership Failure," *HR.com* (January 2009).

———. "Importance of Creating A Field Guide For Newly Hired Leaders," *HR Professional* (February/March 2009).

———. "Importance Of Creating A Field Guide For Newly Hired Leaders," *TrainingMag.com* (Winter 2009).

———. "The Costs of CEO Failure," *Chief Executive* (January 2009.)

———. "Strategies for Defining, Measuring and Clarifying Corporate Cultures," *Talent Management*, May 2009).

Strack, Rainer, Jens Baier, and Anders Fahlander. Harvard Business Essentials. *Hiring and Keeping the Best People*. Boston: Harvard Business School Publishing Corporation, 2002.

Swanson, William H. *Swanson's Unwritten Rules of Management*. Waltham, MA: Raytheon Company, 2004.

Urdang, Laurence, ed. *American Century Dictionary*. New York: Grand Central Publishing, 1996.

Vestring, Till, Brian King, and Ted Rouse. "Should You Always Merge Cultures?" Harvard Management Update (May 2003).

Waldrop, Sharon Anne. *The Everything Human Resource Management Book*. Cincinnati, OH: Adams Media, 2008.

Watkins, Michael. *The First 90 Days: Critical Success Strategies for New Leaders at All Levels*. Boston: Harvard Business School Press, 2003.

Weber, Joseph, and Pallavi Gogi. "Why Wrigley and Perez Need Each Other." *Business Week*, October 23, 2006.

Weber Shandwick. "New Study Reveals Global 500 CEO Ousters on the Rise While North American CEO Turnover Declines." *Weber Shandwick Press Release* (November 28, 1997).

Wiersema, Margarethe. "Holes at the Top: Why CEO Firings Backfire." *Harvard Business Review* 80 (December 2002): 70–77.

Wikipedia Contributors. *Wikipedia, the Free Encyclopedia*, http//en.wikipedia.org/wiki/Big_Five_personality_traits.

———. http//en.wikipedia.org/wiki/moral_character.

———. http//en.wikipedia.org/wiki/Personality_test.

———. http//en.wikipedia.org/wiki/personnel_selection.

———. http//en.wikipedia.org/wiki/Robert_Nardelli.

Yarborough, Tom. *Da Nang Diary: A Forward Air Controller's Gunsight View of Combat in Vietnam*. New York: St. Martin's Press, 2002.

Zweifel, Thomas D. *Culture Clash: Managing the Global High Performance Team*. New York: Select Books Inc., 2003.

Index

abilities, 43–59
  about, 43
  importance of, 43–44
  interviewing executives to
    measure, 44–45
  job description. *See* job
    specifications.
  specialized tools for assessment of,
    55–57
ability vs. personality, 29
accelerated leader selection process
  applicability of use elsewhere, 262
  overview of, 213–214
  steps of, 214–233
actions
  vs. outcomes, 101–102
  speaking louder than words, 65–66
Adelphi Communcations, 239
administrative support, functions of,
  169–170, 253
Alcoa, 240
alignment
  and fit, 81
  today and tomorrow, 92–94
American Express, 238
AOL Time-Warner, 240
aptitude testing, 56
ARA International, 242

Armstrong, Meg, 63, 70
artifacts, 117
assessments of
  abilities, 55-57
  aptitude, 56
  character, 163–164
  culture, 125–126, 184–189
  energy, 162
  intelligence (IQ), 157–158
  leadership team, 181–184
  needs, 106–107, 173–179
  personality, 157–161
  values, 164–165
  See also Appendix A.
assessment tools of culture
  Booz Allen Hamilton, 125
  Crenshaw Associatess Mapping
    the Corporate Lay of the
    Land, 165, 184–191, 199–210
  Richard Barrett Values Assessment
    Process, 125, 165
assessment tools of individuals
  16-Personality Factor Inventory
    (16-PF), 160–161
  Character Interview, 83–84,
    162–164
  Crenshaw Associatess Team
    Topography, 181–182

energy assessment, 162
  Hogan Motives, Values
    Preferences Inventory
    (MVPI), 165
  Hogan Suite of Assessments,
    160–161
  in general, 157–158
  intelligence quotient (IQ) testing,
    55
  Jackson Personality Research
    Form (PRF), 161
  Johnson O'Connor Aptitude Test,
    56, 67
  Myers-Briggs® (MBTI®),
    159–160
  Occupational Personality
    Questionnaire (OPQ320),
    161
  psycho-behavioral interview, 161
  StrengthsFinder® Profile, 56–57
  three-, six-, and twelve-month
    progress reports, 229–233,
    256
A.T. Kearney, 31

Baines, Gurneck, 120
Barrett, Richard, 120, 125, 132, 165
basic assumptions, 117
Bear Stearns, 241
behavior assessment expert,
  functions of, 172
behavior assessment techniques. *See*
  assessments and assessment
  tools.
behavioral-based interviewer, 47
behavioral-based interviews, 49–50
behavioral-event interviews. *See*
  behavioral-based interviews.
behavioral-event questions, 50
beliefs
  defined, 81–82
  importance in selection process,
    83–84

  part of the Character Interview,
    163, 164
benchmarks, 12
benefits of knowing the lay of the
  land, 144–145
Bennis, Warren, 88
The Birth of the Chaordic Age (Hock),
  92
"blind leading the blind" syndrome,
  225
Boeing, 239
Bolens merger vignette, 272–275
Booz Allen Hamilton, 7, 94, 99, 130,
  243
Bossidy, Larry, 77, 103, 123
Bower, Joseph, 130, 243
Boy Scouts (BSA) Law, 86
brainteaser interview questions, 48
Bridendolph, Barb, xvi
Bristol–Meyers Squibb, 241
Buckingham, Marcus, 56
Building Character (Klann), 77
Built to Last (Collins and Portas), 118
Burke, Jim, 123
Business assessment expert, functions
  of, 168, 195
business process summary, 194
business terrain research
  data processing and use of,
    179–181
  developing 174–179
  purpose of, 173–174

Cairo, Peter, 64
CAMCO, Inc., 27
Cattell, Raymond, 160
Center for Creative Leadership, 79
Center for Executive Development,
  94
CEO failures
  costs of, 5–11
  internal vs. external, 3, 130–131
  global statistics, 240

reasons for, 100, 242
U.S. statistics, xi, xv, 3–5, 100, 105
vs. U.S. military, 143
CEO Role Today
vs. ten years ago, 240–241
complexity, 270–271
CEO succession plans. See
Succession Planning.
CEO Succession Study
NACD (2004), 99
NACD (2006), 250–251
Cha, Sandra, 117, 123
Challenger, Gray & Christmas, 3
Character
assessments of, 163–164
bucket, 75–95
changing of, 87
constituents of, 94
defined, 76–77
described, 76–77
difficult to question, 32
elements of, 33
feeding of, 85–86
formation of, 86–87
interview, 163–164, 221–222
malleability of, 190
of the candidate, 31, 32
people who lack, 32
taboos on discussion of, 32–34,
75–76
traits of leaders. See Universal
Character Traits of Leaders.
"Character Is Who You Are"
(Ferguson), 77
Charan, Ram, 77, 103, 123, 239, 242,
246
Chatman, Jennifer, 117, 123
Chrysler, 241
Churchill, Winston, 261
Ciampa, Dan, 222, 227
Citigroup, 241
Clemon, Eric, 134
C-Level, 3

coaching, 38, 88, 99, 123,226–227.
See also executive coaching.
Collins, Jim, 32, 118, 130, 162
Competence at Work (Spencer and
Spencer), 46, 154
competency-based behavioral
interviews (CBBI), 49, 51
confrontations and buy-in, 225–226
The Corporate Athlete (Groppel), 162
corporate calendar, 194
corporate culture. See culture and
subcultures.
Corporate Leadership Counsel
(CLC), 242
The Corporate Library, 4
cost/benefits, 267
costs of leadership failure. See
leadership failures.
courage, 80–81
Covey, Stephen M.R., 132
Covey, Stephen R., 32, 162
Crenshaw Associates, 6, 125–126,
130, 165
Bridendolph, Barb (CEO), xvi
client experiences, 90–91
coaching, xv–xvi, 12,90–91,230
Forward Assessment Consulting,
xv–xvi, 144–147
Mapping the Corporate Lay of the
Land, xii, 125–126, 180, 184–
186, 186–190
Match-Fit Model, xvi, 28–32, 35,
152
outplacemement, xii, xv–xvi, 6, 44,
82, 101, 154
résumé development, 44, 154
www.therightleader.com, 187, 190,
196, 210
critical success factors, 176
C-Suite, 14, 45, 259
Culture
as "soft stuff," xxi, 34, 120–122,
196, 270

Culture (*Continued*)
  assessment of, 125–126, 184–189
  changing, 122–123
  debunking myths of, 116–129
  definition of, 115
  elements of, 115
  formation of, 86–87
  global, 118–119
  importance of, 15
  in business terrain research, 177
  next frontier, 270–272
  Nike and William Perez story,
    xx–xxi, 13, 17–18, 5
cultural myths. *See* culture,
    debunking cultural myths.

Deal, Terrance, 116, 117
deliverables, 13, 18, 36, 101, 107,
    145, 153, 155, 164, 225
design for a new selection model. *See*
    Leader Selection Process.
dimensional type test, 159
directional needs, 36–37, 104–106,
    146, 200, 261
  and executional needs, xii, 37–38,
    102, 173, 187, 254, 264
Disney, 116
Dotlich, David, 64
Drapeau, Anne Seibold, 89
Drucker, Peter F., 89

early wins, 176
EBITDA, 120
Educational Psychology Interactive
    Web site, 77
Einstein, Albert, 151
Eliot, T.S., 1
emotional quotient (EQ), 51
emotional quotient (EQ) and BEI/
    CBBI, 50–51
Emotional Quotient (Goleman), 50
"The Enemies of Trust" (Galford
    and Drapeau), 89

energy
  assessment techniques of, 162
  importance of in selection, 69–70
  of the candidate, 31–32, 69–70
Enron, 240
Epsen Fuller/IMD survey, 243
exceptional severance items, 6–7
Execution (Bossidy and Charan), 77,
    103, 123
executional needs, xii, 37–38, 102,
    173, 187, 254, 264
  and directional needs, 36–37,
    104–106, 146, 200, 261
execution vs. tactics, 103
executive coaching, 215, 224–229,
    234, 248, 263
Executive Leadership Team (ELT)
    defined, 170
executive selection process. *See*
    leader Selection Process.
extended leader selection process,
    145–146, 224, 233, 255, 257,
    265, 268
  overview of, 214
  steps of, 248–250
  when to use, 213, 250, 262
external candidates vs. internal
    candidates, 3, 130–131, 267

fable of the wise old Indian and the
    young brave, 85
fact-finding interviewer, 46
failure
  reactions to, 10–11, 64–65, 87–88
  statistics, xi, xv, 3–5, 100, 105,
    130–131-, 240
  traits of, 63–65
  See also CEO failures and non-
    CEO failures.
false résumés, 33
Fannie Mae, 241
Federal Reserve Bank, 7
feeding of character, 85–86

Ferguson, Reginald, 77
field guide of vital information
    contents of, 192–193
    creation of, 191–192
    See also Appendix C
Finklestein, Sydney, 63, 93
Fiorino, Carly, 5
Firing Back (Sonnenfeld), 155
First 100 Days (Watkins), 225
fit
    and alignment, 81
    clues to lack of, 134–135
    defined, 28
    with culture is key, 15–17
five-factor model, 159
fluidity, 134
forced turnover rate, 240–241
Ford Motor Company, 239
Ford, Henry, 123
formation of character, 86–87
Forsee, Gary, 5
forward air controllers (FACs),
        141–143, 262
forward assessment consulting (FAC)
        team, 146–147, 262
    behavior assessment expert, 171
    business assessment expert, 171
    confidential administrative
        support, 171
    functions of, 170–172
    project leader, 170
    purpose of, 172–173
    research expert, 170–171
    selection of, 169–170
full engagement, 31
fuzzy front end, 13, 213, 220–222,
        247

Gaines-Ross, Leslie, 239
Galford, Robert, 89
GardenWay Inc.
Character Interview example, 83–84
lessons learned re trust, 272–275

GE (General Electric), 25
Genesys Solutions, LLC., 187
ghosts in the office, 179
Girl Scouts of America (GSUSA)
        Law, 86
Global Crossing, 239
global culture, 118–119
globalization, 119
GM (General Motors), 268
Goffee, Robert, 116
Goldman Sachs, 129
Goldsmith, Marshall, 131
Goleman, Daniel, 50, 69
Goodes, Melvin, 116
good-old-folk networks, 32
Good to Great (Collins), 32, 79, 130,
        162
Grasso, Richard, 6
Groppel, Jack, 162
gut feel, 32–33, 144, 268–269

Hamel, Gary, 50
Hancy, Hank, 226
Harmon, Butch, 226
Harvard Business Review, 89, 130,
        134, 243
*Harvard Essentials Guide: Hiring and
        Keeping the Best People*, 45
Hayes, Gary, 157–158
Hayes, Brunswick, and Partners,
        157
Heidrich and Struggles, 246
Hewlett Packard, 5
Hiring and Keeping the Best People
        (Strack and Fahlander), 53
hiring. *See* Selection Process.
Hiring Smart! (Mornell), 54–55
Hiring Success (Hunt), 158
Hock, Dee, 92
Hodgson, Paul, 6
Hogan Challenge Report, 64
Hogan Developmental Survey
        (HDS), 161

Hogan Motives, Values, Preferences Inventory (MVPI), 165
Hogan Personality Inventory (HPI), 161
Hogan Suite of Assessments, 160–161
Home Depot, 5
human capital and bench strength, 177
human cost of leadership failures, 10–12
hypothetical interviewer, 46

IBM, 117
individual assessments, 181–182
individual attributes
  abilities, 29–30,63, 43–59
  character, 32–34, 63, 75–95
  personality and energy, 28–30, 31–32 63–71
In Search of Excellence (Peters and Waterman), 119
insider vs. outsider. *See* internal candidates vs. external candidates.
integrity, 80–81
intelligence quotient (IQ) testing, 55–56
internal candidates, 155, 178, 182, 217, 246, 250–252,264, 267
internal candidates vs. external candidates, 3, 130–131, 267
interpersonal skills as failure source, 65
interview questions, 48
interviewer styles 46
  fact-finding, 46
  hypothetical, 46
  sales-oriented, 46
  theoretical, 46
  therapeutic, 46
interviews

behavioral-based questions, 49–50, 52, 60, 84, 154, 162, 165, 189, 220, 222
brainteaser interview questions, 48
business terrain, 174–179
criteria for, 50
EQ and BEI/CBBI, 50–51
forbidden questions, 57–58
motivational interview questions, 48
situational interview questions, 48
stress interview questions, 48–49
structured vs. unstructured interviews, 47–48
topgrading, 47, 59
traditional or "tell me about yourself" interview, 47
types of, 47–51
interview training, 59, 153–154, 166, 214, 217–218, 249, 253
intuition, role of in Selection Process, 32–33, 144, 268–269

Jackson Personality Research Form (PRF), 161
job descriptions. *See* job specifications.
job specifications 45–46
  disconnect from reality, x, 15, 98–100
  in Extended Selection process, 249, 251
  in Leader Selection Process, 217, 220
  in Traditional Selection Process, 15, 45
Johnson & Johnson, 123
Johnson O'Connor Aptitude Test, 56, 157
Jones, Gareth, 116

Kennedy, Allan, 116, 117
Kidder, Rushworth, 79

King Martin Luther, Jr., 86
KKR (Kohlberg Kravis Roberts &
     Co), 37
Klann, Gene, 77, 79, 87–88
Kluckhohn, Clyde, 115

Lafley, A.G., 123
Landsburg, Max, 247
leader malleability, 18, 190–191, 262
leader selection process, 261–262
   basis for (Match-Fit Model) xvii,
     28–38, 261
   benefits to individuals of, xix
   benefits to organization of,
     xviii–xix
   measurement of success, 263–264
   need for new, 17–19
   paradigm shift required, 57
   and succession planning, 247–250
   ways to improve, 155–157
   See also Selection Process,
     Accelerated leader Selection
     Process, and Extended Leader
     Selection Process,
     Traditional Selection
     Process.
leadership actions/adjustments,
   106–108
leader's character. *See* character.
leadership failures.
   bottom-line impact of, 8–10
   CEO statistics (global), 240
   CEO statistics (U.S.), xi, xv,
     3–5, 100
   human cost of, 10–11
   See failures, CEO failures, and
     non-CEO failures.
Leadership IQ, 65
leader's team subculture, 37, 181,
   264
leaders vs. managers, 88
"Leading by Leveraging Culture"
   (Chatman and Cha), 117

Lee, Blaine, 78–79
level 5 leaders, 79, 81, 88
Liberating the Corporate Soul (Barrett),
   120, 165
Loehr, Jim, 31, 69–70, 162
Lucht, John, 47
Lynn, Adele, 51

managers vs. leaders, 88
mapping. *See* mapping the corporate
   lay of the land.
mapping research, 186–190
mapping the corporate lay of the
     land,
   about, 184
   benefits of, 193
   historical roots of, 184–186
   new research design, 186–189
   purpose of,184
   Specialty Distributors Inc. case,
     189
match-fit model
   development of, 28–38
   need for, xvi, 28–32
   role in selection, xvii, 38–39
   significance of, 32–35, 252
   value of, 63
   version 1, 35–36
   version 2, 36–37
   version 3, 37–38
McKinnell, Hank, 5
Meaning Inc. (Gurneck), 120
meaning of culture, 114–115
Melican, James, 239
Mercer Consulting, 127, 248
mergers and acquisitions
   failure rates of, xvii, 120–121
   applicability of book to, xvii–xviii
Merk, 240
Merrill Lynch, 241
military metaphor, 139–144
Minnesota Multiphasic Personality
     Inventory, 69

missing links to selecting the right
leader, 167–196
*Moral Courage: Taking Action When
Your Values Are Put to the Test*
(Kidder), 79
Mornell, Pierre, 54–55
motivational interview questions, 48
Motorola, 241
movie script framework
directors' cut version of, 51–53
functioning of, 26
original text of, 25–26
Murphy, Mark, 65
Murray, Alan, 4
Mursau, Chris, 8
Myers-Briggs Type Indicator®,
159–160
myths of culture. *See* culture,
debunking myths of culture.

Nardelli, Bob, 5
National Association of Corporate
Directors (NACD), 242, 248
CEO Succession Best Practices,
250
CEO Succession Process, 248
CEO Succession Study (2004), 99
CEO Succession Study (2006),
250–251
needs
directional, xii, 36–37, 104–106,
146, 200, 261
executional, xii, 37–38, 102, 173,
187, 254, 264
new hiring process. *See* Selection
Processes.
New York Stock Exchange (NYSE),
5
New York Times, 17
9-block evaluation system, 123
Nike, 1, 5, 13, 17
non-CEO failures
costs of, 5

frequency of, 65
traits of, 63–65
Nordstrom's, 118
Notre Dame, 33
NOW Understand Your Strengths
(Buckingham), 56

Occupational Personality
Questionnaire (OPQ32), 161
O'Leary, George, 33
onboarding, xvii, 37, 183, 190, 215,
233, 248–249, 261, 269
coach, 222, 224–228, 254–255
organizational culture. *See* culture.
Organizational Culture and Leadership
(Schein), 117
organizational trust. *See* trust.
outcomes vs. actions, 101–102
outsider vs. insider. *See* external
candidates vs. internal
candidates.

partnering with candidates, 57,154,
166, 254
pegs
and holes, 12–13,262
malleability of, 190–191, 262, 269
Perez, William, xx–xxi, 5, 13, 17
performance expectations, 105
personality
and energy, 61–71
assessment techniques of, 157–161
Big Five descriptive model of, 159
in the Traditional Selection
Process, 28–29
defined, 65–66
importance of, 66–68
list of derailers, 64
traits of success (or failure), 63–65
Peters, Tom, 120–122
Pfizer, 5
philosophies. *See* beliefs.
political and regulatory changes, 241

Portas, Jerry, 118
position description. *See* job
    specifications.
post-selection actions, 224–233
  onboarding and executive
      coaching, 224–228, 254–255
  progress reports, 229–233, 256
The Power of Full Engagement (Loehr
    and Schwartz), 31, 162
Power Principle (Lee), 78–79
pre-selection actions, 213–224
  announcements 14, 215, 222–223,
      231–232, 249, 273
  behavioral event interview training
      59, 153–154, 166, 214, 217–
      218, 249, 253
  business terrain research, 173–181,
      218
  candidate assessment instruments,
      55–57, 67, 83–84, 160–165,
      229–233, 256
  character interview(s), 163–164,
      221–222
  commence work, 223–224
  external search, 219
  field guide of vital information,
      221–223. *See also* Appendix C.
  final FAC Report, 221
  first "sighting" candidates, 219
  fuzzy front end and transition
      planning, 13, 213, 220–222,
      247
  internal candidates, 155, 178, 182,
      217, 246, 250–252, 264, 267
  job specifications, x, 15, 45–46,
      98–100, 217, 219–220, 249,
      251
  offer, negotiate, and receive
      acceptance, 222
  onboarding coach meeting and
      briefing, 222
  organization types, 218
  process, protocols, dates, 217

search firm, selection team, and
    FAC, 216
second short-list interviews, 221
short-list interviews, 220
team topography, 181–184, 219
Procter & Gamble, 118, 123
project leader, functions of.
    See Forward Assessment
    Consultant.
psycho-behavioral interview, 161
psychological testing.
    See assessments of and
    assessment tools.
Psychology Matters (APA Web site), 65
public records checks, 54
The Purpose of Education (King), 86

questions, interview types, 48

reactions to failure. *See* failure.
real versus perceived corporate
    needs, xvii, xix, 15–17, 28–29,
    37, 39, 100–102, 106–107,
    130, 144–146, 163, 166, 170,
    173, 184, 186–187, 213, 224–
    225, 247, 252–253, 255, 257,
    264–265, 287
reference checks, 53–54
Renne, Alan, 55
research expert, functions of. *See*
    Forward Assessment
    Consultant.
résumés, 43
review, 261–277
Richard Barrett Values Assessment
    Process, 125, 165
Rigby-Hall, Robert, 153
*Rites of Passage at $100,000 to $1
    million* (Lucht), 47
Ritz-Carlton, 118
Rogers, John, 113, 131
role of ceo today. *See* CEO role
    today.

Rorschach inkblot test, 68
Roth v. United States, 34
Rutgers University report, 7
16-Personality Factors Test (16-PF),
    160
sales-oriented interviewer, 46
Sallie Mae (SLM Corp), 241
Santamaria, Jason, 134
satisfaction and retention, 88–91
Schein, Edgar, 117, 122, 126, 133
Schwartz, Tony, 31, 69–70, 162
S.C. Johnson, 13
SEC. *See* Securities and Exchange
    Commission.
secret searches, 266–267
Securities and Exchange
    Commission (SEC), xvii, 91,
    241
Segil, Larraine, 121
selection processes
  accelerated leader selection
    process, 213–233, 262
  extended leader selection process,
    145–146, 213–214, 224, 233,
    248–250, 255, 257, 262, 265,
    268
  leader selection process, 261–262,
    28–38, 261, xix, xviii–xix
  Traditional Selection Process, 13–
    15, 17–18, 28, 30–31
Selection Team, 14, 34, 55, 104,
    145–146, 154, 156–158, 166,
    172, 176, 180, 184–185, 188,
    192, 194, 199, 210, 269
self-awareness and self-control, 51
The 7 Habits of Highly Effective People
    (Covey), 162
seven habits of unsuccessful
    executives, 63–64
"Seven Levels of Corporate
    Consciousness" (Barrett), 125
severance packages, 5–6
shared values experiences, 90–92

Shen, Gene, 33
Shorter, Frank,214
silos, 204
situational interview questions, 48
six-month progress report, 230–231
Six Sigma, xii, 18, 34, 124,153,
    287–288
Smart, Bradford, 8–9, 47, 59
Sonnenfeld, Jeffery, 155
Specialty Distributors, Inc. (SDI)
    case study, 199–210
  about, 199
  CEO search, 201
  final candidate, 202
  findings, 202–203
  high-altitude snapshot of SDI,
    200–201
  James and the executive leadership
    team subculture, 206–209
  James and the SDI culture,
    203–206
  what to do about James, 209–210
The Speed of Trust (Covey, Stephen
    M. R.), 132
Spencer, Lyle, 46, 50, 154
Spencer, Signe, 46, 50, 154
Sprint, 5
St. James School, 113–114
Stewart, Potter, 34
stock
  price effect, xv, 7, 264, 281
  volatility, xv, 7–8, 11, 20, 267, 293
    Rutgers and University of Texas
    report on, 7
Stoddard, Jack, 113–114, 123
"Strategic Leadership And Decision
    Making," (National Defense
    University), 124
strategy, 175
Strauss, Levi, 125
StrengthsFinder Profile®, 56, 157
stress interview questions, 48–49
structural rigidity. *See* silos.

structured vs. unstructured
interviews, 47–48
style, 36, 63
styles of interviewers, 46
subculture
Bill's Subculture Chasm, 127–129
boss's team subculture, 37, 264
effect on character, 78
importance of, xii, 37–38, 78,
117–120, 126, 264
leader's team subculture, 37, 181,
264
myth of 5, 121, 126–129
success
in a previous situation, 30
traits of, 63–65
succession planning, 239–257
and new leader selection process,
247–250
best practices, 250–256
process adoption statistics,
242–243
reasons not adopted, 243–246
sources of pressure to adopt,
246–247
succession planning best practices,
NACD, 251
succession planning best practices,
new, 251
aggressively manage the process,
253–254
establish the time frame for the
process, 253
fully integrate the executive
recruiter into the process, 255
grow internal talent by planning
and monitoring progress, 252
identify action-based capabilities
and values-based character
traits essential for success, 254
incorporate mapping tools and
character interview into final
interviews, 255

monitor the CEO's transition plan
closely, 255–256
seek feedback for continuous
improvement, 255
select the right forward assessment
consultant, 253
success traits. *See* Universal
Character Traits of Leaders.
Sulkowicz, Kerry, 161
Swanson, Bill, 69

tactics vs. execution, 103
Taking Advice (Ciampa), 227
talents and inherent strengths
testing, 56
targeting information, 144
TAT (Thematic Apperception Test),
68
team assessment, 182–184
team topography assessment, 181
uses of the, 182–184
Thematic Apperception Test (TAT,
68
theoretical interviewer, 46
therapeutic interviewer, 46
three-month update, 230
Topgrading (Smart), 8, 47
Toyota, 120
Toys R Us, 241
traditional or "tell me about
yourself" interview, 47
Traditional Selection Process
steps of, 13–15,
geared to abilities, 27–28
missing steps in, 17, 30–31, 99–102
vs. leader selection process, 18
ways to improve, 155–157
See also vetting improvements.
trust
importance of to success, 8, 88–90,
272–276
organizational, 8, 132
symptoms of lack of, 134–135

trustworthiness, 32, 49
turnover rate, 3, 134, 239–240
twelve-month progress report, 231
Tylenol®, 123
types of interviewer styles, 46
types of interviews, 47–51
types of interview questions, 48
typological test, 159

universal character traits of leaders, 78–81
University of Texas report, 7
unsuccessful executives, seven habits of, 63–64
U.S. Air Force 141, 143
   Academy definition of character, 76
   Forward Air Controllers (FACs), 141–143, 262
U.S. Army, 68, 141, 143
U.S. Marines, 143
U.S. Navy, 143

Values
   and trust, 88–90, 272–276
   as an aspect of character and virtues, 78
   importance of, 78
   Universal Character Traits (values) of Leaders, 78
   See also Appendix B

vetting improvements
   general improvements, 152–153
   participant training, 152
   process management, 152
   relations with candidates, 152

See also Traditional Selection Process
virtues, 78. *See also* Appendix B.
VISA, 92
vision and mission, 175

Waitley, Denis, 99
Wal-Mart, 118
Walton, Sam, 125
Waterman, Robert, 120–122
Watkins, Michael, 222
Watson, Tom, 125
Weber Shandwick, 241
Weil, Sandy, 239
Welch, Jack, 124–125, 287
What Got You Here Won't Get You There (Goldsmith), 131
"What Holds the Modern Company Together?" (Goffee and Jones), 116
Why CEOs Fail (Dotlich and Cairo), 64
Why Smart Executives Fail (Finklestein), 63, 93
Williams, Steve, 226
Wilson, Jack, xiii, xvi, 34
Woods, Tiger, 226
Woodward Personal data sheet, 68
WorldCom, 241
World Kitchen Inc. (WKI), 27–28, 38, 229
"The World's Most Prominent Temp Workers" (Booz Allen Hamilton), 99
www.therightleader.com, 187, 190, 196, 210

Zweifel, Thomas, 121